ALL GROWN UP NOW

A friendship in three acts

KENNETH D. KING

AUTHOR'S NOTE: SOME NAMES HAVE BEEN CHANGED IN THIS STORY, MORE TO PROTECT THE INDIVIDUAL'S PRIVACY, THAN TO PROTECT MY REPUTATION. MY REPUTATION, SUCH AS IT IS, IS BEYOND REDEMPTION.

COPYRIGHT © 2012
ALL RIGHTS RESERVED.

ISBN: 1477698884
ISBN 13: 9781477698884

LIBRARY OF CONGRESS CONTROL NUMBER: 2012911230
CREATESPACE INDEPENDENT PUBLISHING PLATFORM
NORTH CHARLESTON, SOUTH CAROLINA

Dedication:

To Mark, who opened the window for my escape;
to Norma, who kicked me through it;
and to Harry, who provided the moral compass
to guide me along the way.

Foreward:

This is the story of a small-town boy, who dreams of being a "grown-up", and his journey towards *being* all grown up.

Overture:

I'd never kidnapped someone before.

When I told Mark I didn't want to hear from him until he was ready to leave Victor, it didn't occur to me that, if he finally called after all those years, that I would have to take such extraordinary measures to help out. As a sissy boy in Kansas, I got much of my information about life from watching movies. Sadly, though, out of all the movies I'd seen, not one had given me any real, solid information about how to go about pulling off this kind of caper, so I had to make it up as I went along.

Mark's brother, Robert, had called the day before, to let me know there were guns involved, as Victor had a fondness for them, as well as other things like phone-tapping equipment and surveillance cameras. He said that Mark was so traumatized that he was scared to even leave the house, but could perhaps be coaxed out for a short time.

So, I called Mark, using the fiction that I was going to be in Los Angeles on business and we should have lunch. In my paranoia, I even made reservations at The Ivy, just in case Victor *had* tapped the phone and decided to call and check it out.

What I neglected to tell Mark was that lunch would be in San Francisco, where I was living. I only bought him a one-way ticket. But I understood that this might not be a simple snatch-and-run.

So, facing the very real possibility that Things Could Go Horribly Wrong, I *took steps*. I made sure I rented the spiffiest convertible I could get—a black Chrysler Le Baron convertible, to be exact. I also made sure I had on good underwear, as my mom used to say the ambulance wouldn't pick you up without it. (*They'd check first.*) And, I made sure my hair was freshly bleached. My thinking was, that if I got my brains blown out, I wouldn't have to pay for the spiffy car. And, at least I would have gone out in style— good underwear and with my roots done.

As I drove to the airport, I thought about how I now found myself in this situation. This is something that—if Things Went Horribly Wrong—reporters might be soon asking.

As they say— *long story*.

ACT ONE:

Scene 1

Life began for me on May 6, 1980. I regard everything that went before as doing the previews in New Haven before opening on Broadway. That play would have been called *Dances With Land Mines*.

I graduated from Undistinguished University in Oklahoma on May 5, 1980, the first of the siblings to do so. I'm the middle (boy) child, with two sisters, one younger (Kathy), one older (Laurie).

My BS degree was in fashion merchandising with an emphasis on window display. I had begun sewing at an early age—age four, to be exact—for Barbie and my troll dolls. I had traded my gun and holster set to Kathy for Barbie;

I had no interest in boy's toys. This caused both parents no end of concern as we were living in a small town in Kansas at the time.

My Barbie wasn't a teenager like the official Mattel story—mine was twenty-seven years old, drove a convertible, owned only evening clothes, and went to the opera, the theater, and good restaurants. Since my parents would rather have severed a limb than buy Barbie clothes for me, I made all of her fab outfits. One favorite from that time was the strapless, full-skirted, gold damask number—the bodice was made from black grosgrain. She had a slim evening sheath that I knitted out of some gold metallic yarn that a neighbor was throwing out. Barbie got her own mink coat and matching hat when another neighbor gave me an old fur collar, and she inherited an entire set of rhinestone jewelry when Grandma cleaned out her jewelry box. I was always working on something.

Deep down I really wanted to be a fashion designer, but in Oklahoma City (which the locals sometimes refer to as OKC), display was the closest occupation I could imagine doing. The idea of being a fashion designer in OKC, well, I might as well have imagined living on Mars.

But along with this deep desire to be a fashion designer was a real impatience to be a grown-up. Grown-ups had all the fun, like in the movies. They drove cool cars, dined at good restaurants, went to the theater, hung out with glamorous people—life was a dream when you were a grown-up. (It was this idea of what being a grown-up was that I projected onto Barbie.) I joke now that, instead of having an "inner child" as most people claim to have, I grew up with an "inner adult."

Never mind that the examples of grown-ups around me didn't reflect this idea. They somehow didn't count. Grown-ups lived in big cities, had cool apartments, and led glamorous lives; and I resolved at a very early age that I too would be a grown-up. Now that I was graduating from college, I could step onto the path that would ultimately lead to this sparkling new life.

ACT ONE:

During the summer of 1986 was my ten-year high school class reunion. I was debating whether or not to go, whether to spend the money on my new business or just buy the ticket and go to OKC. Mark, during one of our many telephone conversations, (which surprisingly was *not* about complaining about Victor—he actually seemed to be hearing what I was talking about) argued for going. Mark felt that going back to confront the demons that were from my adolescence would go far toward eliminating them. He apparently had missed his class reunions and regretted it.

So I decided to go.

The evening of the reunion was one of those rare days we've all had, when it was a good-hair day, plus a feel-thin day, plus a good-complexion day, plus a good-outfit-day, all rolled into one fabulous burst of glory. It took about three months to get the right outfit for the reunion. I wore a really smart dinner jacket, pleated trousers in black-and-white glen plaid with pinstripes of teal and sapphire blue, a white high-collar shirt with a sapphire-blue paisley silk tie, black cummerbund, and sapphire blue shoes. And Good Hair. Oh, I also wore my new ring. If I could choose to go back to one day in my life and look that way forever, that would be the day.

Graduation night was the only time I wore my class ring. Mom insisted I buy *that* (along with going to the prom, more memories!), so I got the real gold one. I couldn't convince her to pay for it, though, like I did with the prom . . . there was only so far she would go for sentiment. I figured I could melt the ring down later if I got the real gold one. And I did melt the ring down—on the eve of the reunion— in my jewelry class at City College. (I was taking the jewelry class so I could also design jewelry for my fledgling design business.)

Melting down the ring was a symbolic act on the eve of my ten-year class reunion. I wanted to take along a symbol of a time that was hell for me, when I had no choice, and turn it into a symbol of the life I had made for myself in San Francisco—a life where I was doing what I wanted, in the city I wanted, and was not putting up with the small-minded comments of people I didn't care for nor respect. Putting the ring into the fire and watching it melt was really satisfying.

ALL GROWN UP NOW

I arrived at the Holiday Inn, looking good and loaded for bear. Here I was—coming in from San Francisco, an up-and-coming designer, ready for the first person to set me off.

Then came the exchange that launched me into my ten-year high school class reunion. The woman in question was Linda, one of the girls at the high school cafeteria table where I would sit, who I met up with at the door. She started giving me the dish on all the people who didn't come to the reunion. During this monologue she mentioned David Pierce, the other suspected homo in the class. Immediately I was interested and asked what he was up to.

"Oh, it's too horrible! I can't say!" she gasped, her hand clutching her chest.

"What's so horrible?" I asked. Was he committing axe murders or something?"

"Worse!" she said.

"What?"

"He married a man and moved to California!"

I looked her right in the eye, about ten inches from her face, and said evenly, "What in the hell is wrong with that? That's just exactly what I did!"

The color in her face drained onto the white polyester crepe georgette dress she was wearing, and she fled into the crowd.

It was as if the Universe said, "This is it, Kid—SING!"

Nothing in small-town Salina, Kansas, prepared me for my experience in school in Oklahoma City. In Kansas I was an average student, in the orchestra (where

ACT ONE:

I could saw out a competent tune on the violin), a member of the student council, and was involved in the Christmas play. (I was "Little Jimmy Schimmelfinnig.") Though I wasn't wildly popular, I wasn't a pariah either. That changed when I got to OKC.

We were enrolled at Western Oaks Junior High School. (Everything in OKC was named "*Fill-in-the-Blank*–Oaks") The first day at Western Oaks Junior High was a bit frightening. This school was about three times as large as South Junior High in Salina (three floors compared to the one floor at South Junior High), and was populated with lots of kids whose necks were good and red. They all seemed to have a healthy fear of outsiders and could spot anyone who hadn't been there from the first grade on. (Or perhaps it was animal instinct—they sensed that I came from another gene pool, and it made them nervous.) My inimitable fashion sense, which had gotten me somewhat of a reputation in Kansas as a "clothes horse," was to prove a liability, one that definitely marked me as "outsider." Being a chubby, sissy boy and playing the violin didn't help much either.

The second day of school was the first time I heard the word "faggot." It was directed at me, and I extrapolated from context (something that I learned in Kansas schools, which are superior to Oklahoma schools—we even learned to *spell* "extrapolate") that faggot wasn't good. It seems I was carrying my books "like a girl," whatever *that* meant. Again, the clothes—I had embraced the "body shirt," an unfortunate fad in the early seventies whereby a man's shirt was cut with princess panels, those vertical seams usually seen on women's clothes. This supposedly gave a trimmer line but sadly not on me. The one I was wearing on that particular day was a light mauve, worn with burgundy hip-huggers and a wide white belt. From then on, it seemed, I had a tattoo of "faggot" (invisible to me) right on my forehead, and whenever any of the mouth-breathing boys in the school would walk past, knuckles dragging the ground, they would utter it, usually just before spitting out the tobacco juice on me. It was the scarlet "F" that I was never able to see, let alone fully eradicate.

In other words, I couldn't pass as straight. Not then, not now.

Ironically since I've come out, I've not been called "faggot." Other names, yes, like slut, and pig, and whore—but not faggot. (I deserved *them*.) But before I was actually having the fun that we faggots have, I was called "faggot" *a lot*. Why is that?

When people talk of the idyllic, innocent days of youth and wax eloquent about high school being "the best days of our lives," I think "BULLSHIT!" First of all, adolescents can be exceedingly cruel, especially when they encounter someone who doesn't fit the norm. But when that person is a sissy boy with weird clothes, they can be relentless.

The creativity that adolescents express when tormenting any outsider, especially a sissy kid, is really astonishing in a morbid, sick sort of way. I believe that Hitler learned all his tricks from Bavarian youths who took it upon themselves to harass unfortunate *auslanders*. It makes sense of the Hitler Youth—Hitler and his band were searching for new methods of torture and knew where to look. The Hitler Youth provided the Nazi Party with fresh new ideas. It was their "research and development" organization.

Daily spat upon and beat up, my books torn up, homework ruined, four-letter words written on my clothing, school became a time of unrelenting misery for me. (That sounds so overdramatic, but it was the way it was.) I also had the stigma of being somewhat smart, (along with the violin playing) and a good student despite the harassment, which further branded me as no-good.

Add to the mix that, in the eighth grade, I sewed and still played with Barbie. Now, mind you, I knew not to talk about it and did it in secret. I used to get grief from Mom, who would shriek about how I would turn into such a sissy (duh) if I kept this up. But Barbie was an escape for me. As I said, my Barbie was twenty-seven years old, lived in a big city, drove a convertible, only owned evening clothes, went to the opera and theater and good restaurants—in short, a grown-up. I learned sewing by making clothes for Barbie, before I started sewing for myself as a teenager. Barbie taught me my love of fashion. Eventually, though, I carefully packed her up with all her clothes and hid her in the attic. I had a premonition that, if I didn't, one day I'd come home and she would be gone. Mom would have thrown her away while I was at school.

The mind-set at Western Oaks Junior High (and later Putnam City West High School) was one where the smart guys were regarded with suspicion

ACT ONE:

(thought to be ass-kissers at the very least). Being, or at least pretending to be, somewhat of a cretin was considered good form. (Most of the people in this school could have been extras in the film *Deliverance*.) This is where my prejudice against okie accents came from—I automatically deduct twenty points from someone's IQ if I hear one. I only add the points back if I get to know them, and they prove to have a brain.

There was no time off for good behavior—daily I ran the gauntlet at school, nightly I ran the gauntlet at home. Mom was married to Don, who was a one-man chaos machine. I'd be worried that, because of Don, Mom would either be dead when we got home, or if not dead, she would be so wrought up that I'd wish she were dead.

Mom was just a wealth of comfort and understanding during this period. I told her of some of my problems at school (once), and her response was to shriek:

"What are you doing to deserve it? If you weren't such a goddamn sissy, they'd leave you alone!"

Now, *that* was a help! Why hadn't I thought of that?

These conditions continued every year, all the way until I was a senior. I managed to keep my grades up, saw away at the violin, and not get into trouble. Nor did I do drugs or alcohol. I decided that if I couldn't fit in anyhow (I was branded, you remember), I would not even try. So no cigarettes because that's what *they* did. No drugs or booze, again because that's what *they* did. Also I was, and am still, cheap about such things. Spending good money on something I couldn't wear, ride, look at, or tell time with, didn't make sense to me.

Consequently I would wear anything I wanted to school. This was helped along by the fact that, when I was a sophomore, I started making my own clothes. My first project was a blue chambray shirt, and once I was hooked, my garments became more and more unusual. My finest fashion moment (and "fuck you" to the high school) was my outfit for Western Day.

Imagine a sky-blue satin western shirt with sapphire blue rhinestones outlining the yoke, a sapphire-blue western hat, my Angels Flight blue jeans, and very high platform shoes. It's a wonder I got home alive!

Since I didn't fit in, though, it didn't matter—the mouth-breathers were going to have comments about whatever I wore anyway. Strangely, things I wore would filter into the wardrobes of the "cool" kids about a year later. Remember puka shell chokers? Feathered hair? Nylon disco shirts with the pictures printed on them? Fiorucci? I was really given a hard time when I wore them, but within a year, all the jocks were wearing them (except, of course, for the Fiorucci—they couldn't even pronounce it, let alone spell it.). I then had to move on to the next "look," but I stuck with the platform shoes until college. I'm really short.

As far as lawbreaking went, I was a real amateur as a teenager. Since I didn't do drugs or drink, I had to have *some* form of rebellion. My rebellion was driving cars before I was of legal age to do so.

By the time I was fifteen, I had driven about ten or twelve cars. It was surprisingly easy: I would just ask, and more likely than not, someone would hand me the keys or stop the car and get out to let me drive.

There were a couple of times I got caught. The first was the last day of ninth grade. I skipped school (the only time I ever skipped school, actually) and went around with my friend Larry in his mother's brand-new, sapphire-blue Olds Delta 88 Royale—white vinyl top and white interior, bucket seats with the shifter in the center console, Paul McCartney and Wings on the eight-track tape player. How he got it without her knowing, I don't know, but he wasn't legal yet either. So, as I did so many times in the past, I asked him if I could drive.

"Sure! You wanna go pick up your sister and cruise around the lake?"

So off we went to pick up Kathy at home, pulling up and honking, then screeching the tires as we sped away.

When we came home, I got the mail. Looking through the mail, I found an envelope addressed to "Mrs. King," with no stamp or return address. So I did what any sensible teenager would do: I opened it.

ACT ONE:

"Dear Mrs. King," it read. "I thought you should know that I saw your son driving a blue Oldsmobile this afternoon, license plate number blah blah blah . . . "

There was no signature, but it looked like the work of our lard-ass, next-door neighbor Mrs. Knapp, who, instead of minding her own business and spending her time keeping up with her housework (and it showed), snooped on all the neighbors. She had permanent marks on her nose from the binoculars.

The note ended up in the bottom of the garbage can.

I had another friend in junior high named Joe, whose mom and dad were divorced. He lived down the street from me and was a couple years older. Joe had really black hair and really white skin, and, sadly, was rather on the odd-looking side, (he looked somewhat like a vampire with bad acne) which I hope he grew out of.

Joe's dad suffered from guilt about the divorce, which Joe took full advantage of. For awhile, since his mom worked too, Joe would drive us around in her white Dodge Dart, with the avocado-green vinyl interior, after taking her to work. (Little did she know.) This arrangement proved to be too complicated, him taking her to work and picking her up, so his dad was guilt-tripped into buying Joe a brand-new white Subaru.

Now remember, this was in the mid-seventies, so Subaru was a rather ugly and not-very-fast car with next to no cachet. But it was new, had a cassette tape deck, and four-on-the-floor. Joe was in heaven! The two of us would take the Subaru out, tool around OKC and wile away the summer afternoons. He was protective of his new car, but soon I had him talked into letting me drive, and I actually learned how to shift and clutch quite well.

As my grandma would say, if you were doing something you shouldn't be doing, somehow, sometime, it would tell on you. I always thought she was being an old stick. However, one afternoon, while I was driving Joe's car along Twenty-third Street (a main drag in my day), we passed the intersection of Twenty-third and Glade. Joe let out a shriek; I slammed on the brakes and looked to the right, only to see Joe's mom at the intersection.

OH. MY. GOD.

The squealing tires got her attention, to be sure, and once she looked she saw Joe in the passenger seat. She tore out of the intersection in hot pursuit.

I hit the gas and pulled out ahead (which is astonishing given the kind of car I was driving), and by the time we got to the intersection of Twenty-third and Council, Joe and I had switched places and he was in the driver's seat.

We were stopped at the light when his mom pulled up behind us and got out of the car. She stormed up and yelled in the window, "YOU! GET HOME! And YOU! (pointing at me) are in some real trouble, Mister!"

Oh, fuck. I could imagine it now. She would call Mom, or worse yet, come over and tell her in person, and I'd be really busted. I was shaking so bad I thought I'd wet myself.

The ending was sort of anticlimactic. She never said anything to Mom, but I wasn't allowed to see Joe after that—his mom thought I was a bad influence. Imagine that.

The most troublesome driving experience, though, wasn't trouble because of the driving.

I worked at Braum's Ice Cream store. It was the job I got when I was fifteen, and Mom said I'd better have a job "OR ELSE." There was also a girl who worked there named Kathy M., who was Laurie's age. Kathy M. had a really cool, burgundy, late-sixties Chevy Impala, with mag wheels, thrush pipes, and four on the floor, and it was hiked up in the back. One night Kathy M. and I were working, and she offered me a ride home.

ACT ONE:

"Can I drive your car?" I asked. (I asked everyone that.)

"Sure, if you can drive stick."

So I called Laurie to tell her that she didn't need to pick me up because I was riding home with Kathy M. This should have come as good news to Laurie, as it gave her more time to boink Bill-the-mechanic, her boss at the two-pump gas station, where she was the *bookkeeper*.

(A little backstory is in order here. Laurie couldn't balance a checkbook to save her life, but she *did* have big tits and was really easy. The high school boys called her "Meatgrazer" behind her back.

She got this job at a rinky-dink, two-pump gas station as the *bookkeeper*, can you believe it? Mom did; she had an enormous capacity for denial. When she told all her friends that Laurie was working as a *bookkeeper* at this particular gas station—all her friends knew of it—they all looked at her like she was either joking or crazy. Laurie was no doubt taking lessons in bookkeeping—there were many nights that she would pick me up from work, drive over to Bill-the-mechanic's place in the bad part of town, go in and stay a long time. What else could she have been up to? I, of course, sat in the car, waiting and worrying that the wheels would be stolen off of it while I cowered in the backseat.)

Given that backstory, to my surprise, Laurie objected to me riding home with Kathy M. I stubbornly insisted that I was riding home with Kathy M.

A few minutes later, Mom called.

"YOU'RE RIDING HOME WITH YOUR SISTER!" she shrieked.

"No, I'm not!"

"Yes, you are! Laurie told me what a little slut she is, and you're NOT riding home in her car!"

First of all, Laurie calling someone *else* a slut? Really! And second I wasn't riding home in her car; I was planning on *driving* it.

"I've gotta get back to work. I'm riding home with Kathy M. Bye!" And hung up.

So I indeed got to drive her car home, but next morning—boy, oh boy—did I catch hell! Mom was in high dudgeon and cornered me as soon as I was in the kitchen.

"DON'T YOU KNOW WHAT THAT TYPE IS UP TO? LAURIE TELLS ME THAT SHE JUST WANTS TO HAVE A BOY GET HER PREGNANT SO SHE CAN GET MARRIED! DO YOU WANT TO GET HER PREGNANT AND BRING SHAME ON THE FAMILY NAME?"

My conundrum: Confess that, no, I just wanted to drive her car and catch hell; or say no, I'm queer and would throw up if I ever got near a vagina, let alone putting it IN one and catch hell. OR, just keep my mouth shut and catch hell.

I kept my mouth shut. It was all the same to me.

As Mom raved on, I reflected on the fact that *I was the only one in our household who was not sexually active.* Somehow, though, I was the one getting grief about just that topic. Besides, Mom was the one who kept shacking up with her ex-husband after the divorce, so why was she lecturing *me* about "bringing shame on the family name"?

Something good happened in my senior year, though, to relieve some of my torment.

Our school mascot was the Putnam City West Patriot, and we were the "Spirit of '76." Oh boy, what imagination! Stacey Jones was the most popular senior in the class, so she was voted Miss Patriot, the highest honor. (She also happened to date David Pierce.)

ACT ONE:

There were two reasons I took psychology. For one, so I could learn what was wrong with me and how to fix it. I learned a really good bit of info in this class: You have a 40 percent chance of curing your own neurosis. That was good enough odds for me. Besides, grown-ups didn't have neuroses, and since every waking moment I dedicated to getting to be a grown-up, I needed to "cure" myself. The other reason I took psychology was that Mom didn't want me getting out of school until as late as possible. I could have gotten out at noon because I had enough credits, but NOOOO! Laurie and Kathy both got to, but somehow I was different. I think Mom believed I would get into some sort of trouble if left to my own devices. Where did she get *that* idea?

Anyway, Stacey Jones sat behind me in psychology class. One day in about January, we were talking, and she suddenly said:

"You know, you're really cool!"

"Yeah, yeah," I thought. But that comment started something. Stacey would be seen with me in the halls, actually talking to me—something socially risky for her, as I was such a pariah—and actually seeming to enjoy doing it. Then, one by one, the popular people in the school would say a tentative "Hi," then "Hello," and it eventually accelerated to a point where the table I sat at in the cafeteria was frequented by these popular people. Who knew?

A word on this table: I called it the "filler group." We weren't the jocks or jockettes, nor were we the theater group, nor the debate team, or the art crowd, etc. We were the odd handful of people who just wanted to GET IN, GET THE EDUCATION, AND THEN GET THE HELL OUT. High school was *not* the pinnacle of our existence. We, for the most part, didn't go in for extracurricular activities (we all had after-school jobs), and we were not considered particularly good-looking or popular. Having all the popular people visit our table was a really curious experience.

The filler group had some really cool people in it. One of these people was Marilyn Swirczinski. She was valedictorian and had the dual handicap for Okie women: She was really smart and was not really regarded as good-looking, nor was she blonde—she was pudgy with frizzy dark hair and thick glasses. Marilyn was really funny, and I liked her wicked wit, especially when it was directed at the mouth-breathers and knuckle-draggers. The jocks would knock her down in the halls. That was their idea of wit. Oooh.

Another in this group was Janie Friar. Janie looked like Olive Oyl in the Popeye comics but with waist-length hair. (Hers are the type of looks that get better with age—she looks terrific now!) Janie's family was retired military, and her mother was used to doing the protocol thing that a commander's wife did. I remember one night when she held a dinner party for Janic and some of the other members of the group—it was run just like an embassy function with finger bowls, place cards, and everything. VERY grown-up!

Janie was what I would call "a real Joe." She was the one in the science classes who would volunteer for the really gross experiments and not get all freaked out with the dissecting (like I would, sissy that I am). I reconnected with her just a couple of years ago. As I said, she looks really great now, and she's more interesting than I remember her (and she was interesting then). Now she's working periodically in Benin with the women there, teaching them ways to improve hygiene and thus improve infant survival rates.

Janie and I went to the prom together because we were pals, really. I asked her because Mom insisted I go. I didn't want to go, but Mom kept at it. She said, "If you don't go, you will regret it for the rest of your life. You can't replace these memories!" (As if I wanted to remember high school.)

Finally I said, "If you want me to go so bad, you'll have to pay for it! I don't want to spend the money!"

I thought that was the safest dodge, as anything requiring Mom to dip into her pocket would automatically be nixed. It usually worked like a charm.

To up the ante, I said, "And besides, if you want me to go, you have to let me use your car." This was a silver 1976 Cadillac Coupe DeVille with the half-vinyl top and red-striped velour interior—a real land yacht with all the power toys inside. It also had opera windows. Cadillac was anticipating a craze for drive-in opera.

ACT ONE:

To my surprise, she paid for everything! *AND* let me use the car! (So I miscalculated.) I had no choice. Off to Janie's to ask . . .

Mrs. Friar acted like I had proposed marriage! (In Oklahoma, who you took to the prom was usually who you were expected to marry. At the very least you were expected to boink them. I didn't want to do either.) She made Janie this dress—very "Scarlett-pulls-down-the-curtains" green velvet with long, ivory lace sleeves (in MAY!). I'm sure the thinking was that Janie could wear it for the holidays as well, making it a practical, if not comfortable, choice. Poor Janie was sweating like a pig before we left her house. Mrs. Friar took so many photos of the two of us before we left that I worried she'd climb up on the hood of the car to take one through the windshield, which thankfully didn't happen. I was concerned, though; I had just washed and waxed the car and didn't want her up there smudging it.

Thankfully the prom photos were destroyed in a horrible fire that burned their house to ashes a couple of years later, much to my relief. There are now no blackmail photos of chubby me standing next to Olive Oyl, who looked like she had an appointment with Rhett Butler. As for me, I was wearing a white dinner jacket (but *not* a ruffled-front shirt—I drew the line there and chose a pleated-front shirt); shoulder-length, late-seventies hair that was feathered and highlighted with Sun-In; and black (*very high*) platform shoes. I was grateful for the platform shoes—Janie was easily a head taller than me.

Another member of the "filler group" was Steve Richardson, who was my best friend in high school. He was a tall, lanky, tanned guy who wasn't terribly handsome but was, I always believed, too smart for his own good. Steve would go on and on about not knowing if his personality was his, or was just projections of the likes and dislikes of everyone around him. He thought too much, but he *did* have a really cool muscle car that could get up to 130 mph, which he did one evening on a country road with a bunch of us along. I liked his brother Tony, who I called a "gentleman redneck." His neck was red, but he did have manners and respect for women. He was also a real hunk, but I never would have *dared* look too hard at him; he would have beat the crap out of me if I had.

Then there was Steve's sidekick, Jeff Hand. He was a tightly wound, very thin, blue-white-skinned, slightly neurotic guy who *really* loved his mother. He had a yellow Triumph TR6 that he always worked on with Steve, when he wasn't following Steve around like a puppy. It turned out later that he came out, what a surprise.

Jan Burton was another regular member of the group. She looked like Mama Cass (though she couldn't sing like her, but she did sing) and was a part of the religious contingent in the group. I used to visit her mom and dad, who were really nice people but let Jan, an only child, get away with far too much. She was the only one in the filler group without a job. Mrs. Burton wanted her to "enjoy the high school experience," and Mr. Burton felt that she wasn't smart enough to go to school and work. (He was an interesting study—a burly construction worker type who could quote Chaucer at length, from memory.)

This group of oddballs and misfits kept me sane during my high school days. They provided a refuge every day at lunch from all the taunts and threats that I endured from the rest of the student body. Looking back, I think they were way more fun than all the popular people.

Graduation night was the happiest moment of my Oklahoma existence (next to moving to California, which came later). I was GETTING OUT of that damned school and all its small-minded energy. At the commencement, I was sitting in a row with a good mix of popular people and filler group. There were mixed feelings about this; I was happy that I was somewhat liked after all, but there was a part of me that felt like, "WHERE WERE YOU ALL WHEN I REALLY NEEDED YOU?"

It was easy for them to like me after getting Stacey's blessing.

I don't remember much about the ceremony but I do about the party afterward. About a dozen of us piled into the Cadillac land yacht (yes, Mom let me have it again!) to go to Suzanne Hussman's party, then over to Alice-Ann's house to "TP" her trees. I dragged in about six o'clock to find Mom sitting at the table, drinking her orange juice, and reading the paper.

It was also interesting to see what happened to some of the more notable and popular classmates who were at the reunion, like a guy I'll call "Head"—he shopped at head shops. Head was the peace-love-hippy-guy who listened to Cat Stevens and was an artist with long hair.

(He was really, really beautiful with his wavy brown hair, dark eyes, and full lips.) This evening he looked really spiffy and sort of straight.

"So Head, what have you been up to?" I asked.

"I'm in PR for the MX missile defense system," he responded. I had a good laugh. A good, loooong laugh. And noticed he wasn't laughing.

"No, really!" he said.

"But you used to listen to Cat Stevens! And wear peace signs and Earth shoes! What happened!?"

"I'm doing this to make enough so that one day I can quit and concentrate on my art."

I haven't heard if he ever did.

I felt a hug from behind—it was Stacey! She looked really good. It seems she took a gig as a drama professor in Bloomington, Indiana. I remarked that she was so talented, why didn't she go into the theater?

"I didn't want to be a waitress wanting to be an actor," she said. "I'm realistic about the business. This is a good gig for me."

We caught up on things, and finally she hugged me and said, "There were only two people I really wanted to see, and you're one of them." Despite myself, I felt all warm inside. My cynicism said that she probably said this to a number of people, but I chose to ignore it. After all, better late than never. Stacey really did make my last days in high school bearable, and I will always be grateful to her and remember her fondly for that.

Then I saw Marilyn Swirzinski! She looked terrific! Lost weight, got contact lenses, and did really well for herself. We got caught up, and I learned that she became a professor at MIT or something really brainy like that.

"And you know the best thing?" she asked.

"What?"

"I inherited several million dollars! You know the guys who used to push me down in the halls? They suddenly find me very fascinating, and I have the distinct pleasure of telling every last one of them to FUCK OFF!"

Yes, there is a god, and She does answer prayer.

I have not gone to any other class reunions. Don't need to. Coming home from that one gave me the "closure" that we Californians talk about. Once I had this closure, I was able to forge ahead with my life.

Right after high school and while I was going to college, I held down two jobs—one selling clothes at a chain store called C.R. Anthony's, the other job doing windows at one of the other Anthony's stores. Fancy or stylish C.R. Anthony's wasn't, but it was a job; and I jumped at it when I had gotten myself fired from Wendy's Old Fashioned Hamburgers, a firing I richly deserved. (This is why I'll sometimes say that retail is a career for those who can't make it in fast food.)

I took the job at Anthony's because it was the first offer I got. Anthony's was a place where the red states shopped. It carried a good stock of Levi jeans, Haggar double-knit slacks, Munsingwear shirts (when they were still uncool), and Hush Puppies shoes (when they were still seen as geek shoes). Anthony's was a small chain of blue-collar-type stores in the Oklahoma/Kansas area, and the first one I worked for was on Meridian and NW Fiftieth. My new boss was a man named Jack. Looking back, I'm sure Jack was a closet case. There were clues, which I'll get to in a moment.

ACT ONE:

Jack's wife worked as the bookkeeper, his son worked as a salesman, his sister Alpha Mae was also a salesperson. (She definitely was not a sales*lady*.) There were several other family members sprinkled around the place, and two or three non-family employees, of which I was one. If you weren't related, you were screwed work-wise.

Alpha Mae was a sawed-off, roly-poly barracuda with wavy gray hair and cat-eye glasses, who wore her lipstick right in the center of her lips. She was so bold in her stealing of sales that she would snatch sales right out of my hands and ring them up on her number. When I complained to Jack about this regular occurrence, he just said such a sweet thing as Alpha Mae would never do anything like THAT—she was a good Christian woman!

Speaking of good Christians, I really believe Jack was a Lesbiterian. He had this theory that he wanted "something for everyone" in the store, as he would say. This was a small store that carried women's, men's, and children's clothes; shoes; and some domestics such as linens and fabric. So there wasn't a lot of room for anything.

But in regards to "something for everyone" (and Jack's Lesbiterianism), one day Alpha Mae was in the back room checking in an order that Jack had made for the lingerie department. We all heard a shriek from the back room, and I just assumed that she saw a mouse. But we all ran back to see what was up (it was a slow sales day).

Alpha Mae was standing there, pale and shaking, gingerly holding a tiny clothes hanger between her index finger and thumb like it was some sort of venomous snake. She was staring at it, eyes wide, horror-stricken.

Hanging from the tiny hanger was a pair of shiny, leopard-print, split-crotch panties. The opening at the crotch was trimmed with black marabou and tied together with little black satin ribbon bows. In the box were several different styles and colors of the same thing. Never had I seen anything like it (I'm *SURE* Alpha Mae hadn't either), but I got the drift of what type of customer this garment was for—and she DIDN'T shop at Anthony's!

"Why, I'm sure there's been a horrible mistake!" gasped Alpha Mae. "My brother would *never* order something like this!"

In the meantime the rest of us non-family members were amusing ourselves by unpacking and examining these very unusual goods, while speculating under our breaths as to which ones Jack was going to take home for himself to wear. His wife was such a fat-ass (and No-Fun-At-All), that she would never fit, let alone *wear,* any of these.

Holding up the packing slip (heh), which had the style numbers and little line drawings of each item ordered, I said, "No, Alpha Mae. There's no mistake. Here's Jack's signature." And indeed, there it was.

They were sent back. Poor Jack never even got to see them. Pity.

Jack introduced me to the world of window display.

One evening, when it was really slow, he told me to make a new display in the windows. Now I had never done that sort of thing but figured that, hell, I had good taste, I could figure it out.

At the time I was in my minimalist period and did this really graphic, striking arrangement. It was fun, and I got some compliments on it.

The next day I came in and found that Jack had tarted up the display with a profusion of plastic flowers. He had a real fondness for them *(closet case—see?),* and they were strewn liberally everywhere in the store. There were plastic flowers and foliage for all seasons, all of them faded and dusty from years of overuse.

I stormed into the window and tossed out all of the offending shrubbery, and whenever I did windows from then on, it was a back-and-forth, flowers in-flowers out thing. But I was hooked on display.

Eventually I prevailed on the manager of the Anthony's at Twenty-third and Meridian to let me do their displays on my days off—this was my second job. This proved to be a better situation creatively, as the manager had NO interest in plastic flowers (he was hopelessly straight) and just wanted me to take care of the windows so he didn't have to.

ACT ONE:

Thus began my career in window display.

It was in that store that I made most of my design mistakes and embarrassments, so I don't have to do them now. When I look back at some of the things I did in those windows, I blush at the amateur excess. There was the time I suspended everything upside down from the ceiling with fishing line—the entire display, just turned upside down. Other times I'd get creative with spray paint, lacquering the old mannequins with gloss black or silver, trying to make then look up-to-date. Anything I could do that was inexpensive and eye-catching I tried. I had varying degrees of success.

When I look at other things I did on that job—like arranging with different stores in the shopping center to borrow furniture, props, and such—I see the inklings of my eventual self-employment. But I'm getting ahead of myself.

My choice of degree—fashion merchandising—was a real embarrassment to Mom. This was what was referred to in the rectangular states as an "MRS degree." In other words, a girl studied fashion merchandising while she was looking around the college for a husband. She would study until she got married. I was the first male graduate from the fashion merchandising program at my college.

Between my junior and senior year, I made the jump from Anthony's to a department store called Dillard's, the one in Shepherd Mall, which had just undergone a really glam makeover. (Dillard's new look was sooooo glamorous, and this store had really fabulous mannequins—Greneker mannequins that looked so lifelike and glamorous). I wanted to work in department store display very badly, and I heard that there was an opening. Also I liked the idea of having only one job instead of two.

So in my off time that summer, I stationed myself in front of the store manager's office every day for two weeks, even though he had told me the first day I showed up that there were no openings in display. At the end of those two weeks, he called me into his office and shouted in frustration, "THE ONLY OPENING I HAVE IN THE ENTIRE STORE IS DEPARTMENT MANAGER FOR THE LAMPS AND PICTURES DEPARTMENT!"

"I'll take it! I can start in two weeks," I replied. Thus started my career in big department store retail, if not display. It was a foot in the door.

The day I started, I discovered that the store had gotten a new manager, Mr. Probst. I introduced myself to him, explained to him that his predecessor had just hired me, and told him of my interest in moving over to the display department. He was very encouraging and noncommittal.

Two months later the display guy (David, who thought I was cute), had emergency knee surgery, just in time for Christmas trim to go up. Since he had pissed off everyone in the store with his queeny tantrums and hissy fits (this was in the days before the phrase "high maintenance"), David was in trouble. Nobody wanted to help him out. Mr. Probst remembered my interest in doing display, and as they say, "he went out a youngster and came back a star."

This was my first experience in Christmas trim. Christmas is the season in retail that starts in August and goes until December. In my day, preparation backstage began then and continued until the evening of Thanksgiving, when a full night of working made everything magically appear.

To make this happen, there were days of monotony taken up with wrapping fake gift boxes, trimming and lighting trees and wreaths, painting props the required red and green, pulling the Santa out of the box and repairing his moth-eaten beard—the list was endless.

A few weeks before graduation, I announced that on May 6 I would go out in search of an apartment. My aim all through college had been to get out from under Mom's prying eyes and absolute dictates, and live life my own way. It was really getting in the way of being gay and stylish and twenty-two.

ACT ONE:

I had come out earlier that year. I lost my virginity on Valentine's Day, to be exact (I didn't *plan* it that way; it just happened that way), and he gave me a two-pound box of Godiva chocolates as well. So to this day, when I see those gold boxes, I get all nostalgic. I could go into the whole coming-out story, but it wasn't remarkable really—others have told it better. Admittedly it wasn't as easy to be gay in Oklahoma City as it might be in, say, New York. However, I was always thought of as (and called) a big fag, so the only change was that I was actually doing something to earn the title.

"How much do you expect to pay for an apartment!?" Mom demanded sarcastically when I broke the news about moving out. One of her revenue streams (me) was in danger of drying up.

"One hundred dollars a month," I replied.

"You'll never find anything for that!" she screeched. "You stupid kid, you think you know everything! You can't make it on what you've got coming in! You should have gotten a degree in something you could use, like accounting. But NO! You got that degree in, er, whatever you got it in!"

"Fashion merchandising!" I shouted. "I'm going to write it down for you so I don't have to answer this question again. The only time you actually *could* remember it was when you tried to talk me into getting a *doctorate* in it, so I could still stay at home and pay rent!"

"You're so bull-headed; you just want to do what you damn well please!"

"I had to pay for my own college," I said back evenly. "You yourself have always preached that the one who pays has the say. So since I was paying for it *myself*, I felt that it was MY decision!"

(This ambivalence about my college education showed itself graduation night. I was the first of Miss Ann's children to graduate, and summa cum laude at that. So where was I taken afterward as a celebration? Taco Bell. Yes, *Taco Bell*. I was bitterly disappointed but knew not to complain about it. It never occurred to mom that this wasn't quite the venue for this kind of celebration.)

The sticking point in my choice of degree was that I wasn't making all that much money . . . yet. Mom was keeping track of what came into my bank account (what a surprise)—it was at the bank where she worked. Something she continued to do the entire time I had my account there. She grew up in a day when a college degree automatically got someone a big salary and a company car. But Reagan was running for president; she didn't see that the times were changing.

"I'll find something, just you watch!" I insisted after listening to this diatribe about how inept I was.

"Well, let me warn you, young man, once you're out, YOU'RE OUT! You're never coming back! Do you hear? NEVER!" she shouted. It was supposed to be a threat that would scare the bejesus out of me and make me think again about moving out.

It didn't. That's exactly what I had in mind—never coming back.

I should introduce you to my mother, because she is one of the towering presences and influences in my life. Ann King (or "Miss Ann" as I refer to her and her voice in my head) was born during the Great Depression in Salina, Kansas. (*And never let us forget it.*) She was one of six kids of a cold mother and diffident father. Grandpa had a good job as a fireman, but with six children, well, finances were tight. They took in boarders for most of Mom's childhood. To hear her tell it, life was harsh.

"Your grandmother would punish all of us if one of us did something wrong," I remember her saying. "That tree stump in her backyard? She killed that tree, stripping branches off to beat us kids with! We'd all have to line up by age, and she'd start with the oldest. Since I was next to the youngest, she'd have gotten good and wound up, and we got it worse. I was always walking around with welts across the back of my legs."

ACT ONE:

(Mom prided herself on *not* doing that with us three kids.)

Early in her life, Miss Ann was expected to get a job and contribute to the family finances as well as pay for her schoolbooks and clothes. She worked at the dime store downtown in Salina. Like others of her generation, the Depression marked her for life.

After she graduated from high school, Miss Ann went to work for the Bank of America as a teller. Her job carried quite a bit of responsibility; she was to walk to the businesses of the bank's customers and bring back their deposits. Knowing that she would be carrying a lot of money and, therefore, be a target, a family friend in the police department trained her how to use a hatpin. It seems that carrying a concealed gun was illegal then, but packing a hatpin wasn't. Miss Ann learned how to rip a guy's arm veins open with one stab of the hatpin. Thankfully she never used it, but I remember when I was growing up, there was always a hatpin in any of Mom's handbags.

In Salina, Kansas, in the late forties, no respectable young woman had her own apartment, so she lived at home; she was expected to leave home only when she married. Even though Miss Ann was over eighteen and earning a living, the folks still told her what she could and couldn't do, but she now got to pay (rent) for the privilege. That's what she had in mind for me too, actually.

What Mom had really wanted to do was to go to college and be a teacher. I joke even now that there is a God, because She inflicted Miss Ann on only three children, not three generations of them.

"Your Aunt Helen got to go to college, and she just screwed around for a semester, so the folks wouldn't let anyone else go. She just screwed it up for everyone else," Mom used to complain. "The same with piano lessons—Alvera got them and didn't practice, so the folks sold the piano and nobody else got to try."

So even though Mom was happy that I had graduated from college, there was always the mixed message, which I can hear her say in my head to this day:

"You think you're so goddamn smart just because you have a college education!"

Mom always had an inferiority complex about not having gone to college, so I would hear that particular outburst whenever she felt like she'd lost the upper hand. That's what would prompt outbursts like the one when I announced my intention to get my own apartment. I was used to it. It irked me, but I was used to it.

Bright and early on May 6, I went to the Apartment-Lo-K-Tors on May Avenue to find my dream place. I sat across the desk from one of the automaton agents there. After taking all my information, she droned, "Well now, just what kind of place are you looking for?"

"I want something very small on the northwest side of town and close to my work—I work at Shepherd Mall."

"And how much do you want to pay?"

"One hundred dollars a month."

Much to my surprise, this elicited a spell of mirth and chuckles from the automaton agent that made her look positively lifelike! She thought it quite funny that I was wanting this combination of circumstances, and proceeded to tell all the other agents in the office so they, too, could enjoy the joke.

One of them called out, "Hey, honey, I have just the place!"

Silence.

"Could I see it?" I asked.

ACT ONE:

"Sure, hon, when do ya wanna go look?" my new friend asked as she walked over and offered her hand.

She looked like Central Casting had sent her to the wrong audition—they wrote "automaton" on the call sheet, and she read "animation": red-dyed hair up in a French twist; powder-blue, double-knit, bulletproof polyester pantsuit; white patent leather sandals; and Mercurochrome-orange fingernails and matching lipstick, from which dangled a Tareyton, the ash dangerously long.

"The name's Patty! You want ta see the place soon, hon?"

"Right now if I could . . ."

We shook hands, and I could hear the ka-ching sound of a commission earned.

Patty made a phone call and came back with a piece of paper, which was pink and scented with Tabu by Coty. On it was written: 6100 North Villa, manager named Queue.

"You'll ask for the manager; her name is Queue, pronounced like the pool cue," Patty said. "It's REAL small, I'm told, but in a good neighborhood. The old lady who owns the place is a real caution I hear, but I think you'll get on fine."

Off I went to find my new home, which was close by. As I parked on the street, I looked around. This *was* a nice neighborhood! The place was a collection of small duplexes, not an apartment house as I was expecting. After finding the office and introducing myself to Queue (an odd name for an odd woman, who looked and acted like Frances Farmer after the electroshock), we went to see the apartment.

The apartment itself was actually in my landlady's backyard. Mrs. Freeman had inherited the property, which was a farm many years ago. She was very shrewd with her assets and built this series of duplexes as income property long before the area had been built up, and over time, she sold off the rest of the land. After the golf course went in, Mrs. Freeman had decided that with the fence they put up blocking the view, it was a shame to waste such a large parcel of backyard and had a mini-duplex built. (The operative word being "mini.") There were two units here—a one-bedroom and a studio. I would be looking at the studio.

Queue unlocked the door and showed me in. This was indeed the smallest living space I had ever seen. The width of the living room (which was paneled in fake walnut wood grain) was the length of a twin bed (which fit in the "far" end of the room), and the length of this room was about nine feet. That was the big room. The closet was in the kitchen along with the air conditioner. The only way to tell the difference was that the kitchen had the window and the stove. Heat was provided by one small space heater they would bring in when the season changed.

I could put my hand flat on the ceiling, and I'm only five foot six.

However, what sold me about the place (aside from price) was the bathroom window. It was one of those aluminum sample windows you see at the hardware store, the samples you order to measure from. It measured about ten inches wide by eighteen inches high, with an itty-bitty window screen, a sash that pulled up and down, complete with a tiny lock, just like the grown-up windows had!

After I moved in, I made a blind for it using just a placemat I bought at Pier One Imports.

The place came "furnished," a term that almost always means "We had these shitty things we just didn't feel energetic enough to send to Goodwill." I immediately asked Queue if she could have them removed, as I had my own things. Or soon would have.

"It's one hundred dollars a month, with a fifty-dollar security deposit," Queue said. "If you get the deposit to me today, you can take possession tomorrow."

"Done!"

I had some very definite ideas on what I would do after moving out on my own. I decided not to have a telephone for at least a few months. First of all,

Mom would have to sign for it (I had no credit history to speak of), and she would never let me forget it by bringing it up at every available opportunity. She would give you the shirt off her back but would let you know exactly how much it cost, down to the penny. It was never worth the price.

Being without a phone would afford me a blissful respite. Not having a phone meant that I could only be reached at work and only then by being paged. Paging me at work would be inconvenient, and she didn't like inconvenience *at all*; therefore I would hear from her only when it was really urgent. It also headed off any unannounced visits, as I hinted broadly that if she dropped by my new place unannounced she might see something she didn't want to. I never had to suggest what that might be; her imagination did all the work.

It took a couple of trips in Mom's big white Thunderbird, which could carry more than my little red Celica (actually it was so big it could probably carry my little red Celica) to get my things into my new apartment. Another three trips were required for my wardrobe, most of which I felt I needed to smuggle in at night. I didn't want this new landlady to think I was rich or something—just the impression she might get if she saw the piles of clothes, the labels on the shoe boxes (this was when Pierre Cardin was still a "name," and there were a couple pairs of Bally shoes as well), or the full-length, black fur coat I had bought during my visit to New York a few months earlier.

This visit to New York, my first, gave me a glimpse of what Big City Life could be. It was during a work-study trip made through my college—I had gotten a scholarship for it from C.R. Anthony's; they thought they were investing in a future, loyal employee. But it strengthened my desire to be a grown-up and actually *go to* a big city, leaving them far behind.

In high school and college, I had surreptitiously started buying a few necessities to prepare for my first place—an antique chair, a brass floor lamp, a silver caviar server, good art—and Kathy helped as well by buying me a stereo, towels, dishes, and an iron.

Kathy is the sister I love and adore. We are six days shy of being a year apart—her birthday is February 12, mine is February 18. (Laurie's is February

16; it was explained to us that Dad's birthday was May 19. So we know what *he* got for his birthday.) Since Kathy and I were so close in age, we did all of the important development stuff together—walking, reading, coming out—all of the important stuff.

Since Kathy worked in the credit office at Dillard's processing credit applications (another thing we did together—working for Dillard's), she used her "influence" with the furniture department salesmen to help me get a bed for my new place, CHEAP. Actually she told all the salesmen that until I had a good bed "FOR CHEAP AND I MEAN CHEAP!" there would be no credit applications processed. No applications processed, no sales of furniture. No sales, no commissions. It didn't take long; they delivered a new twin mattress and box spring to my new home three days later.

It didn't take long to unpack and get things situated, as I worked in display and was used to "floofing" things up on the quick. Happily, Queue had gotten rid of the yellowed eyelet curtains along with the other "furnishings," so I installed some snappy, tortoiseshell, split-bamboo blinds from Pier One.

It was only after they were up that I discovered that they were alarmingly sheer and provided next to no privacy.

As I was reveling in my new independence and decorating prowess, I heard a knock on the door. It was Mrs. Freeman, I was sure of it. I could see her right through the alarmingly sheer new blinds that covered the door window.

Patty was right. First, the visuals: Mrs. Freeman was (I later learned) eighty-eight years old, about five foot three with that kind of dumpling figure some old ladies get—you know, barrel-shaped body with bird wings and legs. She had gray hair with a little black still in it; black-rimmed, pointy cats-eye glasses (REAL thick), and wore a sort of shapeless, non-descript blouse and pants. Mrs. Freeman (and I always called her that—she had no first name that I know of) wore her bright-red rouge in dots in the centers of her cheeks. The lipstick was similarly applied in the center of her lips, and I got the impression that as a young girl she had seen that particular "look" on

ACT ONE:

Mae Murray in *The Merry Widow*, thought it terribly chic, and never felt the need to change it.

Thinking back, she reminds me of Ruth Gordon's character in the film *Harold and Maude*. Mrs. Freeman was cheerful and full of life, what Southerners would call "feisty." She may have been old, but she *wasn't* "old"—there was a sparkle in her eye and a crispness to her movements that told me she was a force to reckon with. I liked her immediately.

"Hello, young man! I'm Mrs. Freeman," she croaked with a voice somewhat like a parrot that'd had too much whiskey and cigarettes. "So you're the young man that Queue was telling me about. May I come in?"

I invited her in, whereupon she started an inspection of what I had done to the place, commenting favorably on the furnishings (what few there were of them) and how I had it decorated so "cute," and it was so clean and how that was so unusual for a young bachelor man. She was going to have to have her bridge club out here—they wouldn't believe it when she told them!

She didn't hear many of my comments; as I observed and later confirmed, she was deaf as a post. That evening I heard a television playing at full volume and went to investigate; it was coming from her living room. This was very comforting to me, as I realized that I wouldn't hear many complaints from her about noise or comings and goings during the wee hours.

It was the first time in my life that I didn't have to do the "*dances with land mines*," as I had while going to college and living with Mom. Life danced happily along that summer and to a disco beat at that.

It was the summer of Donna Summer singing "Bad Girls," Debbie Harry singing "Call Me," Giorgio Armani starring in *American Gigolo*, The B52s' immortal "Planet Claire," the Village People's "In The Navy," and Hawaiian shirts worn with mirrored aviator sunglasses and tight Levi 501s with the bottom button undone (to show that you were available). My favorite tape, which I played in my car at full volume, was the disco version of *Evita*. I could stay out as late as I wanted and not have to worry about the grilling I would get if I came in late (or not at all).

Being young, thin, and cute, I engaged in lots of fashion excesses in my early twenties so I don't have to embarrass myself now. Feathered hair. Of course. Jelly sandals with "amusing" socks. Had 'em. Italian fishermen's sandals. Uh-huh. Clear plastic jeans from Fiorucci—the crotch fogged up—did it *once*. White, padded-shoulder "new wave" shirt. Oh yeah. Electric-blue painter's pants (not white—too common). Yes, sir. Worn with the double-wrap belts, either the tan leather from Neiman-Marcus or the red nylon-webbing one from Bloomies, and my mustard-gold Nino Cerruti shirt. Skinny ties—*had* to have 'em to wear with the turquoise sharkskin suit with skinny lapels and peg-leg cuffed trousers, and the black shirt! Of course! Burgundy hair. Yeah. Pointy black cap-toe oxfords to go with the blue Eisenhower jacket. Got 'em. Mustard-gold corduroy "new wave" jumpsuit—just like Devo!—with the asymmetrical opening and funnel collar, belted with the asymmetrical, black leather belt. Fab! Body wave for my hair that ended up looking like pubic hair. OH NO! The worst part of having this bad hair was that it didn't go with anything in my wardrobe!

The debacle of the body wave did have its compensations though. My hairdresser Jenny, who really did good haircuts, was mortified! The body wave went horribly wrong; not to put too fine a point on it, but can we say "Brillo"? To make up for this, she got me a lifetime membership card to the new really woo-woo disco/club in OKC called Michael's Plum—a knockoff of Maxwell's Plum in New York, which I had seen earlier that year. Since "the Plum" was ruinously expensive to join, this was adequate compensation for a few weeks of bad hair. It paid many dividends: they had a happy hour that served such good hors d'oeuvres that for the price of a bottle of Perrier (or a glass of club soda if I was really economizing), I could eat dinner. Needless to say, as a boy-on-a-budget, I was a regular, and the above-mentioned wardrobe came in really handy.

ACT ONE:

My shoulders started feeling funny, so I went to the doctor to have them checked out, only to learn that this was what they were supposed to feel like when they were relaxed.

Rumor was going around, that there was a new Dillard's store in the planning stages, so I decided to stay on at Dillard's after graduation (*despite the bitter complaints from Mom about the pay*), until the new store was open to see where I would end up. Then I would decide what my next move would be. If I were to go anywhere with Dillard's, it would be then or never.

During my first summer of freedom, I was called over to the Dillard's in Midwest City, as they were looking for a new display manager. I interviewed with the store manager, who I'll call Bill. He was a closeted gay guy, married, and from the South, with the accent (combined with a queeny voice) that deducts twenty points from the apparent IQ.

The long and short of it was that he offered me the job but at the same rate of pay I was making already as a trimmer. I would either have to move across town (not an option as I loved my little apartment) or lose money to work there because of the cost of the commute. I turned him down, which irked him immensely. (My being openly gay, as well as my spiffy fashion sense, irked him as well, I'm sure.)

When I told him a few days later over the phone that I had decided against taking his kind offer, he asked me why.

"I like where I'm living right now and don't want to break the lease. Working for you would mean incurring commuting costs that I can't afford in light of the salary offered," I said as professionally as possible. What I wanted to say was that I felt I could do better by staying put.

"I had to move for MY career!" he retorted sharply and slightly sanctimoniously in that whiny, queeny Southern accent.

"That was your choice. I choose to stay put."

"I'll remember this! Just you wait!" he shouted into the phone before he slammed down the receiver.

"Oooooooh! I'm scared," was my snappy retort, said to the dial tone.

To most of the folks at Dillard's, I was known as "Tim Kane." When I was being paged, they would hear over the loudspeaker, "Tim Kane, Tim Kane, call the operator please . . . Tim Kane."

When I worked in the lamp department before I transferred to display, I would have to call the operator for a customer carryout. One day I decided to go down on my break and introduce myself to the ladies on the switchboard, to meet them in person. Finding them itself was a challenge as the building was old, and nobody really knew where the PBX room was; most likely no one had ever been there. I found it in the bowels of the building next to the boilers.

The two operators, Anna and Louise, had been working in the basement PBX room for so long that they sounded alike—one only knew who it was on the line by asking, which I always did. There they sat at this big old switchboard, which was bristling with plugs and wires, these two old ladies with big antique headsets on their heads, who looked like they had accidentally embraced punk. Instead of gray hair, one of the gals had apricot and one had light blue. Years of fluorescent light had bleached their skins to a blue-white that would be the envy of any Goth kid. This made their makeup resemble Kabuki, because they were both so very nearsighted they couldn't get a good look at themselves in the morning.

When they saw an actual person in their doorway, Anna and Louise were at first surprised and a little confused, assuming some sort of emergency. I explained, after introducing myself, that I just wanted to thank them for their help and to meet the people behind the voices. Introductions and names were exchanged.

ACT ONE:

"Well, Tim! It's been a pleasure meeting you! Thank you for coming to see us!" Anna drawled. (She was the one with the apricot-colored hair.)

"It's Ken. Ken King."

"Of course! Tim Kane. A very *nice* name!" chimed Louise of the blue hair, smiling.

Hard-of-hearing telephone operators . . .

So from then on I became Tim Kane. I even had it put on my badge.

After my unfortunate and unwise first "boyfriend" (and boss—what a mistake!) David came Brock, a friend of David's, who became my first "steady boyfriend" a few weeks before I graduated. He was the first guy I stayed the night with.

Brock was from an old OKC family (the phrase "genteel poverty" was something I learned later) that put on airs about what a good family they were. They still had the family home (a reduced-calorie version of Tara in an increasingly unfashionable neighborhood), but they didn't have a pot to pee in. Brock's mother always looked at me sort of sideways, the way she might size up a parvenu. She also never invited me into the house. Silly lady, I didn't want to travel with her social set; I just wanted to boff her son and steal his apartment.

Brock had a really cool apartment. It was in this gloomy old pile of a building on North Hudson at Twenty-fourth called the Wendemere, which was built in 1929 when this was a fashionable area. The apartment itself was two stories, and *very Sunset Boulevard*, with the wood floors, stucco arches, cathedral ceilings, and the Spanish wrought-iron railings up the stairway and across the balcony. There was even an arch cut into the wall of the master bedroom that looked down onto the living room.

One could imagine doing the "ready for my close-up, Mr. DeMille" routine on the stairway just for fun.

Brock did the "Rhett Butler" thing one evening, carrying me up those stairs with me (*in my imagination*) pounding his manly chest with my tiny fists, just like Scarlet. It was working really well until he dropped me on the edge of his platform bed, bruising the small of my back and really killing the mood. We had a good, long laugh over this, and I think of it and chuckle even now.

Brock paid only two hundred dollars a month for this place—a steal even then for a two-bedroom apartment and such a cool one at that. He wanted me to move in with him right after we met ("Grow old with me!" he pleaded.), but good sense told me to hang onto my place. Brock was history after three months.

I had finally allowed myself to believe that we might indeed become a couple, and so "the talk" came as a big surprise to me. It was on a Saturday afternoon. I had gotten to his place directly from a modeling gig—I did a little modeling in and after college—and he started with that worn-out phrase, "We need to talk . . . " Looking back I don't remember any reason he gave for splitting, so he probably was just bored. But that didn't matter; I felt like a house had fallen on me.

At the end of the talk, Brock said he wanted to "go back to being friends," at which point I had to remind him that we'd gone to bed on the first date, something I don't do with friends.

Remember that, as a gay teen in OKC, this had never happened to me in high school. I got dumped for the first time right then at age twenty-two. The dating skills and experiences (including being dumped) that my straight classmates had in high school, I missed out on.

So I handled this the same way I learned, growing up with Miss Ann, to deal with showing strong emotions to others—in short, *NOT TO*. After one final kiss, I walked out of his house with head held high; I'd be damned if I'd let him know how devastated I was.

I got in my car, drove the few blocks back to my place, threw myself down on my bed, and had a good cry. Then, as now, I prefer to do my crying in private, offstage—if for no other reason than I don't want someone who has just hurt me to see that they *have* hurt me, nor get any satisfaction from it. In my mind it's like casting pearls before swine.

There's a lesson from this brief liaison that serves me to this day: *If someone uses the word "love" in the first three months, they most likely won't be around in six.*

I discovered later, that, as a send-off, Brock *did* give me something to remember him by– hepatitis.

My job at Dillard's was up and down. After graduating, I was having fun working in display (up) for David, my boss who thought I was cute and whom I made the big mistake of sleeping with (down). The store manager, Mr. Probst (a real doll, so definitely up), liked me a lot as he realized I worked hard (up), but the pay sucked (down). I stayed there because I really enjoyed display (up), we had fabulous mannequins to work with (up), and I figured that if I hung around a little longer, opportunity would knock (up, up, and away!).

So imagine my delight when Mr. Probst was chosen to go to the new Dillard's store at Quail Springs as the manager. He chose me over David to go over for display.

"It was easy," Mr. Probst said about the choice. "David has the better suntan. I know what that means."

And then he gave me a whopping raise. That was my favorite part of the program.

"Oh, by the way, I've hired another guy as well," he continued casually. "He's from California and has experience working in display at Macy's there. You should see his portfolio! You'll like him. Don't worry, though, you'll be equals; I promise. I didn't hire him as your boss."

And that's how Mark and I met.

Mark and I met on September 11, 1980. I remember the date because it is the day my niece was born as well as being the first day of my stint working at Dillard's Quail Springs. This was the first day of the three-week hazing period known in retail as a store opening.

Ask anyone working in retail and they will tell you that the store opening is absolute hell. For the display people, though, it is also an exercise in do-it-do-it-again. At the outset, before the merchandise is in, even before the entire construction is done, we only have blueprints and plans to work from. With incomplete information we make decisions and execute things according to those plans. Then, when the construction is finished, the buyers come in, decide that the entire layout is wrong, and everything needs to be ripped out, moved, and redone. This process can repeat itself three or four times. My experience at this particular opening was that as late as the night before (10:00 p.m. to be exact), another move was initiated.

Back to Mark.

Mark had dark hair and was about my height (short), but he weighed only 105 pounds dripping wet. Mark was Jewish and from a prominent political family in Boston—his father was a judge, rather starchy and cold. Mark's mother, deceased, was the love of his life. Sophie was one of those really fun, stylish, juicy Jewish mothers with good clothes, jewels, and cars. She could stand up to anyone, except Mark's father. One of Mark's brothers was a lawyer, a partner in the family law firm. The other had studied anthropology and worked in a museum.

ACT ONE:

Mark and his partner, Victor, had moved here from Austin, Texas—it seemed Victor was a "troubleshooter" for Rollins Protective Services. They apparently sent Victor all over to whip troubled outlets into shape. (Or that was Mark's story, and he stuck with it.)

During the three weeks it took to prepare for the opening, I was sick with the hepatitis. So not only did I have to deal with the hurt and rejection of being dumped for the first time, I had to deal with this sickness—right when I was on the verge of making a good career move. I discovered I had it the week before Mr. Probst hired me to go to the new store, when I turned bright yellow and was barely keeping up with everyone by sheer determination alone.

I resorted to using "gay camouflage"—raiding the Germaine Monteil counter for a good foundation and a good frosted eye makeup, and hiding my eyes behind really outrageous glasses with tinted lenses. That was one advantage of being cute and faggy and in display—these things were expected of me! The makeup and tinted glasses helped conceal the jaundice, but they got lots of comments from Mark. The comments were of the "gays-in-big-cities-don't-dress-like-that" variety. (He was too polite to say that it all looked too faggy.)

There were several executives from the Fort Worth offices there to help open the store, one of whom was the Big Guy for display. He and Mark got real cozy real quick, as Mark was, I soon found out, a real operator politically, no doubt learned from his politico family. Soon I was shunted aside and became the gofer. It was explained to me that, since I knew OKC and where to get whatever was needed (which was indeed true), it was a better use of my time. I went along with this—what choice did I have? Besides, I was painfully inexperienced. I had a certain talent and drive but no training to speak of, college degree notwithstanding.

In the off-hours, when I wasn't at home trying to store up energy for another go (because of the hepatitis), Mark and Vic and I got to know each other, generally over dinner. Or more accurately I got to know Mark. Victor was usually present, but the vibe he gave off was that he only tolerated me but wished I'd just go away.

During dinners at Mark's place, I got a fuller picture of his life.

Mark was one of those queens who entertains lavishly, and he would prepare three times the food we could possibly eat, all served up on really good dishes—good presentation being the hallmark of the experienced display queen. And if we didn't eat all of it, he turned into the typical Jewish mother. (You know, "EAT! EAT!") I started calling him Mother Mark.

Victor didn't cook. He just ate. And didn't talk much. I assumed he was one of those "men of few words" or just shy. And after dinner he would disappear into their "study" to play "Pong" or watch porn on their Betamax. That was when he wasn't showing me his stun guns, handcuffs, and other boy toys, while sitting *way* too close to me, creeping me out.

They lived in one of the many apartment complexes on North May, this one being a gray, rough-diagonal-cedar-sided apartment block with no architectural distinction, built in the late '70s. Inside was just as bland with the usual "landlord-cream" paint.

But the furnishings!

Mark had really good things and *lots* of them. There was good silver hollowware, a healthy collection of Lalique vases and sculptures, some really good art (names I recognized from my "art appreciation" class in college), and some nice antique pieces of furniture and sculpture (my favorite was an exquisite ancient Egyptian turquoise faience sculpture of Nefertiti that was three inches high, housed in a little glass obelisk). The living room especially tended to be a bit overheated from a decorating standpoint, like those Parisian apartments one sees in *Architectural Digest* with pictures in gilded frames hanging wall-to-wall and ceiling-to-floor. Minimal it was not. I was recovering from my minimal phase in college, and this was an education in piling on the excess—something I love to do to this day.

During our conversations I learned that Mark had met Vic in a bathhouse in Boston. He joked that the first thing he saw of Victor was the top of his head—apparently Victor had an inordinate fondness for large dicks. (Ava

Gardner used to say about Frank Sinatra that there was five pounds of Frank and a hundred pounds of dick. I think this was a similar situation.)

Mark and Vic became an item and eventually decided that they couldn't live freely and openly in Boston because of Mark's family and the political connections. Mark told me later that it was because he felt looked down upon by friends of the family for being gay. I believe that the whispers behind his back were not so much because Mark was gay but because Victor was NOCD—"not our class, darling." Vic was white trash, really, and Mark had mated beneath him.

There was another man in Mark's life before Vic. His name, as I remember, was Preston. I had asked him about a particularly beautiful Russian lacquer box on his coffee table, which, it turned out, was a gift from Preston. That started the conversation.

Preston and Mark grew up together, went to prep school together, studied art together, and were members of the same country club. Preston worked as a curator in an art museum, if memory serves. In short, they were of the same class and had lots in common. (Preston was also very good-looking. I saw a photo of him.) Socially it would have been a good match.

"There was never anything sexual between us and not because he didn't want it," Mark said one day.

"Preston is in love with me and doesn't understand that I'm with Victor now. He has said many times that he'd like to get together, and I'd never want for anything. He'd move me back to Boston, get me a job in the museum if I wanted, but it just wouldn't work," he sighed.

"Has Victor ever given you anything like this?" I asked.

"Are you kidding!?" Mark exclaimed. "Vic wouldn't know a lacquer box from a cereal box. The only gifts he gets me are electronics!"

I thought it strange that Mark would choose a guy like Vic over a classy, rich guy who shared his tastes, but *what did I know?* From recent experience I couldn't keep a relationship together, so perhaps Mark knew better than me.

Anyway they were in Boston. Victor knew a guy who lived in San Francisco named David Burlew and finally convinced Mark to move there. When they landed in San Francisco, they lived in the building that David managed on Sutter Street in the Tenderloin. Mark worked at a place called Community Rentals in The Castro, which was the place everyone went to find an apartment. Since Victor worked for Rollins, he was able to transfer to San Francisco, so the story goes.

After a time (a short time and the beginning of a pattern, it seems), Victor decided that they would move to San Rafael up in Marin County. Why, I can't remember, but Mark did as Vic said. This is where Mark started working for Macy's, at the store in downtown San Rafael. He used to regale me with stories of working there with his assistant, Crystal. Apparently he was the display manager, but it wasn't made real clear.

There were tales of Mark and Vic in San Rafael, but I can only remember sketchy details, such as they lived down by the canal and had an afghan hound. I'm unclear about how long they lived there, but that's irrelevant. Soon they up and moved to Austin, Texas.

Austin, Texas!?

Yes, the Austin branch of Rollins Protective Services was in need of Victor's expertise. As I said earlier, Mark styled him as this troubleshooter who went into troubled Rollins branches and whipped things into shape.

I was more astonished that Mark would give up a promising position at Macy's (in the Bay Area at THAT!) to follow Vic. To me, then as well as now, the idea of sacrificing a career for a man was something foreign and a bit repugnant. I may be a big queen, but I still have the testosterone. (It's a common misconception, especially in the rectangular states, about us gay boys, that we don't have the testosterone and really just want to be girls.)

ACT ONE:

So off Mark and Vic went to Austin. Mark was a bit vague as to what he did work-wise there. But then it really wasn't important, because soon they—again!—up and moved to Oklahoma City, as Rollins needed Vic's help here. And here he was.

While Mark was out scouting for work, he saw the sign Dillard's put out in front of the new store saying they were taking applications. And that's how our paths crossed. It seemed a strange path, one I didn't understand in the least, but it crossed mine and eventually changed my life.

Work went on with the opening of the store, one day blurring into another.

I kept my head down and my eyes open. This store opening was a good opportunity career-wise, and I didn't want to spoil it. Besides, I knew that one day I would be free of this situation, so I decided to learn as much as possible from these people (Mark and Big Guy) while I was there. It was a means to an end.

WELL.

Speaking of learning, I got a big lesson one evening a couple of weeks into the opening. We had just finished early for the day (six thirty), and Mark and I were standing out in the parking lot by my car. The sunset was a really beautiful dark blue, and it was balmy for early October.

Mark didn't have a car; Victor got the car, a douched-out, old faded-blue Ford Torino with ratty black vinyl upholstery, because he made more money. I picked Mark up for work and drove him home every day. For that I demanded coffee and pastry in the morning when I picked him up. I usually had to wait (hence the demand for coffee and pastry), as he never seemed to be able to get ready at the appointed time. He was usually just dressing when I arrived. Mark wore—actually seemed to bathe in—Polo cologne, so now whenever I smell it, I remember those mornings.

"Ken, I have some news," Mark started as we were about to get into the car.

"What's that?"

"Well now, it's for your own good, because you don't have any experience in managing people," he blurted out nervously. "Besides, I want to protect you from the mistakes you could make and teach you everything I know . . . I've talked to Ray (he called Mr. Probst "Ray"!) into making me the manager. It just wouldn't work with two display people of equal standing."

I looked at him gobsmacked! Betrayed! Though I was furious, I kept a straight face. Again the prohibition about showing strong emotion, this time used as a survival skill.

First of all, I was angry with Mr. Probst for going back on his word, but I was even more angry with Mark. He had styled himself as my friend, and this felt like a stab in the back. Trying to sugarcoat it and selling it as a way of helping me was really galling (not to mention insulting), and I decided that I wouldn't forget it. I would even up the score one day, god as my witness. And that's another reason I didn't show any emotion—it would have tipped my hand.

In the meantime, I knew that to declare war wouldn't serve any good purpose, and anyway, I had a lot to learn. I resolved to, again, just keep my head down, go with the program, and learn as much as I could so one day I could get out from under this situation. And bide my time until I could get even.

I did learn a lot more from Mark, who used to teach art in a Boston-area college. Along with the things I learned about display and backstabbing—oh, I mean *politics*—Mark talked about art. More specifically, he talked about the concept of seeing things as opposed to just looking. It took me a little time to grasp what he was trying to communicate, but I understood after an exercise he suggested one day. We were out in the parking lot at work, looking across the street at some trees.

ACT ONE:

"What do you see?" he asked.

"Trees," I replied.

"But what do you actually *see* when you cast your eyes on those objects? If you were from another planet and didn't know what those objects were, how would you communicate to your friends what you were seeing?"

And then I understood. I learned to look at the group of trees as objects formed from a combination of shapes, textures, colors, and lines, with some movement (the wind through the branches) thrown in.

"You can cast your eyes on something—that's called *looking*," Mark said. "When you take in the information presented to you *as it is*, that is what is called *seeing*."

Seeing something as it is. It was a profound lesson, and has had an impact on my life in many different ways.

Scene 2

As I was boarding the plane to do the kidnapping, I started thinking about Mark, me, and our history together. I remembered the first in-depth conversation we had after opening the Dillard's store. Things were a little more relaxed after that, and we had some time at lunch to get to know each other. Somehow conversation was easier when Mark wasn't at home; it seemed that when Victor was there, Mark was a different person.

"Let me tell you about my mother, Sophie," Mark said.

"She was short, loved good clothes and fun cars. Sophie was a lot of fun, and I adored going shopping with her. She liked my taste, and I would help her pick out her jewels and go with her to fittings.

"I remember one spring, when she was driving her white Chrysler Imperial convertible and wearing her new white Valentino coat. She had thrown it into the backseat and gone in to a lunch with one of her friends, and it rained while she was inside. The dye from the carpet bled onto the coat, and there was a big navy blue splotch on it. This caused her to take to her bed for days!"

"The only person she was afraid of was The Judge," he said softly. "And she was afraid of cancer, which she died of."

"She was the glue that held the family together," he continued. "After she died, we all seemed to go our separate ways. The Judge went and married my aunt, his brother's widow, so now my aunt is also my stepmother. And now my cousins are my stepbrothers and stepsisters. David stayed at the family firm. Robert and his wife, Betty, moved to Florida."

He went on to describe the rest of his family. His father (whom he always referred to as The Judge) was a lawyer first, then a judge in the Boston area, so they were a political family. The Judge was a cold, hard man, not ever tender. He had plans for his sons because he saw them as a Jewish Kennedy clan. Mark's decisions in life were a direct rebuke to The Judge's plans, and so their relationship was always strained.

"I had a man who The Judge had sent to jail put a cigarette out in my eye," he said, pointing to a scar on the white of his left eye. "From then on, I had protection while I lived in Boston."

"But you can't be too careful," he said. "There are quite a few people who The Judge sent away who would like to get back at him by attacking me. Even here, I still keep a watch out. Because you can never be too careful. That's why we have the burglar alarm, motion detectors, and the panic button installed at the apartment."

(I couldn't imagine having all that hardware to keep track of.)

There were the two brothers, David and Robert. David, the oldest, was what would be known as "the good son," the one who did the expected thing—which was to become a lawyer and go into the family firm. From Mark's description and constant complaining about him, it seemed David was an asshole. I found out much later, that this was indeed the case.

Robert, the middle son, studied anthropology and eventually worked in a museum in the Boston area before moving to Florida. He was the brother whom Mark liked. The two of them seemed always to be at war with David, because David was executor of Sophie's trust; the inheritance was supposed to come through when they reached the age of forty-five. It was that day, when Mark turned forty-five, that he lived for. There would be plenty of money, and then he could do whatever he wanted.

"What would happen if it wasn't there?" I asked. "I'm my mother's son, and she always said that, unless it was in your hand or your bank account, you don't have it."

"It's all invested in the Marble Head Savings and Loan, good solid stock," he replied. "So there's nothing to worry about. When I turn forty-five, I can do anything I want."

(As an aside, during the savings and loan debacle in the 1980s, this institution was one that tanked. And David, who sold out his private shares early when things were starting to look shaky, didn't sell the shares that were in the trust. Leaving the trust flat busted. Mark never saw a dime. He wanted to sue David for incompetence but never had the money to do it. So he was just shit out of luck.)

People have asked me over the years, just *why* I was so attached to Mark. From the outside, he didn't look like the best of friends. He snatched a job from me. He let me do the work and took credit for it. Then he left town and essentially disappeared. In the later days of our friendship, he was just a voice on the phone, complaining about Victor, and seemed not to be aware that I had a life.

But Mark served as my first "gay mentor." It was early on, during these lunches and visits to his house, that I learned what "a friend of Dorothy" meant. He was the one who introduced me to some of the venerable "gay movie classics," like *The Boys In The Band*, by showing them to me on his Betamax. I learned how to "dish" properly and how to defend myself against bitchy queens. His lending library contained all of the gay books that he considered required reading for me at that particular time, and he pressed one or two onto me weekly. That's how I got my hands on books like *City of Night*, and *Dancer From the Dance*—titles no bookstore in OKC would *dare* carry.

You could say that Mark was like a big sister to me and one who could be really funny, so in my inexperienced way, I looked up to him. (And since I had a difficult relationship with my actual big sister, this felt familiar.) He had studied art on the East Coast and in Italy, had shown his work with artists whom even I had heard of, came from a wealthy and prominent background, had traveled, and lived in big cities. Mark was that "grown-up" I desperately wanted to be. I didn't see, or know, the entire story, or I might have felt differently.

Mark opened a window for this green kid from Kansas. Through that window, I saw the world I had imagined was the world of "the grown-up"—Barbie's world when I was a kid. (This greatly appealed to that "inner adult" I joke about.) It was a world of fabulous apartments, convertibles, theater, art, big cities, travel, glamour, fashion, and opportunity. I got a little taste of it during that trip to New York in college and wanted it desperately—hungered for it, actually.

I was going down to LA to kidnap him, if for no other reason than gratitude for this open window. It showed me my avenue of escape, and Mark held it open while I passed through. Kidnapping him was my way of giving something back, of returning the favor, if you will.

Scene 3

Back in Oklahoma City, life went forward. We got the store open, much to my relief, as the hours were really wearing me out. Working long hours with hepatitis isn't the recommended treatment. Having regular hours again gave me time to recover, so I could go out and misbehave again.

One of my more embarrassing memories of that time happened during the festivities scheduled for the opening week. We were to have a visit from Miss USA 1981, who would be signing autographs. Everyone was in a quandary—who would get to pick her up?

It was decided that I would get to because I was the one who could get my hands on the best car. I hounded Mom to borrow her big white Thunderbird for the occasion. She got the car detailed and waxed in the bargain. This was my chance to meet my first Famous Person. All grown-ups have met at least *one* famous person (haven't they?), so I was really excited.

I met Miss USA, and her handler at the airport. The handler, who I will call Miss Constipation (or Miss C for short, as a shorter word starting with

"C" would be a more accurate name), immediately started demanding a porter for the luggage.

"This is Oklahoma City, ma'am," I said. "I'm your porter for today."

With that, I loaded all of their luggage into the back of the car, and we drove off to their hotel, Miss C complaining all the way.

"Do you want to ride back with the baggage?" I said lightly. I wasn't really joking but smiled real big. Just for effect. Miss USA thought it was really funny. I heard her chuckle from the backseat.

Finally after what seemed like a week's drive through the dead of winter with a broken heater, we arrived at the hotel. They checked in, and it was agreed that I would pick them up in two hours.

At the appointed time, I pulled up in front of the hotel. Miss USA was standing there, dressed in her pageant dress with dyed-to-match shoes, wearing her tiara and banner, holding a stack of 8x10 glossies. Miss C stood at her side, mouth pursed into a tiny sphincter—apparently she was still smarting about my crack about riding with the luggage. I got out, opened the door; they got in, and we drove off.

The embarrassing thing happened in a school zone. We were driving through the school zone when a particularly overzealous cop pulled me over for speeding. I was one mile over the limit.

When he asked, "Where's the fire, son?" in that annoying, Southern sheriff drawl; I replied that I had Miss USA in the car, and we were on our way to the new Dillard's store for her personal appearance. I pointed to her in the back seat for emphasis.

The cop looked into the car (there she was, with the tiara, banner, 8x10 glossies, and all), then looked at me, and said, "Yeah, sure."

And gave me a ticket.

ACT ONE:

Well! Miss C wouldn't let up the entire way back to the store. She ranted on and on about how I could have endangered some poor, innocent school child's life by being so reckless. In the rearview mirror, I could see Miss USA rolling her eyes. She caught my gaze, winked, and made a few funny faces, mimicking Miss C's ranting.

When she got to Dillard's, the first thing Miss C did was to have a word with Mr. Probst. (Actually, she raised Holy Hell with him.) He then had a word with Mark. (Diluted Holy Hell.) Who had a word with me. (Not Twice-Diluted Holy Hell but Major Irritation.) I, of course, was the one stuck with the traffic ticket; what more punishment did they want? And besides, as additional punishment I had to drive the ladies back to the hotel.

The ride back to the hotel was much more enjoyable: Miss C was napping in the back seat *(worn out no doubt from being such a bitch)*, and Miss USA and I chatted about buying vintage clothing. I could understand why she won the title—she was gracious and beautiful (she looked like Susan Anton) and was really nice to me throughout the whole thing.

With the store opening behind me and my recovery from the hepatitis complete, I had a social life again. My friends Penny and Steve, who I used to work with before they moved on to other jobs, would usually come by to pick me up at my little apartment, and we would go out for dinner or dancing. I was a regular at Triples (where my ex-boyfriend Brock worked as a maitre'd until I let slip in front of his boss that he'd given me hepatitis right before he dumped me, and they canned him), and Chicago's. Pistachio's at 50 Penn Place was another favorite restaurant. 50 Penn Place was a very woo-woo shopping center that also housed Cyrk & Co., where I bought my Fiorucci clothes and Godiva chocolates, as well as Orbach's, where Steve worked as the buyer for the fancy foods department.

ALL GROWN UP NOW

I was having the time of my life! No real responsibilities, lots of good clothes, reckless sexual adventures, fun friends . . .

Penny was a big ol' cowgirl from Snyder, Oklahoma, who looked exactly like Jane Russell in *Gentlemen Prefer Blondes*—you know the scene where Jane sings "Is There Anyone Here For Love"? Penny had that outfit as well as the figure that filled it out.

Penny had the almond eyes, the mane of shiny black hair, the TITS—she had a body like a Vargas painting, for sure! She was truly a big girl, an Amazon at six foot three in stocking feet, but she always wore heels. (We wore the same size.)

When we went dancing at the Free Spirit (the Episcopal church-turned-gay-disco) Penny and I would swap shoes. I wore her high heels, and she wore my flats. I wore her heels, so I wouldn't have to dance with her breasts bobbing at eye level all evening, getting seasick in the process. Dramamine doesn't work for that.

The guys there believed that Penny was a drag queen because she was such a BIG girl. One evening she was wearing her black spandex tube top (remember those?). She wore hers with silver spandex capri pants and red patent leather "Candies" mules. After one comment too many about whether or not those were "real," Penny pulled down that tube top, her breasts bounced out in all their glory, and then everyone could see that Penny was, indeed, "all girl." (It also created a stampede for the exit. Several gay men didn't shield their eyes and were turned to stone by the sight of unclothed female breasts. The management carted these unfortunates off to Will Rogers Park, where they still haunt the bushes to this day.)

The low ceilings in my little apartment were a problem for Penny and her high heels. She was forever cracking her forehead on the top of the kitchen doorframe.

No matter how many times I would warn her—"Watch your head!" . . . CRACK! . . . "DAMN! SHIT!"—she never got it. I used to tell her that's what happens when one works as a cocktail waitress; the fumes kill brain cells.

ACT ONE:

"I'm not just a cocktail waitress!" she protested. "I work at Christopher's! In the club! It's not just ANY cocktail waitress job. Come by one night and I'll buy ya a drink. You'll see!"

Not one to turn down a free anything, I accepted for the following evening. Christopher's was one of the "old-money" hangouts in town, an old Victorian house on a small pond (complete with swans) where senators and heads of state had been entertained. Knowing this, I *dressed*.

I arrived just after sunset. (Evening clothes, like vampires, sequins and full leather, should not be seen in daylight.) Since I was pinching pennies (and deathly afraid of the car not starting as its advanced age had made it somewhat crotchety), I studiously avoided the valet-parking man. The door to the club was off to the side, just like Penny told me. I went in and immediately took to the place.

The bar stools were antique barber chairs covered in Aubuisson tapestry. There were lots of very old carpets and Old Masters hanging around (the paintings as well as one old leather master who was wearing his leather under his suit—I found this out later when I went to wash my hands, oh my god!). There were some really plush old mohair velvet couches, worn-leather club chairs, and some tables scattered about. Very old money.

Penny saw me come in and came out from around the bar to greet me.

"Hey, Ken, sit up here at the bar, and I'll get ya a Perrier." She knew my drink.

Soon some scampi arrived as well. Here and there patrons were conversing, waiting for dinner reservations, or just meeting friends. Penny cruised in and out of the crowd like an expensive sports car, dispensing drinks and smart-ass talk. (Penny, like the expensive sports car, was curvaceous and fast.) She was obviously a favorite with the guys, what with that va-voom figure and the shiny, painted-on black dress. The women all stared daggers at her, envying her heat-seeking, cruise-missile breasts.

A very good-looking guy was playing the black grand piano (show tunes, of course!). It was all very civilized. I liked it.

Later in the evening, a distinguished older man (well, to me at the time, he was older. Probably really only 40 or so. It's all relative.) sat in the barber chair to my right, and we started chatting. He was one of those guys I aspire to be one day—witty, good-looking, well-dressed, well-traveled and well-read—very urbane and "mondaine." (I learned the word "mondaine" from a book I was reading on entertaining while researching being a grown-up, written by Elsa Maxwell, that Mom somehow had acquired and not read.) In short, a grown-up.

"Do you know who I am?" he asked after quite a bit of conversation.

"No, I don't. Who are you?"

"I own this place."

"Really? It's a lovely place; you must be very proud of it. It's done up real nice."

"How would you like to never have to pay for food or drink here?" He gave me a look.

Oh boy, one of those. Although he was good-looking and looked like he'd be a fun ride, and I was nothing if not easy. . . well . . . really! There's a name for that type of exchange.

"It's not what you think!" he interjected.

"Well, then . . . what?"

"I'm always looking for a few well-dressed, well-spoken people to hang around and, well, keep the ball in the air conversationally, so to speak," he replied. "As long as you're *dressed* as you are tonight, when you come here you'll never have to pay for food or drink."

ACT ONE:

(No doubt he noted that I didn't drink alcohol, so no worries of a sloppy drunk.)

And that's when I learned that living well isn't always about the money. As long as I looked good, was entertaining, knew which fork to use, and knew how to handle myself, I had a few free meals a month, exposure to a class of people I might not otherwise meet, and a good reason to buy more shoes. It was during this period that I embraced vintage stores—or more to the point the one -and -only one in OKC—and thrift shopping. This, and sewing my own clothes, helped to keep up my fashionable appearance.

I met some really nice people at Christopher's as well as my share of shady characters. One guy, whose name escapes me so I'll call him Ron, stood out in memory for a couple of reasons.

First of all, he kissed like a fish. I didn't find this out at first, because I didn't jump in right away, if you know what I mean. I was infatuated with his car. Ron drove a really cool car—a silver Alfa-Romeo convertible—and you didn't see too many of those in OKC. The evening I met him, he took me for a spin with the top down, which made me want to see him again, if for nothing else, to get another ride in the car.

Anyway, back to his kissing. When we finally got to his house and to that point, I was quite puzzled. Here we were on his sofa; the lights were low. He had closed his eyes and puckered up like a fish. There he lay, with his eyes closed and his lips PUCKERED so tight you'd need the Jaws Of Life to open 'em.

I tried several times and gave it my best effort, but there was no getting past the death-grip fish lips.

He finally opened his eyes, looked at me, and chuckled.

"Heh, heh, heh, it looks like I'm going to have to teach you how to kiss," he said patronizingly.

WELL!!!

Now, I'm told I kiss well. I can't be objective, but I'd never heard any complaints and had done lots of field research on the subject. I like to think I bring a certain zest and enthusiasm to the proceedings.

Insulted by this patronizing remark, I put my clothes back on, told him in no uncertain terms that I hadn't had any complaints so far, and left.

We saw each other casually at Christopher's a couple of times after that; in conversation he told me about his job as an officer in a bank.

"Which one?"

"Penn Square Bank."

Penn Square Bank had quite a reputation in the late seventies as the bank that the oil industry in Oklahoma used. Ron regaled me with tales of loans for millions made on a signature, and lots of high living and various shenanigans that the officers all got in on. It all sounded a little fishy (heh!), so I asked Mom about it.

"You don't know a goddamn thing!" she insisted. "No bank will loan money without collateral. Millions of dollars on a signature! You're either making this up or you're just too stupid to understand what he's talking about!"

Well, she told *me*.

A couple of years later, PBS had a TV special on about the fall of Penn Square Bank and its subsequent ruin of the Oklahoma economy.

(Mom told me that, at her bank, the running joke was "FDIC——branches opening daily." Bank humor.)

Indeed, what Ron had told me was true, and some folks were being sent up the river because of it. On the program they showed a photo of Ron, holding a little card with numbers on it across his chest.

ACT ONE:

After watching that show, I commented to Matthew (my one and only husband) that if Ron was going to be a good bitch for some big, bad convict, he'd have to learn how to relax his lips and jaw.

Mrs. Freeman, my landlady, had a mad passion for bridge. She would play it to the exclusion of every other activity if she could. The bridge group she ran with was equally dedicated, and they would meet every Sunday for a day of bridge and gossip.

The first time I saw this group was on an early Sunday morning. I had just arrived home and was locking the car. (I was also breaking my rule about evening clothes and daylight.) Up roared this big, beige, late-sixties Buick land-yacht sedan with a gaggle of old ladies in it. The chatter sounded like the proverbial hen house. Mrs. Freeman—dressed in a bright pink dress with matching pillbox hat (complete with a little veil), lipstick and rouge in place, big black handbag, gloves, and dressy, black, ankle-high, lace-up orthopedic shoes worn with thick support stockings—came tottering out of the house. A car door popped open, almost spilling some of the hens onto the street, but Mrs. Freeman managed to wedge herself in and get the door closed before they tore away.

I was enchanted.

One time while Mrs. Freeman was hosting, and, after knocking back one too many of her beloved bullshots, fell and broke her arm in three places. Calmly she just told everyone to start the game without her (which they did, hardened fanatics that they were), while one of the ladies took her to get her arm set. When she got back, she washed a few painkillers down with some Sanka and finished the afternoon playing bridge along with the rest of them. Now that's some hardened bridge player! But it was just what I would have expected of her.

When Mrs. Freeman, sporting a cast from her wrist to her shoulder, told me this later that week, I was so traumatized that I wanted to take to my bed!

She told me later that they all rotated around. Each lady hosted a bridge party in their house, and eventually they would get around to her again.

Her next bridge party occurred one Sunday in the fall, right when I was getting back into the swing of things socially. I had been, well, *entertaining* a gentleman caller overnight. We were sleeping blissfully when . . .

KNOCK KNOCK, KNOCK KNOCK!

Opening one eye to see the early morning light, I also saw Mrs. Freeman and the entire bridge group at the front door through the alarmingly sheer blind over the door window.

Oh SHIT!

"Ken, are you awake?" she croaked.

Oh yeah! I was awake.

"Just a minute!" I yelled back.

I turned to my gentleman friend (whose name escapes me, I just remember that he was blond and really cute) and said, "DON'T. MOVE." I rumpled up the covers to cover him up and grabbed my robe.

After opening the door, I said, "Mrs. Freeman, what a surprise!"

"Well, Ken, I couldn't call you because you don't have a phone, but the ladies just won't believe that a young bachelor man can decorate and keep a place up like you do. They wanted to see for themselves."

"Mrs. Freeman, I'm not dressed!" I stammered. "And the bed's not made! It just wouldn't be proper for ladies to see these things...."

ACT ONE:

"Oh, you're shy! There's nothing these ladies haven't seen before!" Much cackling from the ladies.

(I'll bet.)

"Well, we'll come back later in the day after we finish up with our bridge game," she sighed.

And off they tottered, much to my relief. I heard chuckling from under the bedclothes and realized that I had some unfinished business to attend to.

———

I went into my social whirl of Christopher's, the Free Spirit, and the Plum, and included Mark and Vic in my circle of friends. This circle also included Barry Perkins, a really tall, skinny, bitter, bitchy queen who worked in the children's department, and Brad-the-Doll, who worked in the men's department. Brad-the-Doll had a twin named Steve. They both looked like the construction worker in the Village People. Brad was the nicer of the pair as well as the gay one. We could only tell them apart because Brad-the-Doll had a moustache and better clothes. Happily Brad-the-Doll lived right next door to me in Mrs. Freeman's backyard—I'd gotten him in after the first tenant moved away. The five of us became a little "family" of sorts.

Mark would have all of us over for dinner and movies—their Betamax got quite a workout. We all would settle in after dinner for the movie and gossip, and Mark would regale us with tales of Life in the Big City (San Francisco).

(We also hung out sometimes with Penny and Steve, but Penny and Steve really didn't like Mark much and wondered why I didn't either. They both felt that Mark had stolen a position that I had worked hard for and deserved.)

The holidays came soon enough, and for the first time in ages, I had a really fun time. Before I moved out on my own, when I was still in school, holidays were fraught with aggravation, what with final exams and Mom's shrieking about the Social Security checks keeping us from studying in peace, and working long hours in retail, and Christmas shopping. This year, it was a piece of cake, even with the Christmas display workload. And having that little "family," complete with "Mother Mark" as the centerpiece, gave the season a focus.

But as with any family, there were dysfunctions. In this situation it turned around the monogamy issue. It seems that Mark wanted monogamy; Victor didn't. The first inkling I had of this was one Sunday evening when I went out for coffee with Mark, only to hear about the day's drama.

Mark and Vic had gone to the Free Spirit to dance on Saturday evening, and Vic had met a guy, whose name escapes me so I'll call him Bruce. Apparently there was a flirtation exchanged between Bruce and Victor, and then Mark and Vic went home.

Since Mark and I had worked on that Sunday morning, Victor was at loose ends. When Mark came home early, there Victor and Bruce were, buck-naked, in bed. I wonder what they were up to——hmmm.

"So I said to Victor, 'Vic, let's go out for brunch. I'm hungry'," Mark told me coolly. "I looked at Bruce and said, 'Oh, you come, too! It'll be fun.'" The long and short of it was that Mark, Vic, and the trick went for brunch, Vic and the trick being made to feel incredibly uncomfortable, which served them right in my book!

I marveled at how cool he was about it, though. If it had been me, there would have been hell to pay!

"So, do YOU wanna fuck him, too?!" Mark barked suddenly, startling me.

"No! What gave you THAT idea?! Yikes! Ick!" *Just the idea made me queasy!*

"Just asking. You can, you know . . . I won't hold it against you. He's fucked Barry already."

ACT ONE:

In my book that bordered on incest. The idea of those two going at it was enough to put me off my feed! Yuck! And the idea of me and Victor—well, it would be like sleeping with my father, sort -of. Even if he were "hot" (and he definitely *wasn't*), the idea of Mother Mark walking in was just as appealing as the idea of having my actual mother walk in during some louche and embarrassing activity.

It was exceedingly strange how casual Mark was being about all of this, but I chalked it up to how "Big-City Gays" did things. Mark and Vic styled themselves as a stable gay couple, and long -term at that, which supposedly put the lie to those who said a gay union couldn't last. Mark was very insistent on this, claiming it at every opportunity. So being young and naïve, I took them at face value.

Yes, I was naïve in my younger years, but even so, there were things about Victor that made me nervous. He had this disconcerting way of glaring at me when Mark was out of the room, only to look away when Mark entered the room. I couldn't decide if he was undressing me with his eyes or trying to make me spontaneously combust. Vic would also sit too close to me on the sofa, especially when he was showing me one of his "toys," as he called them. Vic had a fondness for stun guns and police-type gear, which he would bring out every now and then.

When Brock dumped me, (before I knew I'd gotten hepatitis from him), he said, "Get used to it. You're either going to be leaving someone or being left by someone. That's the way it is." I felt that was a grim, very "City-of-Night-Dancer-From-The-Dance" assessment of gay life, and I didn't feel it spoke for me. That's not the way I wanted to run my life.

Mark and Vic *appeared* to be different. My only other source of information on being gay was the fag jokes I had heard all through high school and college. That's why I put such store in them as an example.

That said, I suspected that the appearances might be deceiving. I knew that, even though Mark was trying to appear not to be bothered about Vic's horn-dogging, he *was* bothered. And, even though Vic liked playing around, he seemed jealous of Mark.

This aspect of their relationship appeared seemingly out of the blue one evening. Mark and I were in his kitchen preparing dinner. (More to the point, Mark was preparing, I was watching. I chose early which room of the house to be good in, and it *wasn't* going to be the kitchen.)

I had just learned some new dance steps, so I started teaching it to Mark while the lasagna was in the oven. (Donna Summer was playing on the stereo.) Just as we were getting into the swing of things, Vic came home from work.

He stormed into the kitchen, stopped, glared, and said in this strained voice, "What the hell is going on here?"

Mark and I stopped dead in our tracks. (*The hair went up on the back of my neck.*)

"I'm just teaching him some new dance steps," I explained weakly. Mark had gone completely white. This took me completely by surprise—it was disorienting.

Silence.

"I think I should go," I said meekly. And I did.

And Mark didn't mention it the next day when I picked him up for work; actually the both of them acted like it didn't happen. I somehow knew not to mention it either. It was like my teen years, when Mom and her second husband would have had a big blowout. By the next morning, we were all expected to act like it hadn't happened.

I only spent one very cold winter in my sweet little apartment on Villa. The next year I would be in San Francisco, and rain and a leaky roof (not to mention mushrooms growing up through the pile in the carpeting) would be my winter concerns.

ACT ONE:

Mrs. Freeman brought in a heater when the weather changed. By heater I was expecting something with vents and a fan. I was disappointed when she brought this electric space heater. It was the tiniest heater in captivity (about the size of a toaster), which was appropriate, because I would have had to move out if it were any larger. As it was, if I wanted to sew something, I had to move the furniture out onto the front lawn to make enough space to lay fabric out to cut.

The first day or two I left the heater off while I was at work, because I didn't want to worry about fire. I thought I was being prudent. It never occurred to me that this would contribute to a freeze that thawed only when spring came. Sadly the winter got a head start that the tiny little space heater could never catch up to.

The toilet froze over, and I had to keep breaking up the ice to use it. To keep the faucets running I had to leave them on a trickle, otherwise they would freeze solid and there would be no water whatsoever. There surely wasn't any insulation in the walls, so in addition to drafts, there was always ice on the insides of my windows.

During the worst few days, when the wind chill was about 112 below and it was snowing horizontally, the sewer line broke. My toilet (not one to run freely with all the ice as it was) was no more. This was a problem. At first I was hesitant to call, as Queue-the-manager, was notoriously unresponsive to requests for repairs. (She was unresponsive –PERIOD. It was the electroshock.) When I finally called her, she said there was nothing that could be done right now because of the weather, and if I needed to "go," I could go to the filling station at Sixty-third and May.

Great.

So I bundled myself up in my fur coat (fur really *is* warmer, despite what the good folks at People for the Ethical Treatment of Animals say) to make the trek on foot, as there was too much ice on the road to take the car. Mrs. Freeman was looking out her window and waved as I passed. As I got to the street, she called out from her front door, "Where are you going in this weather, young man?"

"To the filling station," I replied, shifting from one foot to the other—the cold was exacerbating my already urgent need.

"Without the car?"

"Yeah . . ."

"Why?"

I told her my dilemma, and she immediately invited me in. After letting me take care of business, she asked me all about what Queue had said and clucked about how you give people a chance to better themselves and they go and do things like this.

I don't know how much it cost (and I'm sure it wasn't cheap), but there was a crew there within the hour, digging up the frozen ground to replace the sewer line. That's how she handled things—straight up and with dispatch.

A few days later when the weather let up, I saw Mrs. Freeman out in her backyard and thanked her for the trouble she had taken. She settled in for a good chat.

"Boy, you remind me of myself when I was your age," she croaked. "You know, when I was a girl, I'd get in so late that I used to have to milk the cows before I went to bed. The sun was usually risin', and many a time I'd be squatted on the milkin' stool, barefoot in my dancin' dress, with the skirt hiked up. You see, I didn't want to spoil my silk stockings or my favorite pair of dancin' slippers! Boy, I had fun . . ." her voice trailed off.

Then she pounced.

"Now don't think because I can't hear that good that I don't know when you come in at night or whether you're alone! I'm hard of hearing not stupid. "

There was a glint of mischief in her eyes that was clearly visible (*magnified, actually*) through the Coke-bottle-thick glasses she wore. She evidently enjoyed the look of surprise on my face.

ACT ONE:

"And the next time we show up unannounced, tell the young man to lay *flat* on the bed before you cover him up. He won't show under the covers as easily."

She paused for effect . . .

"Voice of experience," she chuckled.

Meanwhile, working with Mark proved to be, well, interesting, so to speak. After the opening and Christmas rush, we settled into a groove of sorts; where he would do lots of meetings and talk to the managers of the various departments, while I was on the ladder and in the windows actually doing the work.

Every now and then he would make a display and show me the "Macy's way" of doing things. Even though I didn't want to admit it even to myself at first (he was my friend and I didn't want to be disloyal), it was apparent that I was doing most of the heavy lifting, display-wise. Different department managers made pointed comments about how Mark always seemed to be talking while I was away working.

There was an undercurrent of resentment toward him. Most of the people working there came from the Shepherd Mall store and had seen me working under my old boss David, who was really adept at taking credit for work that he hadn't done. They felt that I, not Mark, should have been the one in charge. Mark was seen as an interloper who took what was rightly mine. I would remind them that he had more experience than I did and that I was learning as much as I could so, that one day, I would be the display manager.

My old boss David who had met Mark while helping open the store, told me one night at the Free Spirit, "He'll be gone soon. He won't last."

"What makes you say that? I just think you're jealous," I shot back, being loyal to my friend.

"I've seen his kind before. You wait and see. He won't last."

I didn't wait long.

In January, retail does inventory. This is a real fire drill, dreaded by management and "associates" (*peons*) alike. During this time Quail Springs was dealing with the usual store-opening problems as well as a tragedy. The operations manager, a gal named Leslie, hit a patch of ice in her car, wrecked the car, and was killed instantly. With that hanging over everyone's heads, the manager of the misses department (half the main floor) quit a week before inventory, leaving with no preparation done.

Mr. Probst called me into his office.

"Ken, I know you're in display now, but we're in a bind. Arlene's gone, and we need you to go in and troubleshoot, you know, get the department ready for inventory. Mark has agreed to loan you out. You already know what to do—you did the lamp department at Shepherd for inventory a couple a times already."

"*Thanks, Mark!*" I thought.

"Besides, between you and me, Mark wouldn't know what to do," he said.

So the week before inventory I was a "fill-in manager," getting all the various departments in the missy area (second largest in the store, next to the furniture department) ready for inventory. In the meantime Mark was out sick with a bad back. I thought it awfully convenient—Mark would probably not be there for inventory.

Indeed.

Boy, did I resent that he was home sleeping, while I was working through the night, along with every other manager. It was the day that lasted from

ACT ONE:

9:00 a.m. Saturday to 6:30 p.m. Sunday. Despite sleep deprivation, everything went swimmingly. My floor finished first to everyone's astonishment—especially the auditors, who couldn't believe a 22-year-old display queen with Good Hair and Great Clothes had organized it so half the main floor was done by noon. That hadn't been done before.

That's when I noticed a shift in how I was treated by the department managers. They noted how convenient it was to have back trouble at this particular time. These people saw me there, right along with them, doing the job at hand in unpleasant circumstances and doing it well. What I saw was that I was indeed capable and was also regarded as such. It was a turning point.

Mark never came back to work.

In early February he called me at the store to tell me that he and Victor were going back to Austin. And soon. It seemed the reason Mark had back trouble was that he had already been packing boxes.

"Why!?" I asked.

"The Austin division is in trouble again, and they need him to bail them out."

"But why don't you just stay here? Big Guy has already been talking about bringing you along, and you have a chance to get to the main offices in Fort Worth!" It seemed like he was throwing away a good opportunity.

"You just don't understand," Mark replied. "Victor and I are married. I have to go where he goes."

"But it should work both ways! Why can't HE give up a little career advancement for a change?"

"You just don't understand . . ."

And really I didn't.

On their last day in OKC, I went over to help the two of them load the truck. It was late at night when we finished and had all the feel of two felons who had to blow town in a hurry. I remember feeling a mixture of confusion, sadness, and irritation as I watched them drive away.

My old boss David had been right on the money.

They hadn't been in town for a full seven months yet.

If ever there was an odd couple it was Darrell and me.

Around the time that Mark and Vic moved away, Barry introduced me to Darrell. As Barry told it, Darrell was someone he had dated, and Darrell was nice and I might like him. Later, when Darrell and I hit it off, Barry had a real jealous hissy fit—it seemed he still had feelings for Darrell. That's when I found out that the blind date was done as a joke on both of us. It was not expected to work out.

You see, Darrell was the "country mouse," and I was the "city mouse."

Our first date was to go to a meeting of an organization that I think was called "Oklahomans for Human Rights," –it was the gay rights group. (Or more to the point the gay men's group—I don't remember seeing women at the meeting we attended.) We had agreed that he would pick me up at 6:30 p.m., as the meeting started at 7:00 p.m.

ACT ONE:

I was in the shower about 5:45 and heard a knock at the door.

"Damn! This is *not* a good time for Mrs. Freeman to come visit!" I thought.

Wrapping myself in a towel with shampoo still in my hair (so she got the message that she had interrupted something), I answered the door, dripping wet. Darrell was standing there.

"I got here early because I didn't know the area and wanted to find the place . . ." His voice trailed off.

I noted appreciably that he was nice-looking, like a budget version of Tom Selleck—shorter and a bit softer but still quite appealing with really kind, sweet, blue, Labrador-retriever eyes. But I was too preoccupied with my present appearance to just invite him in and have him right there.

"Well, obviously I'm not ready, so could you come back at 6:30?"

"Sure . . ." he grinned and said good-naturedly, and off he sauntered.

We arrived at the meeting hall, took places in the front row, and waited for the meeting to start. They did the usual meeting-starting stuff. Then, much to everyone's surprise, one of the board members got up, and, face reddening and veins in his neck popping, started a diatribe about how the others in the group were just using this venue as a social club to meet up with other "A" gays and weren't really interested in the struggle for human rights; and they were all disgusting and he WAS LEAVING! Verbal fisticuffs broke out, and the end result was that the organization self-destructed that evening. That testosterone thing again—it was a group of men, even though they all happened to be gay.

Darrell and I just looked at each other and blinked a lot. Then we got up and left.

I remember vaguely that we went out to dinner, but our first date had really been a bust. Barry had a good laugh the next day at work when I told him about it, and I put Darrell out of my mind.

About a week later I got a call at work and at first didn't recognize the voice. It was Darrell, and he wanted to try again to see if he could have another date. He apologized about the outcome of the previous date in such a way that it sounded like he felt personally responsible for the bad behavior that ruined my good time. I was charmed.

Who knows where we went on that date—I really can't remember. I just remember afterwards, when I invited him home, and how sweet he was. We talked late into the night.

Darrell told me that he was born in Elk City, Oklahoma, a small-town boy with small-town (but not small-minded) values. He went to Vietnam but happily didn't return a shattered man. The government trained him in bookkeeping, so he was able to get a job in Oklahoma City as an office manager in a mortuary. (Happily he never tried to get me to go into the "back rooms" nor needed to himself. Nor did he ever ask me to take a cold bath and lie very still in bed—that came with a later, VERY short-time paramour who also worked in that industry. But that's another story.) Darrell's family was salt of the earth, just like him, and accepted his being gay with equanimity. I met them later on and liked them a lot.

This man was a solid citizen, real husband material. He was enough older than me that he was stable and experienced, but not so old as to be stodgy or of another generation. And he was kind. This is a quality I didn't quite fully appreciate as much then as I do now. I was out of my depth.

We started dating regularly, and at one point I realized he was Getting Serious. This made me very nervous. I was twenty-three (young, with all the stupidity that comes with it) and fickle and buying cool clothes and having adventures and planning my escape from Oklahoma. Marrying him would just complicate things.

I talked to Barry about this, and that's when he told me that the date had been a joke for his own personal entertainment. Darrell and I were supposed to hate each other. The city-sophisticate-fashion-queen would only be bored with the slow-talking-country-hick, who would find the city-sophisticate-fashion-queen tedious and shallow. Barry would revel in the comedic possibilities, like a sit-com only live. He didn't think that Darrell and I would actually start dating regularly, let alone get to the point where one of us might get serious. It really annoyed him.

But I knew I had to say something to Darrell about how I was feeling; at the same time, I didn't want to hurt him. In the interest of fair play I wanted to be as honest as I could. He was a really sweet man, the nicest I had come across at that point, and more than merited fair treatment.

Since I was still regarded as "new meat" in town, everyone wanted to have a ride, and I heard lots of the "I'll call you . . . You're special . . . Grow old with me" bullshit. But when Darrell said it, there was a difference. It wasn't bullshit. When he looked at me, I could see steady adoration in his eyes. It confused and disoriented me. I hadn't encountered anyone like him before.

So one evening we went out to dinner at a restaurant called Aunt Pittypat's, which was in an old house in the historic district (such as it was). We were seated at a banquette where the tables were about three inches apart. I knew this was going to make conversation a challenge, as everyone was sitting practically in each other's laps. But I knew we had to talk. I waited until dessert, though, because I was hungry. (And he was treating.)

"Darrell, we have to talk," I began. "I feel like you're ready to pick out the china pattern, and I'm not there yet. I'm quite fond of you, but I can't say I'm in love with you . . . "

There was a crash at the next table. The couple there was so intent on eavesdropping that they knocked a big pitcher of beer over, which created a Niagara Falls of beer over the edge of their table that completely soaked the carpet and my new pair of Pierre Cardin shoes—the ones I had just paid a week's salary for.

"Hon, that's all right," he said in his sweet Okie accent as I was drying off my shoes. "I realize that ya don't feel as strong for me as I do for you. You don't hafta. Just know that I luv ya."

(I apologize to Darrell for the way I'm writing his dialogue, as in print it looks like the dialogue from an extra in the film *Deliverance*. Darrell wasn't a rube, an idiot, or a product of incest. He was a really good, sweet guy.)

Later we ended up back at his place, taking a bubble bath and making love in his very, very deep, antique claw-footed bathtub, candles burning all around the room. With Darrell I learned the difference between having sex and making love. This particular evening ranks up there as one of the most romantic evenings in my memory, even to this day.

The next day the florist arrived at my humble apartment with a bouquet of orchids.

Barry started acting really squirrelly after my conversation about how serious Darrell was getting. He (Barry, not Darrell) was frequenting the bars and the bathhouse (there being only *one* in OKC, what a surprise! I went there only once—it was built during the Woodrow Wilson administration and cleaned only sporadically since). Barry had the idea he would find a husband there. I used to tell him that the type of man who hangs out at those places regularly probably wouldn't be husband material, but he just dismissed me as one truly inexperienced queen. Inexperience, perhaps, but I did have common sense and a lot of field research to base this on. Guys looking for husbands generally hang out in different venues than guys just looking for some fun.

Also when we spoke of Darrell, there was an edge to Barry's voice. Especially the time I told him about Darrell taking me to The Eagle's Nest. The Eagle's Nest was in the top of the Shartel Tower. Since the tower was cylindrical, the restaurant was designed so it rotated throughout the evening—one of the woo-woo restaurants in OKC and very expensive.

While telling Barry of this dinner, I, of course, left out the part about getting a serious case of food poisoning. I didn't tell Darrell about it either at first. He found out only by accident—he called me at work, and they told him I was home sick with it. Darrell was so upset and felt personally responsible, as if he had put the botulism there with his own hands. He rushed to my tiny apartment to nurse me himself and apologized profusely. I had to remind him that buying me dinner didn't automatically mean that he personally had poisoned me.

"Well! He never took ME there!" Barry spat after hearing about my romantic evening (minus the food poisoning). "Why would he take YOU there?"

"Perhaps it might be because I'm *nice* to him, bitch!"

One day in the early spring after Mark moved away, Barry didn't show up at work. Since he didn't call in sick, everyone at work asked me where he was.

(Straight people think all of us gay boys know each other and keep each other apprised of our social calendars and whereabouts—sort of like air traffic control for fairies.)

I phoned Barry's apartment a couple of times, with no answer, so I went by his place after work. Repeated knocking on the door got me no answer even though his car was there, so I thought I'd go home and stay put. Perhaps I might hear something.

A couple hours later Brad-the-Doll called me from work.

"Get over to Barry's house! He's taken pills!"

"How do you know?"

"I just talked to him on the phone! Get over there; I'll meet you!"

WELL!

Off in the car I zoomed, beating the odds on getting all green lights. I broke into Barry's apartment and pulled him out of bed. He was, indeed, a mess. A real mess.

Trying not to panic, I thought to myself, "OK, what do they do in the movies?" (It's a question I still ask myself. Part of the genetic hardwiring for being gay. That, or perhaps at a young age movies were how I gathered information about life when reality proved inscrutable.)

I remembered that in the movies if someone tried to commit suicide by taking pills, they got the person on his feet, walked him around, and made coffee. So I put on some coffee (a challenge since I don't cook) and hauled Barry's ass out of bed and started walking him around. I'm sure this was a sight, as he was easily a head-and-a-half taller than me.

Barry wanted me to put on some music.

"Music!?"

"Yeah. Donna Summer," he slurred.

So I slung him across my back and tried to get his cheap-ass stereo working. He got exasperated and said, "You're so stupid, you never were worth anything."

I was sorely tempted to drop him right there and leave, locking the door behind me.

Instead I called Don, my brother-in-law, at the hospital. He had a cool head and worked in the lab at Baptist Hospital. Quickly I outlined the situation and read the information on the empty bottle beside the bed.

"You need to get him in to get his stomach pumped and soon!" Don said. "That's not one to mess around with. It's not like in the movies where you can walk him around and pour coffee down his throat."

"Uh, OK."

ACT ONE:

"I'll call ahead and tell them you're coming, but get there now!"

Just about this time Brad-the-Doll arrived, and we poured Barry into my car. Brad-the-Doll followed me over to Baptist Hospital in his beat-up yellow Pinto. The two of us dragged Barry into the emergency room, where the doctor and a couple of nurses were already waiting.

Later, when they had done their work, I was sitting in the room with Barry, waiting for them to admit him overnight.

Then, in walked the policeman.

He didn't look like a friendly one either—I could see in his eyes that he hated fags and was disappointed that a fag hadn't died that evening. I felt my chest tighten and the hair on the back of my neck go on end. Since Brad-the-Doll was nowhere to be seen, I'd have to deal with this one alone. Not something I wanted *at all* to do, but I was blindsided so I had to.

He fixed me with a steely gaze and spat, "So, you're his 'FRIEND'?"

"I'm his friend, with a small 'f,' if that's what you mean."

"So. He tried ta off 'imself."

"No. I'm sure it was a mistake. He wouldn't do that."

"Because if he did he could go ta jail . . ."

"He didn't try. This was all a big mistake."

Barry came to, sort of, and wasn't aware of the policeman. In a fuzzy voice, he said, "I think it would be *grand* to commit suicide by jumping off the Golden Gate Bridge." I elbowed him in the ribs.

"So. The fag thinks it would be 'grand' to jump off the Golden Gate Bridge, huh?"

"I didn't hear anything like that. You have quite an imagination, officer."

I rang for the nurse, and asked her to show the policeman out. He gave one last snort of derision before he left.

"Barry, you stupid son-of-a-bitch!" I whispered. "What the fuck were you trying to do, get yourself thrown in jail?" I was trying to breathe deeply and get the adrenaline back under control when I looked up . . .

It was Darrell. Boy, was he a welcome sight.

Next day I visited Barry in the hospital after telling everyone at work that he had a bout of food poisoning. Barry was in high dudgeon.

"I've had it with this town! I can't even commit suicide successfully here!" he shouted.

"You stupid bastard! Thanks so much for piping up about jumping off the bridge right in front of the policeman. Just what were you trying to prove anyway? Did you *want* to go to jail and be some felon's butt-boy?"

"Oh, go fuck yourself! I'm moving to Austin to be with Mark and Vic. I'll be happy there!"

"Well, fuck YOU! I should have left you there to choke on your own vomit!"

I can't believe I said that, but I was really pissed off. I could have spent a nice evening at Christopher's, but NOOOO! I was hauling a six -foot -two, drugged-up beanpole that smelled of vomit around his apartment.

In the hallway of the hospital I met up with Darrell. He too had gotten a dressing-down from Her Imperial Highness.

ACT ONE:

"Well, ya gotta just let 'im be," he drawled. "Barry's one selfish boy. That's why it didn't work out between us—when things didn't go his way, he'd have a tantrum. I got tired o' that. This is his pattern. He gets to a certain point, then does somethin' stupid, and then moves to another place. It'll happen again, I'm tellin' ya."

So off Barry moved to Austin, Texas, to be with Mark and Vic. We kept in touch with the occasional letter and phone call.

In the beginning I kept in touch with Mark as well. He would regale me with how wonderful his new place in Austin was, and how Vic was doing so well at work, and how it was a really good move. He had taken a job as a display person at the local military base's PX—a strange move, I thought, but perhaps there wasn't a Dillard's there. After the initial flurry of contact, there was silence.

One day a couple months later, after not hearing from Mark, Barry called with the news: Mark and Vic had moved, to where he did not know. It seems that Barry had worn out his welcome (*got thrown out, Mark told me later, probably for boinking Victor one time too many—ick!*), and got an apartment. He had not heard from Mark and Vic for at least a month. So, one day he tried to call, but the phone was disconnected. He then drove over to their place only to find it empty—they had gone, telling no one of their destination.

I felt betrayed and a little lost. This couple was my role model of gay behavior. Yes, there were things I didn't understand, but I had thought that they were good people who gave the lie to the notion that gay people were flaky, transient, and generally irresponsible. It was hard information to digest.

These issues were my only real troubling concerns in that spring of 1981. Since it was generally a time when things were going smoothly for me—work was going well, Darrell and I were settling into a groove, my social life was hopping—I didn't let it cloud up too much of my life. But it did nag at me from time to time.

A few weeks later, Darrel had to move. He was the office manager of the mortuary and, as part of his salary, had an apartment in the back of the property. Part of the reason for this was that sometimes he would have to arrange for a body to be brought to the mortuary after hours, so the owners felt it easier to have someone on-premises. Also, the neighborhood had steadily declined, so having someone on the property at night would offer more protection. The mortuary was closing (partly due to the bad location), so Darrell had to move. He was in a state about this—losing a job as well as a living situation was quite a lot to take.

Happily, though, my next-door neighbor Brad-the-Doll was moving out, so I prevailed upon Mrs. Freeman to ignore the waiting list (much to Queue-the-manager's chagrin) and rent it to Darrell. My argument for this was that he was a really nice guy, and it would be such a comfort knowing my neighbor as we lived so close to each other. Mrs. Freeman made the call over to the office with her usual dispatch, and the deal was done.

I helped Darrell move out of the little apartment and to clear out his desk in the office at the mortuary. As he was finishing up, I was snooping in the office closet and found these really pretty bronze canisters.

"These would make really nice canisters for my kitchen! Would anyone miss a couple of these?"

I had forgotten for a moment where I was.

"No, darlin', you can have as many as you want, but they're sorta occupied right now," Darrell drawled, a twinkle in his eyes. "You'll have ta evict the tenants. That's called the 'unclaimed relatives' closet."

ACT ONE:

By moving in next door, Darrell was close enough that we could see each other easily, but I could go home and close the door if I wasn't receiving. This was the ideal situation. After he moved in, I helped him fix the place up by making draperies and slipcovers. His family brought up new carpet to install, and I got to know them much better while helping move all the furniture. They seemed to approve of me and like me as well.

This said, I was still ambivalent about Darrell and me. Remember, I was twenty-three and fickle (and a bit of a slut), and wary about tying myself down. I had gotten burned by Brock, my first steady boyfriend. And I intended to get out of OKC at the first opportunity. Darrell was the model of understanding and patience. Looking back, I wish I had appreciated him more. Little did I know that men who worship the ground one walks on are few and *very* far between.

Spring was really nice at my little apartment, because Mrs. Freeman started early to plant her garden. She was at it every day, and her work seemed to bear fruit quicker than the neighbors'. Since her backyard was my front yard, I benefited by having a beautiful garden to look at without all the tiresome effort. (Ever since, I've lived in apartment buildings, so I don't have to do gardening. I gave it up for Lent one year.)

There were two wrought-iron lawn chairs in the yard in front of my place and a little table. I could sit out there in the mornings (but never did as I usually woke up just in enough time to get ready and GO) or in the evenings. It was soothing to sit out there, watching the sunset and dodging golf balls that flew over the fence from the golf course next door. I would usually sit there with some iced tea or Perrier and Godiva chocolates, and read my mail before deciding what to do or where to go for the evening and what I would wear.

During one of these evenings, I mused about Harry, who was Mom's lawyer. When I was a teenager, and Mom was going through her misadventures with her second husband and the boyfriend who came after, Harry was the voice of reason. He was the one who gave me hope that life could be more than the chaos it was when I was a teenager.

Let me introduce you to Harry:

We all met Harry when Mom divorced Don, her second husband.

Mom went through the window of a fancy restaurant during their first anniversary celebration. They had gone to dinner at one of the fancy hotels in town, and lots of Chivas Regal had been consumed (by Don) before they left the house. He was already talking really loudly (always the first sign of trouble) before they left.

The story of how Mom actually went through the window was different, depending on who told it: Mom said she couldn't remember; Don said that Mom "fell." But onlookers and the police report said that Don had pushed her through.

If it hadn't been for the drapes, one of the big shards of glass (the building was built before safety glass) would have sliced Mom in half lengthwise somewhat like a guillotine. As it was, the impact left bruises right along a line, starting at the jugular on her left side and continuing down diagonally to the right. This is where the slicing would have occurred had the drapes been open. I think it got her attention.

Going through the window did indeed scare Mom, and she realized that the wedding vows of "until death do us part" were becoming perilously close to fulfilling themselves. That's when she made her first visit to Harry.

ACT ONE:

I remember the photos of the bruises, not taken because she was having Don's ass hauled in for wife abuse but because Don was suing the hotel for: a) defamation of character for accusing him of throwing her through the window, b) false arrest, and c) having unsafe glass in their windows.

Don had studied to be a lawyer late in life—he was studying for the bar exam when he and Mom were "courting" and passed soon after they married. This was one of her excuses for his behavior—such stress studying to pass this test! Everything would be rosy when it was over! Everything will be better then, you'll see!

We had to tiptoe around while he was studying. Such an *attractive* sight he was, sitting around in his cheap, thin, white cotton boxer shorts and droopy black socks, wiping boogers on his law books.

Don's comment when finding out he had passed the bar was, "Now I have a license to steal!" Such were the standards of the Oklahoma Bar in the early seventies. This lawsuit was to be his first real case. Oh boy.

If Mom had indeed fallen, Don was showing no real concern that she seek medical treatment or interest in her well-being; this was his chance to make his mark in the legal arena and "clear his name," as he put it. It seems the manager of the hotel had called the police and filed a complaint about the assault (notice it wasn't Mom who did), and the insurance company for the hotel was pressuring Don to actually *pay* for the damages he caused (and it was such a big window, too!). And then there were all those witnesses. I never heard how it came out.

But the end result of Mom going through the window on her anniversary was the end of that marriage—and that's how we met Harry.

Harry looked like George Burns in the movie *Oh, God!*

Whenever I think of him, I imagine him with a cigar, but that was George Burns. He did have the gold-rimmed glasses, the same voice, the perfect delivery, and the attitude though. Harry was recommended to Mom as a really good lawyer. I liked him because he and I were the same height, and he had a really cool car—a Datsun coupe that was electric blue with a white vinyl top, mag wheels, luggage rack on the back, and white racing stripes.

Harry also had a girlfriend, Donna, who looked and talked like the actress Suzanne Pleshette. She liked nude sunbathing. Harry lived with her but never married her. For a straight man who chose his own clothes, he dressed *way* better than Don, wearing not a hint of artificial fibers, aberrant-looking sideburns, nor brown reptile shoes with black suits. And Harry had a sense of humor.

(As an aside, I really appreciated this sense of humor several years later, after I unknowingly had boinked his new law partner, "Spad"—a big, strapping man who had an enormous dick, I might add, the biggest I had seen up to that point—during a bout of anonymous promiscuity. After finding out that they were law partners during a visit to Harry's office, Harry, after looking slowly first at me, then him, then me, said in a deadpan voice, "No doubt you've come to appreciate Spad's distinguishing characteristic!" Spad joked back that it was all the same for Harry—just another warm, wet place to put it. But I'm getting ahead of myself.)

Harry needed his sense of humor with Mom—he didn't take her too seriously. At times it could be said that he treated her dismissively, but, knowing her, that was what the situation called for.

One day during that time, Mom had to go to Harry's office for something or other, so I had to wait in the lobby with Ruby, Harry's secretary. Stylistically, Ruby was like Della on the TV show *Perry Mason*—efficient in a proper -but -been-around way, a real lady. Ruby's taste ran to expensive, beige tweed tailored suits a la Balenciaga; her voice even *sounded* like beige tweed. She had the apricot-colored widow's peak hair (*very* Suzy Parker), the Revlon "Cherries in the Snow" lipstick, and stenciled eyebrows over the pale-powdered face. The only flaw was the scar on her upper lip—it looked like something from an automobile accident and had disfigured her face just there.

On this particular day, I sat in the lobby of Harry's office, thinking Ruby was cool and waiting for Mom. The door opened, Mom emerged, and Harry looked over to me. He motioned me to come over and said, "Come in. We need to talk".

ACT ONE:

"Goddamn, what did I do now?" I thought.

Being the only son of a widow woman with two sisters, these "talks" were a regular part of my life. They were tiresome, but there was usually no way they could be avoided. Some older male, "role-model" type would feel it was his duty to talk to me and somehow "make a man" out of me. It never involved him actually talking with me or listening to what I had to say. This monologue usually involved some variation of *"Don't be such a sissy! Do you wanna grow up to be a fag?"*

So original—and such a help. *I'd never thought of that! I'll go throw away my Barbie doll and buy a football immediately!* I'd usually respond with my earnest rendition of "Oh really? Thanks, that's such a help! You've been so kind. Thanks!"

That done, he would walk away—chest puffed out with pride—with a sense that he'd actually *done* something that had some value to me. It was absolutely no help at all, and I *hated* it.

So I went into Harry's office, prepared to make all the right responses in all the right places and act appreciative for the effort taken to educate me. It was the expected thing to do. If I didn't act appreciative enough, he might brand me incorrigible or a pansy, and Mom would give me hell for not appreciating the time that nice man took to make sure I was going down the right path. It was just easier to act like I'd had an epiphany.

Mom stood there at his office door and seemed to want to come in, curious as to what Harry was up to. "Go away!" he said to her. "Go talk to Ruby. Ken and I need to talk." Then he closed the door in her face.

Harry sat down, leaned back in his chair, and put his feet up on his desk. Then he gave me a long look.

"I've been watching you for a while, and I see a certain sparkle in your eyes," Harry said. "It's something you could get in trouble with, or something you could have fun with, so that's why I want to talk to you . . ."

I was puzzled. It didn't sound like the usual spiel and didn't feel like it, either.

"Life sucks for you right now!" he continued, the light glinting off his George Burns glasses. "I know that life sucks for you, but you have no choice right now. BUT –it won't always be that way. This is not forever! Your job right now is just to last because *one day* you can leave all this. But not right now. Keep your head down. Make good grades. And one day you can walk away from all of this and create the life you want. Then you can choose."

Nobody had spoken to me like that before. It felt like a lifeline had been tossed to me.

There followed a conversation that lasted about two hours. At points along the way I could imagine Mom cooling her heels outside, absolutely *steaming* with curiosity and grinding her teeth with impatience. I thought of her sitting there, chain-smoking, and trying to make polite conversation with Ruby. Mom always felt outclassed by Ruby, because Ruby had been to college and all Mom had was that inferiority complex about *not* going.

I learned a lot of useful things that day—like how people use the word "selfish" to manipulate someone into doing what someone else wants. Harry told me that the word "selfish" gets a lot of bad press, but like everything else, selfish behavior is a very healthy thing in moderation.

Harry and I were to have other conversations in this vein over the course of my adolescence. Knowing there was someone like Harry, who was sane and keeping an eye on things, gave me a little peace of mind when I was an adolescent.

And, knowing that life like this was not forever and one day I could leave, was what I needed to hear. I remember life being more bearable and feeling less grim. Harry became my gyroscope, which has helped me to keep from getting off course to this day. I'm deeply grateful to him for being there.

ACT ONE:

That's partly why I was thinking about him that particular evening in my little front yard.

As I said, I particularly enjoyed sitting at the table in my little front yard by my tiny apartment, just as I was that particular evening that I was thinking of Harry. It gave me time to just relax and think about what was happening in my life. That evening I sat there watching the birds dart among the plants and dodging the occasional golf ball lobbed over the fence from the golf course. It was one of those balmy but not hot late-spring nights when the sunset is particularly vivid. As I sat there, I also thought about where I was in my life at that moment.

Life was good. I was free to create the life I wanted, just like Harry said. And I chose to have a good life, with no drama.

At twenty-three, I was the display manager of the largest department store in Oklahoma City, working a job I enjoyed. I finally had a goodly disposable income that I spent on clothes and good living, no debts, or real responsibilities. And I was young, thin, and cute which gave me opportunities for lots of reckless adventure and fashion misadventure. Also I had a man who worshipped me, living right next door. I had the life I wanted to have, just like Harry said I would.

I also understood that, while this was a mostly carefree period, it wouldn't last forever, so I had to appreciate it while I had it.

"When I look back on this time, I know, these will be my 'good old days'," I thought to myself as I sat at the table, leafing through the mail. Then I got hit with a golf ball from over the fence.

In the mail was a note, postmarked San Francisco, from Mark, who I hadn't heard from since he mysteriously moved away from Austin, Texas. He wrote that he and Victor were now living in San Francisco, and he included a phone number and address. This letter came around the first of June, so they had lived in Austin only a little over three months after they blew town in OKC.

Little did I know then, that this letter would be a turning point in my life.

To back up a little, on New Year's Eve 1980, I went to a party that proved that all gay people do *not* have good taste. To elaborate, I believe gay men have either exquisite taste or wretched taste—there's no middle ground. (Though I believe this to be changing with the new generation of gay men as we assimilate into the society at large.)

But all gay men believe they have exquisite taste (testosterone again), so sometimes it's hard to tell until you see their dwellings. (This doesn't apply to lesbians. They have a special dispensation, which exempts them from the requirement of fabulous dwellings, bestowed by Saint Sappho or something like that. This exemption also explains the Birkenstock shoes, labia candles, nylon-webbing dog collars, and potluck dinners.)

After beginning the New Year's Eve evening at Penny's place (where they tried to spike my Perrier with champagne, like I wouldn't notice!) we all ended up at this party at a dive gay bar called the Warehouse on NW Thirty-ninth Street near Penn. The Warehouse was one of those places where you don't wear shoes you care about—you could leave them stuck to the floor, or they might get yakked-up on.

As the clock hit midnight, and all the drunks were singing and kissing each other (while I was wiping yak-up off my shoes, totally disgusted with the entire situation), I thought to myself:

"God as my witness, I will be out of OKC by this time next year! I don't know where or how, but I need to be gone by New Year's Eve 1981!"

(Imagine me waving my fist, which held the napkin I'd just cleaned my shoes with, at the mirrored ball over the dance floor.)

ACT ONE:

I wanted to get out of Oklahoma City and just assumed that I would end up in Dallas, where all the upwardly mobile gay boys in OKC ended up. To that end I was working very hard at Dillard's, trying to fill out my portfolio and prove myself, so I could get a position in one of the Dallas stores one day.

⌒

It's safe to say that when I opened the envelope that early summer evening, California wasn't on my radar screen.

As I said, Mark wrote that they were back in San Francisco. I wasn't surprised that they had moved—I'd heard that from Barry already. The surprise was that they (well, actually Mark) contacted me; I had chalked them up as short-term wonders.

On the spur of the moment, I called them and got Mark on the phone. He sounded very glad to hear from me and gave me a recap of the happenings of the last few weeks.

It seems that Mark's display job at the PX was an exercise in homophobia and anti-Semitism, while Victor wasn't happy at Rollins Protective Services any more. They finally had enough of Austin and one day just decided to up and move back to San Francisco. So they did.

Mark glowingly described the city and waxed eloquent about watching the fog creeping in over Diamond Heights from his living room window. They had rented a lovely flat in Noe Valley, very close to The Castro. He told me of the beautiful old houses and how he had a good job as the display director with this small specialty clothing chain.

"Think of coming out sometime! I'll lay the entire city at your feet!" he said just before we rang off.

ALL GROWN UP NOW

Over the next few days I didn't think much about Mark, as I was busy with work and the usual social whirl. I was also having a flirtation with a guy named Jim, who was a waiter at Pistacio's Restaurant. (*So I'm a pig*. Darrell was really understanding about all of this, especially living next door and all.)

Jim was one of the few blonds I've ever gone for in a big way, with his blue eyes, droopy moustache, and the pretty little cleft in his chin. Penny and Steve were with me the evening I made my move and gave him my phone number. Penny was so funny—she acted like she wanted to crawl under the table, even though I warned her in advance so she could go powder her nose if she wanted to miss the performance.

Jim proved to be very resistant to my advances, but we did have dinner a few times and talk a lot on the phone. During one of these talks he told me of the great love of his life, Brian, who looked remarkably like me; he didn't know if he was drawn to me for *me*, or if it was because I looked like Brian. At one point I told him I didn't really care—he could pretend if he wanted. I just wanted to nail him!

I told Jim of my conversation with Mark, which started Jim reminiscing about the times he had spent in San Francisco. It seems he was a dancer with Fred Waring's road show (whoever the hell *he* was), and they went there on tour. (Sadly Jim got stranded in OKC during an illness while on tour, and they replaced him before he recovered. With no job, he was stuck in OKC and waited tables.)

"It's a great city," Jim said about San Francisco. "I would go back there in a heartbeat if I knew I could support myself."

He dug out a book he had on the city, and we looked at photos. (Being in such close physical proximity, I, of course, made another move, which got yet another rejection.)

ACT ONE:

A few days later I invited him over to my place for Godiva Chocolates and Perrier and another try at seduction. We had a civilized time for a while until (again!) he rebuffed my advances.

"I just don't know if I want you for *you* or because you remind me of Brian!" he exclaimed yet again.

I had had enough.

I strode over to the front door (*it took all of two steps to get there, my place was so small*), opened it, looked at him, and shouted, "GET OUT!"

He was dumbfounded.

"Get OUT!"

"You're throwing me out?"

"YES!" At that I grabbed his arm and dragged him up and to the door.

"Wha . . .?"

"When you decide, you know where I can be reached! Until then get out!"

And then I pushed him out, slammed the door behind him, and turned out the light.

The next evening I was still smarting from my last exchange with Jim. So to distract myself before Penny came by to take me to dinner at Christopher's, I dialed up Mark's number.

"Hello!" he said.

"I want to come visit!"

I surprised myself with that one—I hadn't intended to say that.

"Great! When will you come visit? Victor has his birthday in July, why don't you come out then? Of course, you can stay with us! We have an extra bedroom."

"OK, let me see what time I can get off from work."

And after a little more chat, we rang off because Penny was banging on my door. I was slightly dazed with what I had just done.

Thank heaven for travel agents. I would never have gone through with this trip had it not been for a very understanding travel agent who held my hand and made all the arrangements. She explained all about getting on the plane and how it all worked—I had never dealt with all that myself.

With my visit to California fast approaching, I started to prepare. First of all, Darrell brought over the *San Francisco Chronicle* to read to get a sense of what was happening.

"I thought you'd like ta see what's happenin' there before ya go," he drawled. "The best way is ta read the newspaper, so I got ya one."

Darrell was considerate like that. We both looked through the paper before we went to dinner and read with astonishment an installment of *Tales of the City*. What so amazed us was the topic: Michael picks up a policeman at the Twin Peaks bar and talks about how guys with no taste in decorating an apartment are usually the best lays.

Well! Our jaws were on the ground, we were so astonished! Talking about such things in a major newspaper! Such a place this was!

I also started poring through all my back issues of GQ to see what it had to say about what was being worn on the West Coast.

Then there was the issue of hair—what style was I going to go with? Jenny, my stylist, said all the boys in San Francisco were wearing a really short brush cut, which she would blow out so it stood on end and finish with a little butch wax. (I hadn't worn my hair this short, nor butch wax for that matter, since the fifth grade. Mom used to take me to the barber to have my head shaved the last day of school so she wouldn't have to do too much hair washing during the summer. I HATED it and swore at the time that I would *never* choose to wear it like that. Indeed.)

The color I chose was Clairol's dark warm brown. I decided any blond highlights would look too cliché, as I wasn't *from* California, just visiting. The warm brown, combined with my green eyes, would be just the right look.

But the finishing touch . . .

Since this was California I was visiting, I had to have a good suntan. (I wasn't clued into the Northern California/Southern California thing yet.) So I decided to do all of my tanning in one weekend. I was thankful that Brad-the-Doll had moved. It was safe to sunbathe—Brad-the-Doll was so good-looking that I would never have shown that much flesh in our combined front yard had he still been living there. He might have come home from work and seen me! (And Darrell had *already* seen the merchandise.)

Mrs. Freeman was quite amused when she happened upon me while doing her yard work and spritzed me down with the garden hose for some laughs.

Thankfully I got Mom's complexion—I never burned. I used to brag that I could stay in the sun for WEEKS and not even turn pink—it just turned tan. Unbeknownst to me, though, the hole in the ozone layer was especially large that day. The first day of my tanning marathon turned me red as a fire truck.

This was a new experience. Even the breeze across my skin hurt. That Saturday evening before I went to bed, I slathered every lotion and cold cream I could lay my hands on over every square inch of skin. When it hit my skin, it melted like butter hitting a hot skillet. With all the oil and red skin and waves of heat coming off me, I looked like hot asphalt in the desert at sunset.

So there I was that night, beached stark naked and oily on my bed with the lights out (*even light hitting my skin hurt*), practically glowing in the dark I was so red.

And then there was a knock at the door.

"Who is it?" I shouted.

"It's me. Jim."

He paused. "I had to see you."

"*Oh, GREAT! Isn't THIS fine timing!*" I thought.

"Why?" I shouted again, expecting yet one more disappointment.

"I want you. Tonight. Right now."

Well, what's a boy to do? I was already oiled up, so I got up and opened the door! (But I didn't turn on the light—*that's* for sure!)

He grabbed me and held me close (*ouch*) and said, "Oh, you feel so hot! I was wondering what it would feel like when I finally got to hold you."

(*Ouch. Ouch again.*)

"It's you, Jim . . . see how hot you make me?"

What else was I gonna say? His timing was perhaps a bit off, but this was a bird in the hand, so to speak! Besides I wasn't sunning in the nude, for heaven's sake!

Then he kissed me. (*Ouch. WOW! What a silky moustache!*)

ACT ONE:

You can guess the rest.

⌒

The day came to fly to San Francisco. I talked to Mark and told him which flight I would be arriving on. He said that, along with my other things, I should pack a jacket.

"A *jacket?*" I thought. "This is the middle of summer! He's just pulling my leg. If I show up with a jacket in the middle of the summer, he's just going to have a good laugh."

Besides it was 107 in the shade at five in the afternoon! Just the thought of carrying a jacket to the airport gave me heat rash.

So on the plane I went and off to my big adventure. Beforehand Mark had said that I should bring my portfolio, as he was looking for an assistant and would try to get me hired on. I brought some good clothes, so I would look good for an interview. This was set up for a couple of days into the visit—I was visiting for a week.

When I got to San Francisco, Mark and Vic picked me up at the airport. When we went to get the car, Mark asked, "Do you have your jacket? It's thirty-eight degrees out."

"You're kidding! I just know you are. Of course I don't have a jacket! It was 107 in the shade when I left."

It was indeed something like thirty-eight degrees and foggy. Perhaps I'm exaggerating a bit but not that much. Somehow I, like others who don't live in California, thought that San Francisco was about thirty miles north of LA, and that the whole area was warm and balmy all the time—hence the perception of "sunny California." Right off I made the typical tourist mistake: bringing summer clothes to San Francisco.

Most tourists are alarmed by the cold, but I was delighted!

"Just think! A place where I can wear a sweater in the summer—I've found paradise!" I thought.

Happily I didn't bring shorts. For some reason when I travel I'm reluctant to bare my legs, even though they're attractive enough (knock-knees aside). So with a borrowed jacket from Mark, I was ready to take The City (he also told me that the phrase was capitalized) by storm.

When we arrived from the airport at Mark's flat, I noticed that the two dogs were gone. Now Vic's dog, B.J., was one dog I could live without, but Mark's dog, Danielle the yorkie, was gone, too. I asked Mark about it over coffee the next morning, and he got a bit teary.

"They didn't allow dogs in this place, so we had to give them away" was all he could manage. I charged ahead and asked why they couldn't have waited until they found a place that would allow dogs.

"We had a truck full of our stuff, and we needed to get it back, or they would charge late fees. Vic and I decided at the last minute to move, so we just packed the truck, drove here, and took the first place we could get. They didn't allow dogs." Vic came into the kitchen, and the look that passed across Mark's face told me not to discuss it further.

ACT ONE:

My first look at the Golden Gate Bridge was later that morning. I wasn't really awed by it, clueless guy that I was. (It was the fog. I didn't get a long view of it.) I guessed it was the Golden Gate Bridge by the color, but Victor, who was driving to Marin to check out a burglar alarm for a customer, wasn't quite the tour guide one would want. He seemed resentful at having me fobbed-off on him by Mark, who had to work. His lack of enthusiasm rubbed off on me.

Later Victor took me down to The Castro to a restaurant called Welcome Home, where we had brunch, and Vic greeted people he knew and cruised those he didn't but wanted to. I was in culture shock, as I'd never seen the likes of a place like this.

Remember, I hit town in July 1981 when the place was still in full swing. AIDS was just being whispered about as the "gay cancer" and later that year was called "GRID" (gay-related immune deficiency), but for most of us, it wasn't on the radar screen yet. So I got into the swing of things.

The first time I went out on my own to The Castro was a real eye-opener. As I was walking down the hill on Castro (Mark and Vic lived at the corner of Twenty-second and Noe), I looked over to see, standing in a window at eye level, a guy stark naked for all to see. Moreover he was doing the one-man-one-hand show! I'd never seen a sock puppet show like *that* one!

Later I went to the Elephant Walk on Eighteenth and Castro for a Perrier, only to find that one ordered Calistoga—that was the "done" thing to do. I was told this by this really nice man who bought me one. (He also asked me to come over to see his dungeon. I laughed, thinking he was joking. The more we talked, the more I was sure he wasn't joking.)

"You're from out of town," he commented casually. "I can tell."

"How?" I asked.

I was wearing my electric-blue painter's pants with a red Calvin Klein shirt, my double-wrap belt from Neiman-Marcus, and my Italian fisherman's sandals. Looking back, I now think, "Duh. Not a single item of black."

"It's the suntan," he replied.

"Really?"

"Yeah. Guys here don't have tans. It's the fog."

At the time I thought of all the wasted effort of tanning, but later I realized that it was because I wasn't wearing the "clone" look of the early eighties: T-shirt, Levi button- fly jeans, black combat boots, moustache, and bomber jacket. At least I didn't commit the unpardonable sin of wearing WHITE JEANS. Mark told me in no uncertain terms that owning, let alone wearing white jeans branded one as horribly "East Bay" ("suburban" and definitely uncool to the rest of the world, Concord or Union City to those in the Bay Area) and wouldn't be tolerated in polite society. Besides, he explained, white jeans make even the smallest ass look huge.

That vacation was a blur, but I remember dancing at Dreamland and later smooching at a bus stop on Market and Second with a guy named Sandy I met through Mark. This was really a big transgression for little ol' me from OKC! Sandy showed me around The City a day or two. One memory I have is of watching them take down the old City of Paris department store, astonished that someone could demolish a building like that!

I also met Sandy's roommate, David Burlew. David was the guy Vic knew from the Navy and the person he and Mark connected with the first time they moved to San Francisco.

David Burlew! I still think of him with a sigh. What a doll! I still have a photo of him, nude and sleeping, like an exhausted modern-day Pan. Elfin is the best adjective. David was slight of build, about my height, had dark hair, and brown eyes that twinkled. (His nickname was "Beer Can.") It wasn't too long before we got together to misbehave.

The day of the job interview arrived. I took the M train to Stonestown to meet Mark, who would introduce me to his boss, Bob Vaupin. Bob was my age but had done really well for himself it seems, as he was named the director of stores.

The firm was called Roos Bros., formerly Roos-Atkins. Roos Bros. started out in the late nineteenth century as a nice men's and women's clothing store, and through the years, it had come along as one of the better clothing stores in the Bay Area. In the fifties they merged with the Atkins chain (hence Roos-Atkins) but by the late seventies had fallen on hard times.

A group of investors bought ten of the Roos-Atkins stores with the aim of turning them back into the Roos Bros. of old, a sort of regional Brooks Brothers. Part of this image renovation was presentation, and Mark was hired to help do that. Bob asked him to get whatever he needed, so Mark said he needed me as his assistant.

The interview was really casual and short. Looking back I'm embarrassed that I handed over my "portfolio" in an envelope. It was just a stack of pictures of my displays with a rubber band around them. Thankfully the work spoke for itself. Bob said he would be making a decision in a few weeks.

I really had to think about working for Mark again. Since I had worked under him in OKC, I knew what I was in for. He wasn't a bad person nor an unkind one, just someone who liked to take credit for the work of others. I knew what the situation would be—while I was toting the barges and lifting the bales, Mark would be schmoozing with the manager and drinking coffee.

Now don't get me wrong, he did work, but his efforts always felt a little, well, thin.

Knowing this I had to look at it as a means to an end. This opportunity could get me out of OKC. However galling it would be to give up being the one in charge (like I was then at Dillard's), it would be advantageous on a number of fronts. Besides it wouldn't be forever—Mark had this pattern of moving on unexpectedly.

The flip side to this situation was that Mark was really ill. He had been seriously ill from May until just a week or so before I arrived there and was still weak. With neuropathy in his legs and feet (as a result of his illness), he was having difficulty walking. He would be troubled with it for the rest of his life.

So here Mark was, ill and desperately needing me to come on board. He knew I was a hard worker and had drive and a bit of talent. My hard work would let him off the hook, because physically he wasn't recovered and was barely keeping up appearances, not gaining any ground.

I desperately wanted out of Oklahoma and was willing to trade some autonomy and swallow some pride to do it. At least in this situation, I wouldn't get the surprise—"I'm your boss now"—but was going into it with eyes open and by choice.

As all good times do, this vacation ended. I went to the airport on a clear, sparkling, gorgeous, glittering jewel of a summer day in the Bay Area, all sixty-eight degrees and sunshine. This was one of those days in the Bay Area where it doesn't get any better or more beautiful, and makes one want to sing opera while driving really fast in a convertible with the top down. It was a glorious send-off, a memorable last look.

ACT ONE:

When the plane touched down in Oklahoma City, it was ninety-eight degrees with ninety-eight percent humidity at nine thirty in the evening. The contrast was not lost on me.

"I can't do this any more!" I said to myself. "I'm outta here!"

Back at work I was inspired by all the display work I'd seen in San Francisco. I embarked on a storewide campaign to make this Dillard's store the best-looking one in the Oklahoma City area *at least*. The store looked pretty good already but was nothing compared to what I'd seen on vacation.

There were ulterior motives for this as well. I wanted to round out my portfolio with some more good work in preparation for either moving to San Francisco or Dallas or wherever I was going to end up.

While I was in this prolific display mode, I would call California every day on my morning coffee break. When I got Bob Vaupin on the line, I would ask him if he'd made a decision yet. He would say no he hadn't, and when he did he would let me know.

I'd thank him and call again the next day. This went on for two weeks. It was a tactic that worked when I wanted to get into Dillard's, so I thought it might work again here.

(In case any of you are wondering who was paying for all of those long-distance charges to San Francisco, remember Anna and Louise, the two hard-of-hearing telephone operators from Shepherd Mall? They still liked me. I would just ring them up at Shepherd Mall, ask nicely, and *they* would put the calls through. And they were *sooo* nice about it too!)

On the fifteenth time (I think) that I spoke to Bob Vaupin, he shouted, "ALL RIGHT! I give! You're hired!"

"When do you want me there?"

"Call me tomorrow. I'm sure you've gotten into the habit already, so it won't be any problem!"

"Done!"

With that I went down to Mr. Probst's office. Happily he was in.

"Could I talk to you for a minute?" I asked.

"Sure! Sit down . . . What's up?"

"I've been offered a job in California, working as Mark's assistant."

"You sure you want to do that?"

"Yeah, I'm sure."

Mr. Probst looked at me, seeming to size me up. "You know, I'll give you $5,000 more a year to stay." (This was in 1981 Oklahoma dollars—a 40 percent increase in pay.)

I let a beat skip. "You've been holding out on me. If you can make that offer right now, it's been available all this time."

He skipped a beat. "You're a smart one. Are you really going?"

"Yeah. Your offer just confirmed it."

"OK." He sighed and looked at me. "Now that I know I've lost you, here's some advice. Ask them to pay for your move."

"You can do that?" I gasped.

"You can ask for anything you want. They'll either say yes or no. But more importantly, Ken, get out of retail as soon as you can!"

ACT ONE:

"Why do you say that?" I asked, slightly taken aback.

Ray (I right then started calling him Ray) told me of the retail treadmill of inventory and spring and summer vacation and inventory and back-to-school and Christmas and inventory again, in an endless cycle that traps people.

"You've *got* something," Ray said. "I'd hate to see it snuffed out by the retail trap. Get out! Use it to get where you need to go, and then GET OUT!"

I've been lucky in life. When I need a sign, I get it. This time was no different.

After telling Ray about the job offer, I started to get second thoughts. What if I couldn't do it? How am I going to live in San Francisco with the cost of living there? Is this the right move for me? Am I biting off more than I can chew?

These were all questions that I asked myself the rest of that day, making myself crazy until I could call Bob Vaupin the next morning.

When I spoke to Bob the next morning, he told me he needed me there in ten days.

"Will you pay for my move?" I asked.

There was a heavy sigh. "Yeah! Jeez! Just GET HERE, OK?!?"

"See you in ten days!"

I was still wavering as to whether or not this was the move for me. So, as I do in these situations, I asked for a sign. Now! And none of these "still, quiet voices" for me, but a REALLY BIG SIGN (preferably neon) that I can't miss. I asked the universe for a really big sign and was thinking about it after my conversation with Bob, as I went downstairs to the weekly managers' meeting. I went into the conference room, took my place, and steeled myself for yet another one of those weekly water tortures called "meetings."

There was something in the air that felt very different. I just chalked it up to me being anxious about this job offer, but Ray wasn't there yet and he was always punctual. After about fifteen minutes, we all started to get restless.

And then in walked Bill. You remember him, the manager of the Midwest City Dillard's? The closeted gay married man with the queeny Southern accent? The one I turned down? The one who said to me that he would "remember this"?

He looked around the room slowly.

"I have an announcement," he stated, in that same whiny, queeny, Southern-accented voice. "Ray Probst is no longer with the company. I will be assuming the post of store manager as of a week from today."

And then he gave me a look. And I knew.

I had my sign. My time there was over.

ACT ONE:

It's funny how things happen really fast when it's time for them to do so. I had ten days to finish up my job, get my apartment packed up and closed out, say my good-byes, and drive out to San Francisco.

Mom, of course, was her usual encouraging self when I delivered the news.

"YOU CAN'T MAKE IT IN CALIFORNIA!" she screeched. "You stupid kid! You gave up a $5000 a year raise to do WHAT—run off to California! You'll NEVER amount to anything!"

"Excuse me, I have to go home and PACK!" I shot back as I snatched my car keys off the kitchen counter and stormed out, Kathy following in my wake. We went back to my place, where Kathy broke the news of her decision to move out into her own place. She had just signed the papers that afternoon.

"Great!" I said. "Since you don't have any furniture, why don't we just take everything over to your place, and when I need to send for it, I'll just have them pick it up there."

It was agreed that this was more easily dealt with than Kathy's breaking her news to Mom. When she did, Mom hit the roof! Two of her kids abandoning her in one week! This is just how she would see it. Because it was, indeed, all about her.

This was a woman who didn't make a move on her own in her life. No college because the parents said so. She married Dad to get away from home and married Don to get out of Kansas. Mom never would have moved to San Francisco in her life, so of course, she would say that I couldn't make it. Again that didn't make it any easier for me to take—I was *really* pissed off by what she said—but there you have it.

So life skipped along those last few days as I emptied out my apartment into Kathy's new house and went to a succession of going-away dinners. One morning Mom called me at work with some news.

"I quit my job today," she said quietly.

As she told it, her boss yelled at her in front of a customer, which she didn't like, so Mom went over to the president of the bank and quit. This put them into a bind—she was the only one who knew how to balance the bank. Mom never liked working for this bank to begin with, and I (foolishly) thought she finally had enough and gotten a backbone.

"Now you can get a job you really like!" I responded. "You never liked working there. I know they're over a barrel, but however you play it, you have a chance to work in a better situation. You've mentioned several offers you got in the past—call them and tell them you're in play."

Then the other shoe dropped.

"You know," she said cagily. "This isn't a very good time for you to be leaving . . ."

"Oh, I get it. You quit your job to try to guilt-trip me into staying here!"

"No, that's not . . ."

"That's not, hell! It's *never* going to be a convenient time for me to move, but in case you hadn't noticed, I'm not living my life for your convenience!"

"You NEVER think of anybody else!" she screamed. "You were ALWAYS so goddamned stubborn; you've always wanted to do what YOU goddamn well pleased!"

"Isn't that the point? You MADE your choices, now I'm making MINE! I'm GOING to California!" I shouted back. With that I slammed down the phone.

And yes, she expected me to call the whole thing off, stay in OKC, and hold her hand until she got this mess sorted out. That was the most exasperating part. But I'm my mother's son—she called it "bullheaded" when describing me but "strong-willed" when describing herself. Where we were different, though, was that I wanted to use that stubbornness to move forward; she wanted to use it to keep things as they were.

ACT ONE:

The time to go drew near. I gave notice at my apartment. On my way out of the apartment office, I stopped by to tell Mrs. Freeman. She was sitting on her front porch and offered me some iced tea, and we chatted. She surprised me with her response to the news of my move.

"Boy, I went to California once and hated it. If you hate it, I will personally pay for your move back because I don't think you'll like it," she croaked confidently.

I thanked her for the offer and told her I would stop in before I left town, as I had a couple days left in the place before I went.

On my last day at work, I didn't feel like working. My car was in the shop for service, and I was worried that it might throw up some expensive problem. What was more irksome was that nobody seemed to be concerned that it was my last day. My assistant, Lana, wanted to keep making displays, and I didn't hear a thing about how people would miss me. It was really pissing me off.

Finally about four o'clock, I could take no more. In disgust I thought about how hard I'd worked, only to be ignored when I went away. I paged Lana.

"Lana, could you take me to get my car from the shop? I'm blowing this joint!"

"OK, but could you give me a few minutes? I'm right in the middle of something."

So I hung up the phone and moped for a few moments, when I heard my page. I called the operator, and she said, "Chuck from Operations needs to see you in the credit office."

"What the hell is *this* for," I thought as I went downstairs.

Chuck met me in the office, where he said, "We need to go into the computer room to pull up your account and see if you're current."

Now I was really mad—was this it? Checking on my account before I go?

He opened the door to the computer room, and I heard everyone yell, "SURPRISE!"

And it indeed was a surprise. They all kept it such a secret that Lana's fast thinking kept me from bolting before they got me in the room.

It was a good time. I heard from everyone just how well I had done. As I suspected their regard started all those months ago when I helped out on the inventory, staying throughout the entire thing right alongside everyone else. Presents of clothing and cash were given along with the usual speeches. Thinking about it even today, I'm grateful.

The days before my move to San Francisco passed in a blur. As I said, I had ten days between when I accepted and when I had to be there. There was a lot to be done—Darrell was game for all of it and a tremendous help. I reserved the last free evening for him. We had dinner out and went to the bars. In the Circa (a sort of piano bar on NW Thirty-ninth Street), we ran into Brock, of all people. Remember him? The ex-boyfriend who gave me hepatitis?

"I hear you're moving!" he shouted over the drunken, off-key singing.

"Yes, I am," I replied and introduced him to Darrell. Darrell had heard about Brock and the hepatitis, and got a look on his face that resembled a Rottweiler baring his teeth. This was in direct contrast to his usual, sweet, golden-retriever expression.

"Well I thought something was going on," Brock said airily. "The people at Dillard's called me and asked if I wanted to have my old job in display back, but I turned them down."

ACT ONE:

"Hey, don't knock it!" I replied coolly. "It was good for me. Here I am, going from working in display at Dillard's to San Francisco to take a position as the assistant director of visual merchandising for a chain of upscale specialty stores, while *you*, dear, are a maitre 'd in a second-rate restaurant."

At that I said evenly, "Come, Darrell," turned on my heel, and swished out of the bar.

There was a look of astonishment on Darrell's face as he followed me out. He had never seen that side of me before.

Sitting with me in the car, he said, "Do you do that often? And what's an assistant director of . . . uh . . ."

"First, no, I don't do that often, only when it's necessary. Second, it's a nice title for a glorified 'pin-pusher.' That's the side of me I hoped you'd never have to see."

"Well, darlin', he had it comin'. Now let's go home . . ."

Early the next morning I was to leave. I had said all my good-byes and arranged with Brian, Mom's next-door neighbor, to drive out to San Francisco with me. He was my age (we graduated in the same class) and had lived for a time in Walnut Creek, one of the Bay Area suburbs. It was a free trip out there for him and would provide company and another driver for me. I had stayed in OKC until the very last minute, so we had to drive continuously to get to San Francisco.

All my furniture and such was now at Kathy's new house, and the majority of my wardrobe I packed into the car. Some of it I strapped to the luggage rack on the trunk, but most rode in the backseat, as the shocks in the back couldn't handle the weight, and the tires rubbed in the wheel wells. The Celica was old—it had 190,000 miles on it—and my fear was that it would die on the road, and someone would find my bleached bones and wardrobe in it somewhere in the desert.

Early that morning Kathy and Mom saw me off. I almost sideswiped Kathy's car going out the driveway because I was crying so hard. They weren't tears so much of sorrow but of anxiety and anticipation; this represented a big step for me, and I felt a bit overwhelmed. I did stop crying as we passed out of the OKC city limits. The big adventure was on!

We were on the road continuously for thirty-eight hours, stopping only for gas and food. The Medfly roadblocks heralded our arrival in California. This was during the time of the dreaded Mediterranean Fruitfly, and roadblocks were set up to confiscate all fruit and plant products coming in from out of state. There were two fruits in this car (at that point, *this* fruit was feeling more like a vegetable), but we were not the right variety.

We crossed the Bay Bridge at 8:05 p.m. on August 21, 1981. It was just getting foggy, but to this day I still remember the light and how The City looked. Soon we were at Mark and Vic's, where I would be living until I had enough money to get my own apartment.

As a welcoming gesture, they had invited over David Burlew.

My job at Roos Bros. began on Monday the 24th. As I said earlier, my official title (that I still use on resumes) was "assistant director of visual merchandising." Translated into real language, it meant peon display person. My job, along with Mark's, was to travel to each of the ten stores, which were spread out from Santa Rosa to San Jose, and do displays in them. My little Toyota was appointed to be the display commute/transport vehicle for all of this commuting. Vic was still driving the douched-out Torino.

On that first day, I was introduced around and met Dave, the old trimmer kept on from Roos-Atkins days. Dave would be working with Mark and me, doing the displays for all of the stores. His style, which Mark derided as old-fashioned, was of the old-time haberdasher school.

ACT ONE:

Being twenty-three and stupid, I also thought that he was old fashioned and that he took way too long to do things. Soon, though, I developed a real liking for Dave. He was the real article, someone who really knew his craft and could do it blindfolded (which he proved to me one day). While Mark was off in meetings and schmoozing, it was Dave-the-Trimmer and I who did the work.

Dave-the-Trimmer was from the days when display work was one of those "apprentice-journeyman-master" trades. He had mastered all of the old-time display techniques, such as rigging a suit form complete with the cuff blocks, rigging the shirt forms with the flying shirttails and cauliflower sleeve treatments, wiring neckties to lay just so, weighting the hems of garments to make them appear more luxurious—Dave knew all of that old haberdashery stuff. What I learned from him was that I needed to know more about the craft of display. This knowledge made it possible to push forward into new territory without having to reinvent the wheel.

Happily Dave showed me lots of tricks, and I learned volumes of what was considered proper and "good form," especially in the area of men's proper dress. His pet peeve was the roll line on a suit coat. I pressed a lapel flat one (and only one) time, only to be lectured on why they called it a *roll* line, operative word ROLL.

The other thing he was specific about (to the point of measuring) was that when rigging a suit, there should be exactly one-half inch of linen (shirt cuff) showing below the cuff on the jacket. And he always called the shirt "linen"—it was the proper term.

Our display room in the main store in Stonestown was shared with the tailor shop. I was delighted by this, and over time I peppered the old Sicilian tailors with questions about what they were doing and how to do it. At first they waved me away as an annoyance. One day I brought a couple of things in that I had made, and after they carefully examined them (without saying anything about them to me), they warmed up to me.

Whenever they were working on something more exotic than the usual trouser cuffs or such, I'd hear, "Hey, BOY!" And I knew to get over there fast as they had something cool to teach me. This is how I learned the beauty of a properly pressed garment—you can save bad sewing with good pressing or kill a good garment with bad pressing—and how to achieve that beauty with a good iron and all of the pressing hams and tools. I learned what all of the different scissors were for, why there were different types of hand-sewing needles and threads, and when hand-sewing was better and a stronger finish than machine sewing. They even taught me reweaving to repair rips and holes, which I really put to good use with all of my vintage clothes.

These tailors also had their pet peeves, which I learned as well. One was: *touch their tools and die*. Each one had a funky tool—a weird knife sharpened *just so* for ripping, a pin cushion that they favored over others, or a point turner whittled for them by a favorite uncle—and if that tool came up missing, it was a Big Deal.

Being older now I have my own pet peeves, some of them learned from Dave-the-Trimmer and those old Sicilian tailors.

I discovered over time that the Roos Bros. organization was an exercise in ignoring common sense. The stated goal of the company was to recapture the golden name of a bygone era, to reestablish a venerable San Francisco retail institution. Common sense, then, would dictate certain things.

Like printing new sales slips and shopping bags saying "Roos Bros.," instead of waiting until all the "Roos/Atkins" ones were used up.

Or changing the signs on the stores to say "Roos Bros.," instead of keeping the old "Roos/Atkins" signs and covering them with painted canvas signs.

Or upgrading all the stores gradually but equally, instead of blowing all the upgrade money on one store.

ACT ONE:

Or making sure that any print ads in the media were distinctive enough to be noticed, instead of being so tasteful and unobtrusive (read: invisible) as to be missed even by those looking for them. I could never find the ads in the newspapers. It was kind of like those cartoons that look the same but have hidden images—but at least in the cartoons you could eventually find something.

Or more close to home, hiring someone who actually knew what he was doing to run the display department, instead of someone who could talk a good game (Mark).

Or hiring someone qualified to be his assistant from an overflowing talent pool right in town, instead of moving in some unknown quantity from the middle of nowhere at great expense (that would be me).

What I'm taking a long time to say is that my ticket to San Francisco was the result of a ponderous lack of common sense, and for that I'm extremely grateful.

I got lucky.

The first big push we had after I started was getting the Stonestown store updated. It was going to be the flagship store and already housed all of the main offices. For those not familiar with San Francisco, Stonestown was an open-air shopping center built in the early 1950s (and looked like it); it was one of the first of its kind.

When it was built, this area of town (south and west) was relatively new construction. (Later on in the mid-eighties, the whole shopping center was torn down to build an enclosed mall.) Roos/Atkins was one of the older stores in Stonestown, and it looked like it too.

For this renovation, the Powers That Be hired a consultant, Bob Hartman. Bob had worked at Macy's Union Square managing the window crew, and Clark Stone, who had been the Big Cheese at Macy's before hiring on as the Big Cheese of this gig, brought him in.

I learned a lot from Bob, some of it about display.

My education began during this Stonestown crunch, when we were working through the night to get the store redone for the grand reopening. Bob and I had to transport a large table from the loading dock downstairs up to the front door. Since it was too large to get up the stairs, we had to drive it there in the big panel truck. This was about two in the morning.

In the truck on the way down, Bob casually asked, "Would you like some coke?"

"No, I drink Tab, thanks," was my reply.

He stopped the truck. Then he turned and looked at me.

"Coke."

"No, Tab. Or Diet Pepsi. I don't like Diet Coke."

"COKE," he said meaningfully. And then he sniffed.

A beat skipped. Then another. Light dawned.

"OOOOHHHH!" I gasped, shocked. "You mean you do that *AT WORK?*"

"Yes," he answered flatly.

I was scandalized! This was news to me! Looking back on it, though, this was really sooooo early eighties, and coke was really the "done" thing then. Sort of like a handshake. (The other "handshake" I learned about was the casual blow job or other that I would catch Bob at in the back of that big panel truck.)

A moment of silence.

ACT ONE:

"Well . . . ?" he asked.

"I'd really prefer a Diet Pepsi."

Whereupon Bob started up the truck, shaking his head and muttering about me being fresh off the boat from Oklahoma.

Working with someone really experienced like Bob showed me the glaring gaps in my display knowledge. I discovered that an Okie accent helped me fill these gaps. Though I had studiously avoided developing the accent while I was in OKC, when Bob would ask me to do something that didn't sound too familiar, I would drawl, "I'm sure we call it 'somethin' differnt' where I come from." This way I could usually tease enough information out of him to figure out what I needed to do.

I really hit the ground running when I moved to San Francisco. As I mentioned earlier, it was at the tail end of the merry-go-round that was the gay scene in the late seventies, Sylvester was still "feeling mighty real," and AIDS was still known as the "gay cancer," and not on most peoples' radar screens. So being young, thin, and relatively cute—and a bit of a slut with good clothes—I was out there with all the rest of them, dancing in the clubs and screwing in the bathhouses. My first time in a bathhouse was with Mark and Vic.

It was during my vacation. They wanted to take me to the Club Baths on Ritch Street. Mark assured me it would not be scary or tacky, that I didn't have to do anything I didn't want to do, and that the place itself was actually quite tasteful, even had a small café—very civilized. (Which it was.) I went out of curiosity and horniness, and also to see the two of them in this place. I thought it exceedingly strange that they, a supposedly monogamous couple, would be going there. But Mark said that "all the couples do it."

At one point during the evening, I (unknowingly) walked past the door to their room. It was open. I saw Mark sitting there, looking *not-at-all* happy to be there, towel draped just *so*, looking like bait. Victor was occupied with someone else. Thankfully they didn't see me, and I hurried away.

(And, to make a long story shorter, I hooked up with a guy who looked like the Olympic swimmer Mark Spitz, oh my god! and I've been a convert ever since.)

I had all sorts of adventures that first year in San Francisco. Some were of long duration, and others were one time or one night. It was really very different than OKC!

The main difference I noticed was that in OKC, if a guy wanted to get laid, he would generally be expected to spring for dinner. So I could count on a few dinners during the week to help economize. In San Francisco a guy could get laid in five minutes, just by making eye contact and saying a quick "Your-place-or-mine?" It wreaked havoc with my budget.

One (non-sexual) adventure I remember was my first visit to The Stud. This was when The Stud was still on Folsom Street, back in pre-history. I remember the place as being one of those where you didn't wear shoes you cared about—my new, off-white, Candies clear-soled oxfords got absolutely trampled, it was so crowded. There were all these early-eighties New Wave types there with the occasional punk thrown in. Lots of "looks," lots of Important Hair. I, of course, was trying my best to do the "clone" look but could never really break the fashion code on that one, especially since I didn't like combat boots. Really my taste at the time ran more to mohair suits with skinny ties and pointy shoes.

Anyway I was standing at the bar (well, actually I was held in place by the crowd at the bar—I could have raised my feet off the floor and not fallen down), being chatted up by this guy wearing (of all things) a gray pinstripe suit. He of course was wearing it ironically (you could just *feel* the quotation marks), what with the black army boots, torn T-shirt, and the hair he cut himself with nail scissors.

Finally he said to me, "Well, how do you like my photographs?"

I had noticed them hanging on all the walls above the crowd, these grisly, *very* up-close photographs of dead rats in traps, their eyes bulging and tongues lolling, cropped at interesting and arty angles.

ACT ONE:

"Indeed! Your photographs? Like you own them, or you took 'em?"

(I tried to sound politely interested. It wasn't easy.)

"I took 'em!"

"Really! What an, uh, *interesting* treatment of the subject matter."

"You wanna go to my place? You're really cute," he purred lecherously.

Not wanting to be the subject of a new series of potentially grisly photographs, I politely declined and got the hell out of there.

It took only a month for me to get into an apartment. The studio apartment I rented was in Noe Valley, basically one room with kitchen and bath with skylight. They said it had "partial view" of Diamond Heights, which meant I saw mostly the roof next door and a little sliver of Diamond Heights. There was a little balcony/fire escape with sliding doors off the kitchen, where I fantasized I'd put a little table and chair so I could eat my breakfast every morning. That didn't happen, primarily because of the fog. But it was a nice fantasy.

Eventually in this place, I would experience not one but two floodings from a leak somewhere. (The water would rise up through the carpet not drip through the ceiling, as one would expect from living on the top floor.) The landlords were enthusiastically cheap and never got around to fixing things, so I endured mushrooms growing up through the pile in the carpet before it was all over with.

The mushrooms appeared on my first birthday in The City. Mom had called to ask what I was up to.

"I'm sitting here, looking at the mushrooms that are growing up through the pile of the carpeting" was my response. There was silence on the other end of the line. Mom, no doubt, thought that I had either gone crazy, was doing drugs, or had joined a cult.

Anyway, I was glad to be out of Mark and Vic's place. They were nice to have me stay with them, and Mark was especially helpful about getting me established. But not having a place of my own was troublesome to me, especially since I was cutting a swath of sexual devastation across the scene. While I was living with Mark and Vic, I made sure I was a good guest—you know, washing all the dishes and laundry, buying dinner occasionally, getting lost for large blocks of time so they could be alone. Mark wanted me to stay longer, but Victor very pointedly *didn't*.

There was another reason I wanted to be out of Mark's place. It was the little camera in my bedroom.

At first I didn't notice it, just thought that it was part of the burglar alarm system that Vic had installed in their apartment. This alarm system reminded us of its existence with a "beep" every time a door or window was opened.

The camera was a little black box, placed high up in one corner of the room, near the ceiling. As there seemed to be visible hardware in every room, at first I didn't pay it any mind. But one evening, when I got to looking more closely, I saw what looked like a lens. (Which freaked me out. Big time.) From then on I dressed in the bathroom—there wasn't one in *there*.

Mark said it was a motion detector. Uh huh.

Vic offered to install a burglar alarm in my new place for free. I politely declined.

ACT ONE:

It took until the end of December to get my furniture shipped from Oklahoma. In the meantime I had all I really needed: a borrowed bed (from Mark), a borrowed Stickley sofa (the most uncomfortable, expensive antique piece of furniture known to man), a folding chair, and a telephone (a black Trimline—very stylish and touch-tone, which was still an extra charge back then).

One thing I noticed when I moved out of Mark and Vic's house was that, except for picking Mark up for work in the morning (Vic still got the car), I was dropped from their social life. At first I was a little puzzled and hurt. Here I was in a strange city, and Mark and Vic were the only people I knew besides David Burlew. And he was really, really busy being a bigger slut than I was.

But it dawned on me one evening that I would have to start meeting people on my own and not relying on Mark and Vic for all of my social interaction. I started spending lots of time down in The Castro, and since it was over the hill from where I lived, I'd ride the 35 Eureka bus over and back—it let off a half block away from my apartment.

Waiting for the 35 Eureka bus at Castro and Market one fall evening, I started a conversation with a rather distinguished-looking older gentleman—white hair and beard, dressed all in black—who introduced himself as The Bishop. We continued our conversation while riding the bus, and it turned out that he lived one block up the hill from me on Valley Street.

"My clerical name is Father, but you must call me The Bishop," he said as I eyed the gold bishop's ring on his finger; it had an amethyst the size of a robin's egg set in it. When I asked him about the ring, he told me that he was the North American bishop for the Roman Catholic Synod of the Syro-Chaldean Rite, an order of monks based in Baghdad. Being a fallen-away (*really* fallen-away) Protestant, it sounded legit to me—what did I know from Catholics? That was his story, and he stuck with it the entire time I knew him. And when I say I knew him, well, let's just say I eventually *knew* him.

As an aside, one time I asked him The Question: Shouldn't you not be *doing this*? His answer, which I've later heard elsewhere quoted from Catholic law, was that they are vows of *chastity*, not celibacy. Chastity means *not getting married*. And since it wasn't *my* vow that was getting broken, I didn't care one way or the other. *So there.*

The Bishop was establishing a monastery here in San Francisco, just as soon as he could get money from Baghdad to buy a building. The building he had his eye on was this big Beaux Arts pile on Guerrero Street that was painted bright turquoise and had big, round bay windows and a ballroom in the basement. The war between Iran and Iraq was making it impossible to do just that, but he was confident that the conflict would be resolved soon. (Remember, this was in late 1981. We all know how *that* turned out.)

"We'll go to dinner soon!" he said grandly as he got off the bus at his stop. Thus began my education in the big city.

The Bishop lived a block away from me in a late-sixties house set into the side of a hill. This place was crammed full (and not artfully so) of all sorts of stuff. There were some really good, antique, gilded "Louis-Louis" pieces, as well as some gloomy-looking, heavy Spanish Inquisition case goods with lots of hob-nails and hardware on 'em—tortured furniture for people who torture people. Along with the furniture were lots of books (in a variety of languages), religious icons, and cat hair. I mention the cat hair because *everything* in that house was covered with it, and the smell of cat pee permeated the entire place. The cats, one black and one white (named "Black Kitty" and "White Kitty"), especially liked sharpening their claws on the Louis pieces. They had ripped the needlepoint upholstery on a couple of the gilded bergere chairs to shreds already and were working on the settee. (Later additions to the decor would include an assortment of very pretty, young Cambodian boys and even more cat hair.)

There was one bedroom in this house I still think of with awe. It was crammed cheek-to-jowl (no exaggeration) with silver. Not plate. Silver.

ACT ONE:

Flatware and hollowware, front to back, ceiling to floor, packed so you couldn't walk in but had to remove things to get through. There was a sterling flatware service for twenty-four with all the esoteric forks and such. There were silver bowls you could bathe a baby in and platters you could serve him up on as well, if you were so inclined. Just astonishing! Since I was new to The City, I just accepted it all without question, assuming that I had run into one of those eccentrics whom I had read about in Armistead Maupin's "Tales of the City" books.

Then there was Virgo John, The Bishop's driver, who lived in the in-law apartment in the basement. Nobody knew his real name, not even him. Virgo John was a shell-shocked Vietnam veteran who looked like Rudolph Nureyev. He drove The Bishop around in this old '66 Cadillac limousine that looked like someone had slathered it with Elmer's Glue and rolled it in silver glitter. When we would go out, we either rode around in this glittering barge of a car or Virgo John's fire engine-red '67 Buick Riviera.

Going out with Virgo John was always an experience akin to Russian roulette. Since he was shell-shocked, one never knew what to expect. He could be charming and funny, and the outing could pass without incident. Or it could go horribly wrong—one never knew. My first experience with his particular brand of craziness coincided with my first taste of sushi.

We took the glitter barge to a sushi place down on Polk Street, with me all the while thinking, "Just try to divorce yourself from the fact that this is raw fish. Just experience it for the taste and texture it is, and for God's sake *don't look like an out-of-towner!!* I had already practiced with the chopsticks at home for the event—I was too new in town (and, therefore, too insecure) to ask for a fork.

The Bishop ordered (he always ordered, probably because he always paid as well), and we presently were served an assortment of the finest sushi (or so I was told—I wouldn't have known) so I could have a good, well-rounded first experience. As I was gagging down the first piece (thinking "goddamn this tastes like raw fish"), Virgo John started hyperventilating.

"Bishop, this is RAW FISH!" he muttered between breaths, while staring wild-eyed at his plate.

"Yes, John, it's sushi," The Bishop calmly explained.

"IT"S RAW FISH! RAW!" A more agitated tone.

"Yes, John, that's how they prepare sushi." The Bishop was still speaking calmly.

"OH! MY! GOD! IT'S RAW FISH! AAAAAAAAHHHHHHHH . . . !"

The scream signaled that Virgo John was having a flashback to some horrible concentration camp somewhere in Vietnam, no doubt triggered by the raw fish. As he was screaming at the top of his lungs while staring in horror at the food (I could relate—it scared me to look at it too), I should have felt sorry for him. However, my only thought was:

"Great! A diversion!"

At which point I scooped up all the sushi off my plate and tossed it under the table. (I also wanted to scream about what I had just eaten, but I thought this a more sensible response.)

That action was lost in the pandemonium as Virgo John was grabbed by two of the Japanese waiters and three of the other patrons, dragged screaming from the restaurant, and flung onto the sidewalk while The Bishop sheepishly paid the check.

Mark enjoyed hearing tales of my exploits in The City, and he especially liked hearing that I was dating a Catholic bishop (his being Jewish and all). You should have seen his expression, though, when I told him about the member of the motorcycle gang I was also seeing at the same time. Now *there's* a story! But I digress.

Being the bishop's Cute Young Thing for a season was educational and fun, but it did have its drawbacks, which I'll get to later. I got to go to all the shows,

ACT ONE:

learned about new cuisine, saw all the sights, and listened to The Bishop hold forth on many different subjects, of which he seemed to know quite a bit. He also regaled me with stories of his various careers. There were some things that didn't quite gibe though, like his claim to have studied draping with Paul Poiret.

The Bishop claimed to be sixty and this was 1981, so that meant he would have been born in 1921. Poiret, for those of you who haven't studied fashion history, was prominent in the 1914-1919 period but lasted into the early thirties. The Bishop must have been really young when he studied with Poiret. Looking back, this was my first inkling that The Bishop might be a vampire, hence much older than he presented himself to be.

There were other tales as well: he was an air traffic controller at one time, another time he owned and ran a nightclub in San Francisco, he had traveled all over the world for various enterprises . . . it went on and on. Comparing notes with Susan later, the stories she heard were completely different from the ones he told me. Add up all the time it would take to do these and put it end to end, and there is only one possible explanation: vampire.

(Well, two explanations really, but "fraud" is such a strong word. And I don't recall seeing any mirrors in his house.)

Speaking of Susan, we met through The Bishop, ushering at the Opera House. She had been friends with The Bishop for years while ushering with him. Early on The Bishop decreed that to be a fully rounded person I was to see a lot more ballet and opera. Since I had no money for this but did look good in a dinner jacket, he got me on as a guest usher in the Dress Circle at the Opera House. The first opera I attended was a grim, brooding, dark Russian drama called *Lady Macbeth of Mtinsk* by Shostakovich. (No costumes. No "hit tunes.") Even though I had absolutely no idea what was going on (this was the days before supertitles), I was hooked. I guest-ushered a couple more times before I got my permanent pass.

"I just talked to Henry!" The Bishop gasped on the phone one evening soon after my last guest-ushering gig. "I have your permanent usher's pass for you!"

"Uh, ok," I said, completely underwhelmed.

"You don't understand! People wait years for a permanent pass. Henry must really like you! You must have made a good impression."

Henry Watson, head usher of the Dress Circle, looked like a Black Alfred Hitchcock, with the bald head, the protruding lip, and the protruding stomach. He was tall (about six foot four) and looked like a real badass (useful for a head usher), but I found out over the years that Henry was a real softie. I used to give him headaches over the dress code—it said dark suit, white shirt, and tie. There's quite a bit of variation one can introduce within that framework—like red shoes, for example.

Or jewelry.

Or "amusing" jackets.

Or hair colors that don't occur in nature.

Henry finally gave up after the patrons told him how much they enjoyed the spectator sport that was "What will he come up with this week?" In short he liked me.

So once a week I would dress up and go off to the Opera House to see the opera or ballet or whatever was playing. Sometimes we would do penance and have to work some real stinkers like the Chinese rock singer (imagine Prince songs sung by your cat, accompanied by lots of cheap spandex and a low-budget laser light show) or the Meechum Choir (a singing group from Hunter's Point that drew more ushers than audience—their idea of good singing was LOUD singing, and their production values were in the negative numbers).

Whatever was showing, Susan, The Bishop, and I would hang out and talk before the performance and during the intermissions, sometimes with Susan's husband, George, who always thought The Bishop was a phony but was too much of a gentleman to mention it.

Susan and George are an interesting and, I've always felt, glamorous couple. Susan was born in London to an upper-crust family. She survived the Blitz and was sent to a Catholic school for girls (even though she is Jewish) in the countryside until she was expelled for bad behavior. It seems that she wouldn't wear her gas mask, though she was constantly being nagged to wear it during air raids. So during one air raid, she *did* wear it—just the mask, nothing else—and was promptly expelled. This was the beginning of a trend. Susan did as she pleased and didn't give a whit about what other people thought of it.

Susan left high school to make her way as a columnist on Fleet Street, where she reported on the doings of all the bright young things in London. To supplement her income, she was an artists' model ("Undraped, Darling Angel! Of course!" she told me), when she wasn't staying at her parents' apartment in Paris or getting engaged.

"Darling Angel, I got engaged a *lot*! It was the thing to DO!" she explained with a mischievous glint in her eye. "One could do a *lot*, if one were engaged. Not that I misbehaved, good heavens no!" Then she laughed.

George is a real gent, born in Oakland on the wrong side of the tracks. He and his brothers opened a jazz club in the Tenderloin called the Blackhawk, which is mentioned in all the jazz history books. They hosted all the greats.

Billie Holiday's last gig was at the Blackhawk. Susan told me once that, at Billie's last gig, she knew when buttoning Billie's dress and aiming her at the stage that the end was near. Billie was too far gone.

The Blackhawk existed in the early 1950s along with other now-legendary nightspots in San Francisco. There was The Hungry i, where Phyllis Diller got her start doing comedy. Then there was The Condor, which Carol Doda made famous in the early sixties by wearing Rudi Gernreich's topless bathing suit there—and broke that particular taboo. The Blackhawk was one of these famous places, the go-to place for jazz, and anyone who was anyone went. There are classic recordings of jazz greats done at the Blackhawk. It was a Big Deal.

Johnny Mathis got fired from the Blackhawk; as Susan still says, "He doesn't discuss that period of his career." Since it was housed in one of her previous business addresses, famed Madam Sally Stanford was at the Blackhawk on opening night (which, by the way, featured Tempest Storm taking a milk bath while Johnny Mathis sang "Oh Promise Me." It's no wonder he doesn't discuss that period.) The venerable Ms. Stanford, who ran a string of "houses" and later went respectable and became mayor of Sausalito, told George that night that all the people present who had claimed to be in that room when it was her establishment *never were*. They were just bragging. And she would know.

George and his brothers were also the original founders and partners, along with Saul Zaentz of Fantasy Records. Saul Zaentz went on to produce films and sold Fantasy Records to David Geffen, as I remember. Susan and George have a painting over their sofa that George proudly tells people about—it was used on the cover of one of the first albums they produced for Fantasy Records. It was this association, along with the Blackhawk, that made Susan and George members in good standing with the jazz community.

Along with jazz musicians, Susan met Herb Caen, who frequented the Blackhawk during its (and his) glory days. Herb Caen was the "inventor of three-dot journalism," as they used to say. (He was San Francisco's version of Walter Winchell.) Herb and Susan had an ongoing acquaintance from the

Blackhawk days on, and Susan was in Herb's column many, many times over the years.

"Darling Angel, one isn't *truly* a San Franciscan until one has been in Herb Caen's column!" she once declared to me, right after my one mention in his column. (Which, by the way, was for making the red hat for Elton John's Diet Coke commercial—the one called "Nightclub," which had all sorts of dead movie stars electronically inserted into it—that caused quite a stir. *So there.*)

Susan and George met through what Susan called "The Jewish Princess Network." She was visiting San Francisco in the early fifties and wanted to stay. Through connections on the "network," she met and married George within two weeks and got her green card.

"I married George for my green card, but it worked out quite well," she confided to me at lunch another day. "He's really funny and kind, and we've really had fun and a good life together—what more can one ask?"

George's version of the story is a little different but quite charming. He told me one evening over dinner that he was invited to a party for one of the jazz greats (I can't remember which one, but he knew them all from the Blackhawk), who had a house in the Oakland hills. The house was considered quite avant-garde for the time, this being the mid-1950s—there was a very large tree growing up through the living room ceiling.

Anyway he and Susan were introduced at this party, and he was immediately smitten.

"She looked like an English version of Elizabeth Taylor, so beautiful and refined," he said. "I thought that she was a really solid person and that if I could marry her, we would be very happy."

He went on to tell about some of their early years. George, as well as running the Blackhawk, played cards in a card room on the Peninsula, the part of the Bay Area south of San Francisco. He approached the management to see if he could get a game going and develop a customer for that game (I guess that's what you would call it), and if he developed a business, then he would get a percentage.

The first day Susan was recruited to be one of the card players (even though she didn't know how), so they would have enough people to play. At one point, one of the (paying) players asked her a question. Panicked, Susan excused herself, and locked herself in the ladies' room.

"She's changed a lot since then," George observed, smiling.

And, indeed, she had. Aside from this momentary lapse, Susan has walked through life with her head up and her spirits high. Over the years I've seen her through some serious health problems as well as more than her share of troubles. She remains the same brave, true spirit that showed up wearing only a gas mask, posed "undraped" for artists in London, and found her green-card husband in San Francisco.

One time we were talking about the spinal surgery she had had some years before. The doctor had told Susan that she might not walk again.

"Darling Angel, I insisted that this was *not* an option!" she exclaimed. "There are roles on the Opera House stage that I've not performed yet, and this *simply* wouldn't do!"

Susan does what are called "supernumerary roles." These are the roles for mute actors that advance the action but don't require lines or singing. She had done some in the past but had others she wanted to do, and no surgery was going to stand in the way. So not only does she walk, but when a particularly demanding role comes her way, she tells her doctor that she's doing it and what action is required, and then gets him to show her ways to do it without injuring herself. *Not* doing a role because of her back, well, isn't even considered.

ACT ONE:

Actually Susan's crowning achievement was Lady Capulet in *Romeo and Juliet*, ("Darling Angel, my costume looks like they got their money *last week*!" she exclaimed.) For the opera *Mephistopheles*, she got her photo into *Vogue* magazine with her performance of the old woman peeling apples or "the visual metaphor in the second act" (her words). So Susan got into *Vogue* before I did.

"Darling Angel, never complain and never explain" is her motto.

The Bishop was visiting Cambodia regularly when I knew him during the early eighties. As I was not really well versed in world affairs (fashion and gossip were more my speed then as now), it didn't occur to me that this would be unusual. But we did not have diplomatic relations with Cambodia yet (as I understood it). Still The Bishop went.

During this time he also started his retinue of Cambodian boys, who were in this country as refugees. They eventually took my place as the Cute Young Things; at twenty-four I looked too old. They looked really young and cute, and The Bishop *was* Catholic, you understand.

With The Bishop's Cambodian phase gaining momentum, I fell from favor as The Bishop's Cute Young Thing. I saw it coming (I mentioned that there were drawbacks earlier) and even welcomed it after one particular event.

The Bishop had a friend named Ruell who, at the time I met him, was opera diva Montserrat Caballe's driver. He was very dashing and I think a bit of a roue'. (I believe he also owned the house The Bishop was living in.) One evening when Ruell was in town, he, The Bishop, and I went out to dinner (riding in the barge with Virgo John driving). Ruell kept referring to "the chippie," and it slowly dawned on me that he was referring to me. (It felt really strange being referred to in the third person while still present.) Ruell was speaking about me as if I was some sort of airhead kept-boy. It wasn't the "kept-boy" part I resented (I was flattered to have someone think I was cute enough to be kept), but I did resent the "airhead" part. (Testosterone speaking again.)

And what's more, The Bishop was keeping up with the conversation, also using the third-person singular.

That's definitely a drawback to being (whoever's) Cute Young Thing—the operative word in the situation is "Thing." The function of a Cute Young Thing is to look good—the only thing Cutie pays is attention.

I didn't want to be regarded as a "thing" or thought of as an airhead. (I'm a brunet. And there's that testosterone.) It felt dirty. I will admit to being a slut, but I'm not a whore. It's another thing entirely.

I was also tiring of the role of "audience," which is an important function of Cute Young Things. Yes, I learned quite a bit from The Bishop, but when it is all said and done, I got the impression that he really didn't care to know of any of my opinions or experiences. I think it may have surprised him that I actually *had* any opinions or experiences. So after that evening in the car with Ruell, I started refusing invitations that would involve The Bishop spending money or having the opportunity to speak unimpeded for any length of time.

Soon thereafter The Bishop had two pretty young Cambodian boys on his arm, part of the above-mentioned retinue. They all adored him and called him "Father," and hung on his every word. (I joke that when I turned twenty-four, he traded me for two twelve-year-olds—Catholic and all.)

The Bishop and I remained friendly for a number of years, and he would ask me along for any number of outings. With Susan as my "date," I got to experience some interesting times that otherwise I would not have seen.

Like the Cambodian wedding.

The Bishop claimed that Chandara, one of the cute Cambodian boy retinue and his current favorite, was a crown prince of Cambodia. (Chandara sold

ACT ONE:

stereos at The Good Guys.) Chandara was to be married to the girl he had been betrothed to at birth, and The Bishop would be performing the wedding.

So Susan and I took ourselves off to a crowded apartment on Turk Street in the Tenderloin one Saturday morning for this wedding, which was to be an all-day affair. It was quite a feast for the eyes. Susan and I didn't get to see the procession (we were wedged into the back of the apartment by the crowd and couldn't get a look out the window), but The Bishop led the procession up the street from the bride's dwelling to the groom's. They were followed by the couple's families (I think) and well-wishers, all of them dressed in traditional Cambodian clothing and carrying brightly colored parasols. The apartment was draped in fine textiles and decorated with any and all finery that the community could round up; and the couple was dressed in beautifully colored wedding clothes, complete with hair and makeup. As the day progressed, they did two more costume changes.

The entire population of the building was there—this was one of those "vertical villages" we were hearing about in the papers in the mid-eighties, where an entire building would eventually rent out to a certain Asian group, this building being the Cambodian "village." This was a red-letter day for this building: their prince was getting married!

In the evening there was a feast at a restaurant in the Tenderloin (Vietnamese as there were no Cambodian restaurants yet in The City), where Susan and I sat, looking at all of this food that didn't look like food by western standards. It was a safe bet that none of it was kosher either. Then they brought the large platter heaped with an enormous mound of squab.

"Why am I reminded of Union Square right about now?" I asked, eyeing the huge heap of small blackened carcasses.

"That's it! No more! We're leaving, Darling Angel!" Susan shouted, and laughing, we ran off into the night to dish the day and search for dinner.

Years later I was in Wisconsin visiting a friend when, on the TV news, I saw Chandara. He was older, of course, but was talking with a reporter. The sound was off so I couldn't hear what he was saying.

"OH MY GOD! That's Chandara!" I shouted.

"Who?" Pam asked.

"I went to his wedding! That's Chandara! He used to sell stereos at The Good Guys!"

"Yeah, sure. Sit down."

The text at the bottom of the screen identified him as a crown prince of Cambodia.

Christmas of 1981 in San Francisco was a little different than the year before—Brad-the-Doll was still in OKC; Barry was somewhere in Austin, Texas; and it was just Mark, Vic, me, and David Burlew. We all went out to the DeLancey Street Christmas tree lot on Turk Street to get Mark's Christmas/Hanukkah tree and strapped it to the roof of the station wagon that Motorola had provided Vic as a company car. He had, by this time, left Rollins and moved on.

Somehow this didn't mean that Mark and I could start using the douched-out Torino for commuting to the stores, even though Vic wasn't driving it. I complained that the commute was fast wearing my car down, and I had had to hock my jewelry to get a new set of ball joints just a month before. I was sweating my trip back to OKC for Christmas—if I didn't have on my rings, Mom's eagle eye would notice, and Questions Would Be Asked.

I had committed to going back to OKC for Christmas, if for no other reason than to get Miss Ann to shut up about the move. As the trip got closer, I was actually glad I'd be going—the mood around Mark's household was strange, and I couldn't get a real fix on what was going on. There had been one incident in the car on the way to work that was particularly disturbing.

ACT ONE:

Mark came out of the apartment just as I was pulling up—unusual for him, as he was usually still dressing when I arrived. He got into the car and was wearing sunglasses. It was foggy so he didn't need them, but I didn't give it much thought.

As we drove away, he said, "Ken, I have to get away from Victor."

"Why? What happened?"

"I just have to get away. If I don't, something terrible will happen."

"Mark, what? What happened? If you need to, you can stay with me."

"I can't talk about it right now . . ." He said in a wobbly voice.

So I let the subject drop.

The next day when I mentioned it to him, he acted like I had been imagining things. Leaving Victor? Problems? There were no problems! What are you talking about?

I remember feeling a little crazy about it. I *knew* what he had said the day before, and now here he was, acting like I was imagining things. It was like the times when I was a teenager, and Mom would act like Don, her second husband, had *not* beaten her. Would I trust my ears or him? Crazy-making. That's what it was.

After the first of the year in 1982, it was apparent that Roos Bros. was not a moneymaking proposition; stores were closing and people were getting laid off. One of the first to go was Dave-the-Trimmer, who had been around forever so he had seniority over me. Mark made the case to the Powers That

Be that he was old, slow, and since we had fewer stores, he wasn't needed. I felt sad to see him go but kept my mouth shut, as I needed the job. Mark and I did the job after Dave-the-Trimmer left, or really I did the job and Mark schmoozed. He was still suffering from the neuropathy and couldn't work too hard.

Then in February—*why is it always February? A year before in February he did his disappearing act from OKC!*—Mark called me outside one day while we were working at the Stonestown store.

"Ken, I'm leaving. They're abolishing the visual merchandising director position and wanted to make me a trimmer and fire you, but I volunteered to go. So you'll have a job and a little raise that I talked them into giving you, but you won't be visual merchandising director."

I, of course, expressed my shock and sadness about this turn of events, but also suspected there was more to the story—especially the part about abolishing Mark's position. There was a moment when I considered quitting in solidarity but thought better of it. Mark had a husband to help out financially; I didn't.

The next day I asked Bob Vaupin, the guy I pestered for this job, out for coffee. We went to the little cafeteria across the mall.

"I brought you out here because the walls have ears," I said. "I understand that you could fire Mark and keep me cheaper than you could fire me, even with the little raise I got." It was a hunch I had.

"Yeah," he said.

"I'll take the small raise, but I also want one other thing. Mark told me you had abolished the position of director of visual merchandising. I want a letter on company letterhead sent to all the stores and a copy for myself for my portfolio, saying that I have been promoted to director of visual merchandising. I know I'm just a glorified trimmer, but I have to think of my resume—this has to look like a step up. This will make up for the difference between the raise and what Mark was making."

ACT ONE:

"Done," Bob said. "Anything else?"

"Yes. Know that I'm not going to quit out of solidarity to Mark. He has a husband, and I don't. Also I don't want to make you people look bad, so I can look good like he used to do, and I don't want to play politics. I just want to make some good windows and displays to round out my portfolio, so that when this gig goes bust, I can get work elsewhere. Deal?"

"Deal."

I had my letter later that day and was sure to go over to Mark's house that evening to show it to him and happily announce the good news.

Remember that October evening at Dillard's, when Mark snatched the display manager job out from under me?

I still did.

As I said to myself at the time, I'd remember this, and one day I would even the score. I still had that score to settle, and I regarded it as settled the minute I saw the look on Mark's face.

ACT TWO:

Entr'Acte

There was plenty of time to think on that flight to Burbank.

Really, I believed that I would never hear from Mark again, especially after our last conversation. As it was I hadn't laid eyes on him in nine years, and boy, oh boy, *that* was one depressing visit. He and Victor were living in this crappy little house in Long Beach. Quite a lot of his antiques were nowhere to be seen, the place was covered with a film of stale cigarette smoke and regret, and the whole conversation consisted of how miserable he was. From then on, until our final conversation, we had what I called a "telephone friendship." He never came to visit, and I never went to visit; we talked on the phone. So I really couldn't imagine what Mark even looked like now, let alone what kind of person he had become. The voice on the phone made me think that the person I was going to bring back to San Francisco was a shadow of the man I first met in Oklahoma City.

During our "final" conversation, I said what I needed to say. I wasn't helping Mark by listening to him complain, and the frustration of not doing any good was making me crazy. So I had to make a break with him.

However, through the years I thought of him often and hoped that he was OK. My fear, though, was that he would end up as a sordid headline: "*Gay Man Found Beaten to Death—Long-time companion disappears.*"

I also contemplated the headline the papers might soon use, if Things Went Horribly Wrong: "*Fashion Designer Found Shot to Death In Botched Kidnap Attempt—Was wearing clean underwear and had his roots freshly done*".

Act Two:

Scene 1

Mark and I kept in touch after he left Roos Bros., and I understood that talking to him about the job was off-limits. But as I had had my revenge, I stayed off that topic—there's revenge and then there's unkindness. I know that sounds like a peculiar concept, but that's how I am.

Soon after Mark left Roos Bros., he and Vic moved from their flat on Noe and Twenty-second to an apartment on Corbett Street in Twin Peaks. It was one of those concrete apartment blocks put up in the 1960s, one that lacked any charm whatsoever. Mark's job was to be the manager of that apartment building—or so I was told. He never held another real job the rest of his days in San Francisco.

After they moved, on my first visit there, I noticed that more of Mark's antiques were missing. Some of the silver was gone too—sad. When I asked about them, Mark started to answer but Vic entered the room. The subject was very abruptly dropped.

Right about this time I met Matthew. I refer to him as my "trophy husband" because he looked really beautiful naked. Really. Beautiful. Naked.

Really.

Beautiful.

Naked.

Mark wanted to meet him, so we went over there for dinner. This was the Mark I remember, bringing out all of the good dishes (but not as many dishes as I remembered from OKC) and cooking a whole restaurant-full of food.

Mark was his usual Jewish-mother self, the anxious host, always jumping up and making sure that everyone had what they needed. I was used to that—it's how he entertained. He was polite to Matthew but seemed to be keeping a distance.

Victor, however, was giving Matthew the hairy eyeball the entire time. He also kept shooting Mark looks, which seemed to make Mark nervous; then Mark would be *more* the anxious host—it was a downward spiral of sorts. I was oblivious to all of this, because that was they way Mark and Vic *were*. I was used to it.

Matthew was polite, made all of the necessary conversation, kept away from Victor, and seemed to enjoy himself. But in the car on the way home, he let me know what he really thought.

"I don't know why you hang around with them," he said. "There's something creepy going on there, and I don't know what it is. But I was really uncomfortable the entire time. Victor looked like he wanted to jump me, and Mark looked like he wanted me to leave *because* Victor wanted to jump me."

There was no response I could give—except that, well, that's just how they *are*.

ACT TWO:

I met Matthew through Susan, who worked with him at the Greyhound corporate offices. She had invited him to guest-usher at the Opera House a few months after I started ushering there. My gig with The Bishop was winding down, and I was establishing some sort of social life outside of Mark and Vic, so I was up for meeting new people, especially cute guys.

Matthew showed up wearing an obviously borrowed suit, shirt, and tie, and worn-out military oxfords. Poor Matthew was desperately in need of a trim (black moustache and hair), but otherwise he had a rugged, but slightly geeky, Marlboro Man charm—sort of like a young Clark Gable, complete with the jug ears. We sort of sniffed around each other during intermissions and exchanged phone numbers. At the time I was still living in Noe Valley, which was too far away from the Opera House to walk, which meant that I had the car. So I offered to drive him home (it was sort of on the way) after coffee.

To my surprise, we didn't go to bed that night—quite unlike me, to be sure. We had a real serious goodnight kiss in the car, but that was it. I couldn't wait until our next date.

That occurred a few nights later, when he came over to my place. We had a bite to eat and eventually ended up naked. Now Matthew was one of those people who, in clothes, looked sort of nerdy, but out of clothes, *well* . . . *!* I was astonished to see before me this lean, wiry guy who looked like a hairier version of the guy in the Calvin Klein underwear ads that were just coming into the market—you know, the ones that Bruce (I'm-not-gay-really!) Weber photographed with the model wearing just the white briefs, posed against stucco and shot from below?

It was a surprise to see this gorgeous vision in white briefs, and from the very first, I was a bit glamoured by his charms. Looking back, I really didn't think much past them at first (his charms *and* the briefs).

Matthew had just returned to the States from being stationed in Japan with the air force, where before his term was up, he suffered the hazing that gays in the military get once the knuckle-draggers discover the truth. He was originally from San Antonio, so that's where all of his belongings had been shipped and stored.

There were also an ex-wife and a child back in Minnesota, where she was originally from. It seems she didn't go to Japan because they separated just before he was stationed there, and they divorced while he was away.

Matthew moved to San Francisco after divorcing and sort of went wild, what with lots of drinking, no doubt some drugs, and lots of sex. The sex wasn't so much a problem in itself (everyone was doing it *a lot* then—it really was like a handshake!), but Matthew chose risky situations (like giving a blow job in a doorway across from the police station at high noon) and druggie friends to carouse with.

Matthew lived in a studio apartment on Fulton Street near Webster, in a building right across from the Projects and a block away from the notorious Pink Palace. Matthew slept on the antique Murphy bed in this apartment. I did too, when I was there. It made lots of noise, sort of like a big Morse-code machine—tap-tap-tapping to telegraph to the downstairs neighbors that we were at it again. It drove one of the neighbors crazy . . . but I'm getting ahead of myself.

Soon after we started dating, his son, Peter, came to visit. Peter was nine years old at the time and slept on the Herculon sofa in Matthew's place. Having Peter around was a bit weird for me; I always regarded being gay as a blessing in that I didn't have to deal with children. Now I was fast becoming a step-ma-ma.

Thankfully Peter liked me, because if he hadn't, it could have been hell. His mother in Minnesota (St. Paul, actually) was mad-as-hell about the divorce, even though she knew that Matthew swung both ways before she married him. It puzzles me to no end why women persist in the notion that once a bi-guy has had the "love of a good woman," he will forsake men forever. What rubbish! Then when the old hankerings return, these gals get all upset because the guy can't switch it off.

The Ex sent long letters venting her spleen about how-could-he-leave-her-after-all-they-had-been-through-and-what-about-their-son. At the time Matthew made her out to be sound irrational, but looking back, I can better understand why she was angry.

ACT TWO:

But I had a look at the other side of the bisexual question as well. When Matthew and I got together, I really didn't think much about the flip side of the coin—we were banging like rabbits every night for the first six months or so. Then he was living with me, and I had to address the issue after I was into the relationship for a while.

The bisexual issue showed itself in several ways at different times. Matthew had this ongoing attitude that since he had actually put his penis into a vagina he was more of a man than I was. I'm what some gay men call a "thoroughbred": a "Kinsey six," never had sex with a woman, not even a kiss, and proud of it. Whenever Matthew would start with that "more-of-a-man-cuz-I-fucked-cooze" attitude, my response was something along the lines of "When you can hang drywall, fix the broken spring on the garage door, and tune up the car, we'll talk." (When we split up, I'm told by Andie, the woman he briefly took up with, that he would meet her at the door wearing high heels and panty hose. That pair of pumps of mine had gone missing—I had wondered where they went off to.)

Occasionally Matthew would go into his fantasies about "having a woman in." I would counter that with *my* fantasy of "having a woman in," which involved her scrubbing windows and floors while I watched from the sofa. (You missed a spot!) That would usually put an end to the discussion for a while.

Every now and then Matthew would use the "if you haven't tried it, how do you *know* you wouldn't like it" argument. My response (after suppressing the inevitable wave of nausea) was, "I haven't tried drinking poison (driving my car off a cliff, poking my eyeballs with sharp sticks, yanking out my fingernails with the pliers, etc.) either, but I know I wouldn't like it. One has a feeling for these things."

What I'm trying to say is something that will be regarded by some in "our community" as not PC. Bisexuals should mate with each other, and leave those of us who can make up our minds alone.

Matthew was living on very little money, and his neighborhood was really dicey. I lost four trunk locks on my car to denizens of that neighborhood and did what my friend Sandra calls the "Park-and-Run" whenever I would visit. For this very reason we spent increasing amounts of time at my place.

The event, though, that spurred me to invite Matthew to move in with me occurred late one night in October of that year. He was sleeping and awoke to the sounds of someone raising a ruckus by stomping on the roof, directly over his bed. Forgetting where he lived, he got up and went up to the roof to investigate. Foolishly he opened the door to the roof, when . . .

This wild-eyed man on the roof charged at him, screaming how he was going to kill the faggot. Well Matthew high-tailed it back down the stairs, missing a few on the way, and breaking a toe. He barely got into his place and the door locked behind him before the guy crashed into the door.

It was the downstairs neighbor. He had finally been driven crazy by the Morse–code tapping of the bed.

Police were called, the emergency room was visited, and Matthew was out of work for a month. This caused him to miss a child support payment, which caused the ex to take him to court. His bank balance was seriously into the negative numbers, and he was scared to leave the apartment.

With the ex-wife hounding him for money and his homesickness for his belongings in San Antonio, I offered a possible solution: Come live with me (in my studio apartment, what was I thinking!) until he had saved enough money to pay first and last, and get his things moved out here. I reasoned that it would take no time at all if he didn't have to pay rent, and would afford him the chance to get into a better neighborhood. My one rule was: NO TRICKS IN MY PLACE.

So the day before Thanksgiving he moved in. And promptly broke a crystal vase that Kathy had given me—this was an omen, but naïve I certainly was at the time, and I didn't see it.

He looked good in those white briefs, so I chose not to see this red flag.

ACT TWO:

Our first Christmas in 1982 was spent apart (like all the others). I went to Oklahoma City, and Matthew stayed at my place. He had plans to go to Susan's house for their annual Not-A-Christmas-Party for all the non-Christians they knew. Susan requested that he bring two frozen Sara Lee Boston Cream Pies.

I called him Christmas evening to wish him a merry-merry and noticed that he sounded a bit distracted. I didn't think much of it, until he mentioned that he had gotten mugged.

"MUGGED!?" I shouted. "What happened?"

Matthew had taken the J-Church streetcar from our place to Sixteenth and Church, where he planned to walk over to the BART station. As he got off the bus, this guy walked up to him and calmly said, "I've got a gun. Give me all your money."

"Did you see the gun?" I asked, incredulous.

"No," he replied.

"Then why did you give him your money? If it would have been me, I would have *wanted* to see the gun to be sure I was really being held up at gunpoint!"

Then the alleged gunman demanded Matthew's bus transfer, leaving him no way to get home except on foot. But the final insult: he demanded that Matthew give him the two frozen Sara Lee Boston Cream Pies.

As the gunman hopped on the bus (with the pies), he turned to Matthew and said, "By the way, Merry Christmas!"

A couple of weeks later, one of Matthew's friends let slip that Matthew had, indeed, had a trick in (in my bathtub and in my bed, to be exact!) while I was in OKC.

"See?" I said. "God punished you! Serves you right, getting robbed for having a trick in when I asked you not to!"

But he still looked good in those white briefs, so I chose not to see this red flag.

Earlier in 1982, I had my car rear-ended by a MUNI bus driver in his Buick land yacht. I was coming back from the Roos Bros. store in Marin, a couple of weeks after Mark had been let go. I was stopped at a light on Park Presidio and got totally creamed in the back end of my little red Celica. This was the one and only time my new title came in handy. We both got out of our cars, and I walked back to survey the damage. I also asked him for his ID, which he didn't really want to give me.

"Hey, man, you're makin' me late for work!" he shouted.

"Give me your driver's license and your Muni ID number, and I'll move on," I said evenly. Talking evenly was a challenge—he was a foot taller than me and outweighed me by about 200 pounds. I could well imagine him beating the crap out of me. There was no choice but to just brazen it out.

"No, man, I won't."

"OK, then I'm calling the police."

"No, man, don't do that!" he pleaded. "You're makin' me late for work!"

"Listen," I said. "I'm the director of visual merchandising for the ENTIRE chain of Roos Bros. stores. I'M late for an important meeting because YOU hit my car. Now I'm going to take as much time as I need, and I'll call the police if I feel I need to!"

At that point I headed for the pay phone across the street. While I was on the phone with the police (who were not helpful, as I wasn't injured—yet) he came forth with all of his IDs.

ACT TWO:

Later, when I contacted the insurance company, I was afraid that they were going to total the car because it was so old. Someone recommended this body shop on Twenty-fourth Street in Noe Valley, and that's where the car ended up.

The proprietor was a German man named Dieter, who wasn't too hard on the eyes. He seemed to take a shine to me (I looked especially fetching in my teal tuxedo shirt, the painted-on jeans, and my favorite Pierre Cardin shoes), so when I told him of my concern, he said, "Vee vill see dat dis does nacht happen!"

(My apologies to all English-speaking Germans for this rendition of your accent.)

Later in the week when I went by the garage to check up on the car, Dieter told me that the insurance company had decided to repair the damage. (I'm sure there was some fast-talking on Dieter's part.) Of course there was one hitch: since the damage was from the doors back, the insurance company wouldn't pay to paint the whole car, just the rear end. As the rest of the car looked like tomato soup (red fades so quickly), I would have a two-tone car.

Dieter's German precision and perfectionism was really offended by this, so he suggested that, to make a good job of it, I should repaint the whole car. However, I didn't have the dough to be spending on paint jobs, so I had to think fast.

Sighing, I said, "Dieter, just do the primer on the back. I guess I'll just take it to Earl Scheib to make it all one color." (For those of you who haven't heard of Earl Scheib, this was the absolute bottom of the barrel of the discount auto painters.) Then I sighed again helplessly, eyes downcast, thankful that I had worn my very tight "Gilley's I-Rode-The-Bull" jeans.

Poor Dieter cringed at this offense to German precision, and I could hear him grinding his teeth. But I just kept my eyes downcast, my hands hanging limply at my sides in a little gesture of surrender. I let another little helpless sigh escape.

It only took a few moments.

"Vee vill see vat ve can do," he finally said. "Call me next veek."

The following Saturday Dieter called and said, "Your car iss reddy! Come down and pick it up!"

When I walked into the body shop, I could *not* believe my eyes! Dieter had painted my little Celica Ferrari Red! You know, the blue/red, with no hint of orange that hurts the eyes to look at in bright sunlight? The paint was shiny like glass, and Dieter had even cleaned the vinyl top so it was white again, polished the mag wheels, and replaced the white pin striping. It looked like a new car!

"And this is where I'll have to put out", I thought, wondering just how that particular transaction would play out. Miss Manners didn't comment on that one—would it happen right there, or would we make a date?

I wondered.

"Dieter, how . . . ?" I asked. "And how much do I owe you for this?"

"Ach, it's nutting! Jussst left-ofer paint from another job!"

And I didn't even have to put out for this, even though I would have, gladly!

Matthew was the first one to put a scratch on it.

I was backing the car out of the garage, and Matthew was waiting by the garage door to pull the door down. I had gotten only half way out when he started pulling the door down, so that the garage door smacked down RIGHT ACROSS THE HOOD OF THE CAR!!!

ACT TWO:

Thinking he had just hit a snag, Matthew started pulling down vigorously on the garage door handle, which just made the fresh crease across the hood deeper. I started honking and calling him some very unkind names.

It took a few moments, but Matthew finally noticed the (rather large) object that was hanging up the garage door.

"You stupid sonofabitch! Didn't you think to look at what you hit? Goddamn, look at this crease! This is an expensive paint job, you stupid-ass jerk!" I shouted as I surveyed the damage.

But he still looked good in those white briefs, so I chose not to see this red flag.

Since we were living together, I started calling Matthew my boyfriend. (It seemed like a legitimate assumption.) I discovered, much to my dismay, that he wasn't seeing it the same way. It started when I noticed that he wasn't interested in sex. (This was quite the opposite of the situation at the end of our relationship, but I'm getting ahead of myself.)

I would try to initiate, and he would give me the cold shoulder. Assuming I had done something wounding (Matthew would always let me know when something I did reminded him of his ex), I badgered him until he finally talked about it.

"I AM NOT YOUR HUSBAND! I AM NOT YOUR BOYFRIEND!" he shouted. "Just because we're living together doesn't mean we're married!"

Well. You could have knocked me down. At the time I felt really wounded, but looking back as I write this, I'm thinking, "What an ungrateful ass-wipe!" He was all right with my paying for his lodgings so he could save money, but didn't want to commit to anything except being "good friends." That moment was when I knew he wouldn't be the one I would grow old with.

(So, you ask, "How long did you stay with him?" Five and a half years. What an idiot, huh?)

But he still looked good in those white briefs, so I chose not to see this red flag.

———

In February of 1983, Matthew had saved enough money to get a place and have his things moved out from Texas. He asked me one Sunday morning if I would be interested in moving in with him. My first reaction was to say no, which I did. He gave me this wounded look and left the apartment. I knew I had hurt his feelings, but this was my gut reaction.

For a few days he and I didn't talk much. He started looking for an apartment, and I began drawing classes at City College. One night I got home from class, unlocked the door, and came in—the lights were out. I felt a hand clamp over my mouth, and I heard Matthew whisper, "Don't make a sound."

"Well!" I thought. "This is a new game! I'm going to be the young beauty ravished by the intruder! Oooh!"

"I've called the police," he whispered. "Someone's broken in next door—he's still inside."

I could hear someone next door, obviously ransacking the place. We both stood in the dark, listening. The doorbell made both of us jump.

ACT TWO:

It was the police. The entire SWAT team came in, guns drawn, and swarmed through my place—out onto the little balcony, inside the front door, everywhere. I, of course, was *mortified*! The place was a mess, and oh GREAT!, The entire San Francisco Police SWAT team comes to visit. I busied myself trying to tidy up.

Matthew was much more sensible in this situation. He grabbed me, pulled me to the floor, and said, "Goddammit, get DOWN! We could get SHOT!"

"Well that would be mercy killing—I'm dying of embarrassment as it is! Look at this place!" I shouted.

The SWAT team broke into the place next door, chased, and finally caught the guy. He was taken away in handcuffs.

A little background about the married couple next door: When I moved in, they were newlyweds. She was an erotic dancer at the Mitchell Brothers O'Farrell Theater—the X-rated place in the Tenderloin that had a fantasy undersea mural painted on the outside—and he was a projectionist there. They met when he saw her do a bride striptease.

I'm not making this up.

When she came out in that wedding gown and commenced to gyrate and strip, he fell in love—HARD.

Really! You can't make up this kind of stuff.

I used to ponder her dancing career. Since my living room window was at a right angle to her kitchen window, I could watch her cook Sunday breakfast in the nude (not even an apron!), whether I wanted to or not. And I wanted *not* to. She was built like a boy – two pennies on a plank, as my grandma used to say.

As I can't remember her name, I'll call her Penny.

One day I drove Penny to work. I drove up from work one afternoon, and she looked so panicked standing in front of the building that I asked what was wrong. She was late—the cab hadn't shown. So I offered to drive her to work, and as we drove along, I chatted her up about her job.

"Like, you know, the management encourages us to go and like basically mingle with the customers after we dance. They want the customers to know that we are, like, uh, intelligent people, as well as, ya know, beautiful and, uh, talented dancers."

Indeed.

After awhile the marriage went on the rocks (what a surprise). Penny started seeing some low-level thug, and Mr. Husband moved out, heartbroken. (He really loved her, poor guy. Did I mention that he wasn't too bright?) A little time went on, and Penny decided that she was tired of the thug as well, so she gave him the heave-ho.

But Mr. Thug was having none of it. Hence the break-in.

I didn't hear anything from Penny for a couple of days, as she was staying away. Finally one afternoon I ran into her in the hall and asked about what was happening. She told me she had decided not to press charges.

"Why?" I asked, incredulous. "He broke into your house and ransacked the place. Don't you think he might do you some harm?"

"Like, he's threatened my family if I do," she mumbled.

"Well, girl, working at a place like that I'm sure you can find some sort of "protection," if you know what I mean."

ACT TWO:

"It's cool, man. It's cool. I know what I'm doin'."

It was about three in the morning, two weeks later. I awoke to hearing Tara, my downstairs neighbor who lived directly below the "happy couple," pounding on the door and screaming, "Goddammit, shut the hell up! People are trying to sleep!"

I heard the door open and a man's slurred, druggy voice say, "Hey, it's cool. We'll be quiet. It's cool."

I waited until Tara got back into her apartment and phoned down.

"Ken, I can hear everything that goes on in that place, the floors are so thin. I'm hearing him saying things like 'I'm gonna cut you up' and 'I'm gonna put you inna hospital,' so I've called the police."

So another visit from the SWAT team, along with the ambulance and the medics—it was quite an evening. I didn't go out into the hall to watch all this. It was just too close to home. It reminded me of those nights when Mom and Don battled when I was a teenager.

The next morning, though, when I left for work, I wasn't prepared for the sight. It looked like the Sharon Tate murders revisited. There was blood *everywhere*! Smeared along the walls, on the carpet, all the way down the stairs! It was too gruesome!

That evening I told Matthew we could look for a place together. Noe Valley was getting too weird for me.

My requirements were: two bedrooms, central location, and my part of the rent three hundred dollars per month. What we ended up with had a real tony-sounding address: 33 Elgin Park #9. A double-digit address in a park, right? Top floor of a building like a penthouse, right?

The reality was grittier than that. This was a piss-yellow and flamingo-pink, poured-concrete building from the fifties that had no Architectural

Distinction whatsoever, inside or out. Thankfully I had good furniture, as this place cried out for accessories!

I had a little housewarming party, where I invited my new friends. Some of them were people I'd met at Roos Bros., like Diane and Rick.

Guess who didn't show up? This was the beginning of a pattern. Mark would always enthusiastically accept an invitation but then had some sort of excuse to cancel at the last minute, one that didn't make a lick of sense, but that was that. It was extremely disappointing, and I really didn't understand —it wasn't as if Mark had an actual job that he had to get up for, or had to do late hours for!

"He's a flake," Matthew said as I got off the phone before the party. "I don't know why you keep in contact with him. Especially lately he never seems to be available, and if he does set a date, he always cancels."

Our new apartment building was right next to the Central Freeway, just before it crossed over Market Street. We were close enough that I could read license plates on the cars that passed by on the lower level from my bedroom window.

The neighborhood, which all was in the shadow of the freeway, was not the best, to put it mildly, but the rent was cheap and the landlord was very hands-off. At first I asked myself *WHAT AM I DOING!?* because of the noise from the freeway, but believe it or not, I got used to it. I just convinced myself it was the sound of the ocean.

This ocean had a beach as well. It was our roof. We had that really good view of the freeway, which was still a double-decker then (this was before the '89 earthquake). As I said, we could see the cars on the lower level from the apartment, but the retaining wall on the upper level was high enough that only really tall vehicles could see over the railing onto our roof. It was quite private up there.

The roof was littered with stray car parts, which landed there from the various auto accidents on the freeway—that's how close we were. Many were the evenings when we would hear squealing tires, then a crash, then miscellaneous thunks and clunks on the roof. We could have had a side business dealing in used car parts.

But on sunny Sunday afternoons, having access to the roof saved a trek to the beach, where it might be either crowded or fogged in. We had sun and privacy. And the "sound of the ocean."

One particular sunny Sunday afternoon, Matthew and I were up on the beach, sunning in the nude. What with the sun, the tanning oil, and all, one thing led to another, and we got up to misbehaving. Things were going along swimmingly when I heard a truck's air horn blasting.

I looked up to see that traffic had jammed on the upper deck, marooning a (very tall) TOUR BUS directly opposite our building. This bus was listing to the right, as *all* the tourists from god-knows-where were plastered to the windows, ogling the two naked faggots who were fornicating right there in broad daylight. I even saw a couple of flashes from cameras.

What's a boy to do? We just laughed and waved.

In the meantime, my gig at Roos Bros. was winding down. A few months after Mark was "let go," there was a change in the Top Brass. The New Guy was known in the retail industry as an "undertaker." (And believe me, he looked the part.) The handwriting was on the wall, so I started scrambling to get another job in display and set my sights on Macy's. In the early '80's, Macy's California was *the* place to be in display, as it was regarded (rightly) as the top of the industry. There was a particular vision and the money to support it, and all the display queens wanted in.

Mark suggested that I contact Bob Hartman—you remember, the consultant who had been the first to offer me cocaine and while working, at that?

He still had connections with Macy's and could possibly get me to the right person to talk to. Mark made the first call, and I followed up. Bob had talked to the "human resources" person in display for me; he also happened to be named Bob, Bob Williams.

Auntie Bob, as we in display called him behind his back, was one of those queens of a certain (very old) age who "permed" his (thinning, obviously dyed) hair and wore leather trousers with his Armani jacket. (He sounded like a Hefty bag when he walked; leather trousers on a saggy, deflated ass will do that. But what did I *really* think of him?) Mr. Williams and I would be meeting at a bar in the Financial District called Sutter's Mill.

Auntie Bob held court every evening at Sutter's Mill and also was reputed to do the casting couch routine. I never got to the casting couch (I must not have been his type, thank God! Ick!), so when he hired me, I was relegated to the Pleasanton (Siberia) store. (Rumor had it that the downtown display crew was pulled from the casting couch ranks.) Taking this new job in Pleasanton meant an hour-long drive each way.

My new boss at the Pleasanton store was named Carmel Dole. He claimed he was part of the Dole pineapple fortune, but I never saw any evidence of that. He also claimed that English was his first language (he was born in Hong Kong), but I never saw any evidence of that, either.

Before I met Carmel, I thought the name sounded real classy—you know, like Carmel Snow at Harper's Bazaar in the fifties. The reality of Carmel was drastically different. Carmel was a pear-shaped, pockmarked Asian man with a bad haircut, flat ass, bad clothes, horrible taste, really bad teeth, and disgusting table manners. He was also crazy. (And also gay. I desperately *didn't* want him on our team.) Combine this with an accent that made most of what Carmel said unintelligible, and I had the recipe for the Work Situation From Hell.

Thankfully I worked with two really good guys, Loren and Craig. Craig was dark-haired and silent and slyly funny. Loren was tall, sandy-haired, and larger than life. They both were really good display trimmers, and I learned quite a bit from them.

ACT TWO:

It was here at Macy's, under their watchful (and sometimes bitchy) eyes, that I learned the craft of display. Thankfully I had my own skill set, gleaned from my upbringing as the son of do-it-yourselfers, but when they got done with me, I was a fully accredited member of the trimmer ranks.

From them I learned how to mix paint to match a color. From them I learned how to do a mean painted finish. Loren taught me the finer points of composition as it relates to display, and how displays that will be viewed from all sides have to be composed differently than those viewed from one angle (such as a display window). He also taught me how to cut hair and how cutting a mannequin wig is different than cutting hair on a head—wig hair goes on in rows, so layering is more problematic. Cut the wrong way, and instead of a smooth effect, you got what looked like shingles.

Craig was the one who taught me the concept of overstatement—that if one did a display that someone might have in his own home, the point (*of buying more merchandise*) might be lost. If the display overstated, either fashion-wise or in home furnishings, it would look more glamorous or appealing than what the customer had already. That was the point: to "romance" the merchandise, as he would say, to make it desirable and wanted.

They both also emphasized the idea of having a customer in mind when making a display. Know what this customer did, where the customer went, what events, restaurants, social gatherings she attended—to have a picture of who she was. For example, a customer who went to the country club for lunch wouldn't wear certain things, like budget jewelry or white high heels. We even had names for some of the mannequins, and certain ones "didn't do" the budget dress department. Others less glamorous would get duty in the maternity section after being stuffed with a pillow.

Some of what I learned from Loren and Craig was about display, but the most necessary skill I developed was being able to think on my feet and get off as many good lines as they could. And Loren and Craig were really good at that, so I had to work *hard*!

My first success in the one-liner department came one day while Loren was talking with the manager of cosmetics, Evelina. Now Evelina looked like Erma Bombeck and talked like Joan Rivers and walked around the cosmetics department in pink fuzzy slippers. She was scolding Loren for not taking as much time as she felt necessary in her department. When dressing down people, she could get wrought up into an operatic frenzy, which she was building up to in this particular tirade.

When it appeared that Evelina was just about to break into her aria, I interrupted and said to Loren, "Never mind her, she just found out that her upper arms don't fit into puffed sleeves anymore."

Both of them stopped and stared at me—stunned. They had never heard that kind of comment from me before.

It was Evelina who spoke first. She glared at me for a few moments and then broke into a big smile. "That was good!" she laughed. "You're going to get along fine here!"

Oh, I also got a new name— Muriel. Loren was Donna Louise. And Craig was just Craig—we needed at least *one* butch.

The three of us banded together to cope with Carmel, whose work habits were, shall we say, erratic. Carmel would show up about eleven o'clock after offering up one excuse or another. Craig always said that Carmel's lover tied him up each night before bed, and it would take until mid-morning for Carmel to chew through the ropes. I disagreed with that theory, arguing that if Carmel were, indeed, chewing rope so frequently, his teeth wouldn't be so fuzzy.

If we wanted to get any particular project done, we came in really early and tried to be done before Carmel got there. Work ground to a halt when he arrived and only got up to a snail's pace after that, what with Carmel's interfering. It galled him to think we could actually produce, and quickly, without him. There were many occasions where Carmel would slam on the brakes if

ACT TWO:

he came in and found us mid-project, and several times he had us completely undo what we had done and start over.

Once Carmel arrived we would have to stop and take a break with him, so he could "give us our instructions for the day." This usually involved us watching him eat a bagel with cream cheese and peanut butter, and then loudly slurp down a tall glass of hot tea. He chewed loudly and talked with his mouth full, so we would have to dodge the bits of food that would spew out of his mouth as he talked. (The peanut butter and cream cheese would also add another layer of fuzz to his teeth.)

At first I was oblivious to what Carmel was saying, as I couldn't make out a word of it. For the first three months, Carmel would yell at me because I couldn't follow directions, but I wouldn't just come out and say that I couldn't understand what he was saying.

Then one day Carmel was talking and I understood! It was what I imagine it's like when one is learning a foreign language and first understands it without trying to translate into one's native tongue. Loren noticed the expression on my face.

He pulled me off to the side and hissed (in true women's-prison-film style), "You're one of US, now, Muriel! MWAH HA HA HA HA HA!"

For better or worse, I knew I had arrived.

Speaking of the language barrier, Donna Louise, Craig, and I developed the "Carmel Dole Unabridged Dictionary of the English Language." It was for the new people who might come after us, so they could learn that particular dialect instead of puzzling it out, as we had done.

ALL GROWN UP NOW

Here are a few entries, culled from the section on "Christmas Trim":

Treem: (*trēm*) –1. Noun, singular. Generic term for objects used by display people to make a display or parts of a display. Plural, treems. 2. Verb. The act of assembling or otherwise arranging a display, as in "He is treeming the Christmas tree."

Bee Lice: (*Bē Līss*)—Noun, singular and plural. Electric cord, usually green in color, with tiny clear-glass bulbs attached. When plugged into an electrical source, the electricity causes the bulbs to glow brightly. (They are known in the trade, as "B-lights.") Such a pretty treem.

Brouse: (*brŏwss*)—Noun, singular. These objects were made of metal and green plastic, and designed to mimic pine tree branches. Plural, brouses. Brouses were usually put into pots with bee lice and other Christmas treem, used to treem doorways or archways, or otherwise spiff up the place in a holiday sort of way.

Bouse: (*bŏwss*)—Noun, singular. These objects were usually made of red velvet or satin ribbon and were usually tied onto the brouses or the reeves (see below). They could also be attached to boxes that would have been covered with festive holiday paper to mimic gift packages. Plural, bouses. Not to be confused with blouses—that's the ladies' garments.

Plop: (*plăp*)—Noun, singular. Non-merchandise objects used to enhance displays. These could be anything from silk flowers to the two gross of plastic doll arms Carmel bought for cheap. Plural, plopss.

Reeve: (*rēv*)—Noun, singular. These round, large donut-shaped objects are usually made up of brouses attached to a Styrofoam base, and trimmed with bouses and other treems. They usually had bee lice on them as well. Plural, reeves. Not to be confused with Christopher Reeves, the actor.

When we were packing up the Christmas treem and plopss after the season, we got temp workers to do some of the heavy lifting. The temp workers we got that first year I worked at Macy's were the living

ACT TWO:

inspiration for the cartoon characters Beavis and Butthead. Donna Louise had given them the CliffsNotes translation of this portion of our dictionary, feeling it was her duty to help them understand some of what was being said.

As Beavis and Butthead were packing up all of the treems, they used the "Carmel Dole Dictionary" spelling for labeling the cartons, which Carmel thought tremendously funny. He was laughing at them for their stupid spelling because he didn't realize —the joke was on him.

While living with Matthew, I got to meet his family. The first foray into dealing with the in-laws was a visit his parents undertook, driving in a camper from Texas to San Francisco. When they called and told us of the impending visit, Matthew told me that they said they would be here "Thursday". I, of course, interpreted this to mean the *upcoming* Thursday (a logical assumption) and commenced an affairs-of-state housecleaning, just to make a good impression.

Thursday came and went, then Friday, and the weekend. By Sunday evening, after being "on receive" all that time, I became exasperated and insisted that Matthew call the Highway Patrol. I reasoned that something bad must have happened to make them that late.

Monday evening the parents called to tell us that the Highway Patrol had, indeed, contacted them and that they were arriving in a couple of days. When I questioned Matthew about WHAT THE HELL WAS GOING ON?!?, he seemed unconcerned and not a bit surprised.

"They said they were coming on 'a Thursday'," he replied.

"Well you neglected to make this tiny but very important distinction. When MY family says they are arriving on "Thursday," they mean the upcoming Thursday. Most people would make the same assumption!"

I stopped staying home waiting and arrived back from the Opera House one evening (it was a Friday, actually) to find Matthew's mother drinking tea at the dining room table. We got along just fine, but she herself didn't see why I insisted that Matthew call the Highway Patrol—they *said* they were coming on "a Thursday." I let the matter drop.

During this visit, I won his mother's everlasting affection when I gave her a really fab haircut. She was needing one and wanted to get it cut in San Francisco. So she asked Matthew to recommend someone, and he recommended me. The results were so successful that, a couple months later, she sent Matthew a wig and asked him to ask me to give it the same haircut and style—and then ship it back packed so it wouldn't get mussed. It seems she wanted her hairdresser to see what I'd done, to learn from it.

As for travel or other social arrangements, Matthew's siblings were similarly inclined to be laissez-faire about dates and commitments.

One Thanksgiving, after we had been together a couple of years, I got it in my head to actually cook Thanksgiving dinner. We thought we might invite his brother Joseph, and his, well, "wife" George, who I really enjoyed. George was always such a girl that I referred to him as my sister-in-law. (The "wife" thing became actual fact several years later when George became Georgette. But again I'm getting ahead of myself.)

I also wanted to invite Matthew's sister, Frances, and her homophobic-jerk-husband, David, who both lived in Livermore. Before I did, however, I called Joseph and George and asked if they would be comfortable, as David was really a homophobic-jerk-husband. Both assured me they would be OK with all of this. So I extended the invite to Frances and David.

ACT TWO:

When Matthew and I arrived home from the grocery store with the turkey and all the trimmings, there were two messages on the answering machine—you can see where this is going. It would be just Matthew and me at dinner.

Exasperated, I yelled at Matthew about "your family" and made him put the groceries away while I sat on the sofa and called Mark to commiserate.

We were talking when from the kitchen I heard a loud WHIRRRRRRRRR! It sounded like my electric saw.

"Uh-oh, I gotta go, Mark. He's up to something in the kitchen, and it sounds like it involves my electric saw," I said as I walked into the kitchen.

It *was* my electric saw. Matthew was attempting to saw the frozen turkey in half with my electric saber saw.

"WHAT THE *HELL* ARE YOU DOING?" I shouted over the din. "STOP THAT!"

That's when Matthew patiently explained that he was sawing the turkey in half so we could cook half and freeze half. I'm not too expert in the kitchen (one must choose which room to be good in), but even I knew that we could cook the whole bird and freeze what we didn't eat.

So the one and only turkey I ever cooked had a terrible chest wound.

For someone who had an IQ of 140 (although I never saw documentation of that fact), Matthew could be amazingly dim.

These were some more of the red flags I chose not to see.

ALL GROWN UP NOW

Work was driving me crazy. I was spending all my waking time either obsessing about my Crazy Boss or working with him. Looking back, it was a blessing in disguise, as it forced me to remember what Ray Probst at Dillard's had said before I left OKC—you remember, to get out of retail as soon as possible. I realized that, if I were to stay at Macy's, I would be working for crazy people like Carmel forever. Also, looking at the situation in The High Offices (where the courtiers' ass-kissing and office politics recalled Versailles during the reign of the Sun King), I surmised that there were only a limited number of positions, and the people holding them were hanging on for Dear Life.

Besides, it really galled me that anything I created was property of someone else, i.e. Macy's. (It's called "work-for-hire" in the artistic fields.) This was the situation when working in display: If you do good work, the Main Guy in display gets to claim it. If the Main Guy hates it, you get in trouble for doing it.

All of this aside, I was having fun working with Loren and Craig. Being in display was really a fun job and provided opportunities for fun with fashion and props. One "series" we started was the cocktail hats made from dust masks. It was the perfect base to work with—a little cup shape and an elastic to hold it on the head.

In the display shop, we had a case of dust masks, supposedly to protect us if we worked on something dusty. Nowadays there is a sticker on these masks that says, "*This mask will not protect your lungs. Misuse may result in either sickness or death.*" Back then, even with no warning stickers, we knew they were worthless. So we made cocktail hats from them. Every spring and fall there was a new "line," and if someone was having a birthday or promotion, they got a cocktail hat. It was all for a laugh and great fun.

The best part of the fun was tormenting Carmel, who had high blood pressure and could get really wrought up about us wasting money on such foolishness. Unfortunately for us, though, we couldn't get him wrought up enough to bring on the stroke—we hated him that badly.

We once had an opportunity to kill Carmel and make it look like an accident (it would have involved him "falling" several stories to smash against the marble floor), and we *almost* did it. But since homicide is not a career path (and I believe in reincarnation and don't want to cross Carmel's path again!), we decided to let Carmel live. After that, though, the three of us embarked on a program of injuring him whenever the opportunity presented itself. There was a period when Carmel was either always wearing an Ace bandage or using a cane, and he would remark on how accident-prone we had become.

Loren steered Carmel into a manhole once, while dragging around Christmas trim. Since Carmel was walking backward, Loren, who had seen the hole with the cover off, steered him until he just dropped in, just like in the comics. Then Loren feigned surprise and let Carmel stew down there, while he "went for help." After a refreshing coffee, we finally got around to hauling Carmel out of the hole.

My favorite was dropping a fully loaded china cabinet over on him. I had it pulled out from the wall, Carmel walked behind it, and oops! It tipped over (OOPS! How *did* that happen?), pinning him to the wall, blackening an eye and cracking some ribs. The explosion of crashing glass and china was really gratifying.

Well he was making *our* days miserable. Tit for tat.

About this time my car dropped a transmission. Since the car was kaput, I had to take public transportation to Pleasanton, making the commute two hours each way. Since I wasn't making that much money (Macy's was a prestige job, but trimmers at The Emporium, which was the down-market department store in the Bay Area, made more), I had a problem scaring up the dough to get the car fixed.

Right about that time, Mark came through with Mrs. Thames. She was Gordon's mom and had lots of money. Let me back up a bit and introduce you to Gordon and Mrs. Thames.

Gordon was a spoiled, rich kid monster, who was my age (twenty-six at the time). He met Mark and Vic at a bathhouse in Austin, Texas, and became their "ward," so to speak. My understanding of the situation was that he had a big dick, and that was all Vic was really interested in. So that's why he became their ward—so Vic could blow him and Mark could get him out of trouble. Gordon had a lot of money but no brain to speak of—he didn't have to have one. Other people functioned as his brain, Mark being the more recent recruit. Gordon moved from Austin to San Francisco just to be with Mark and Vic.

When Matthew and I met Gordon for the first time, it was at a bar called the Café San Marcos in The Castro. It was an upstairs (and upscale) bar, with a stainless steel and brass floor, clear acrylic barstools upholstered in brown leather, deep club chairs upholstered in taupe ultrasuede, lots of smoke-glass mirror on the walls, and pinspots on very arty floral arrangements of exotic tropical flowers, Bird-of-Paradise being the prominent flower. (1983, remember.) And a dress code. You know the place.

Anyway we were to meet Mark, Vic, and Gordon there. Matthew wasn't a fashion queen (by any stretch of the imagination), so I had done my best to dress him in the least geeky outfit I could cobble together from his limited wardrobe, supplemented with some of my own accessories. We arrived first. They all came in a few minutes later and sat down. Matthew and I were stunned into silence by Gordon's appearance.

Gordon was wearing a dark, dull-blue silk shirt, open to the waist, and dark trousers and shoes. The open shirt revealed some gold chains in his chest hair. Any of these chains could have been used to tow a car out of a ditch. (This was not hip-hop; it was late Tom Jones.) His hair, which I believe was naturally a strawberry blond, was wildly and very artificially streaked with red and yellow blond. But the makeup!

Mark told me that Gordon bought the Erno Lazlo makeup tester setup they normally used at the sales counter and would take at least two hours to put on his face. This was in the time before Tammy Faye Baker became known for her makeup abuse; I sincerely believe Gordon got there first, and Tammy Faye was a follower.

Poor Matthew, he had never seen anything like this before. He kept whispering to me questions, like "Is that gold and green on his eyes?"—which I thought was a little bit hilarious because Matthew was color-blind, but I still got the point.

Gordon could well-afford to spend so much time working on his maquillage. He didn't have to work, really. He had a job, one his daddy got for him at Bechtel, but I think his boss decided that Gordon didn't need to actually come in to work—it was easier just to send him the check. Which usually went up his nose.

On to Mrs. Thames:

Mrs. Thames married Mr. Thames, but it was Mrs. Thames who had the money, as the story was told to me. Mr. Thames worked for Aramco and Bechtel, doing God-knows-what. They had loads of money, so they didn't have to raise or otherwise deal with Gordon—they just threw money at him, and things seemed to take care of themselves.

I met Mrs. Thames on one of her trips to San Francisco. Mrs. Thames was seeing an oral surgeon about a tooth problem.

The Mr. And Mrs. seemed to have a weird relationship. I remember Mark telling me that, at a party one evening, Mrs. Thames got drunk and loudly reminded Mr. Thames (in front of a bunch of people) that he had married up when he married her, not the other way around.

So after the party, he put her in the car. Then he got in behind the wheel.

He fastened his safety belt.

And then crashed the car into a wall—throwing Mrs. Thames through the windshield. Hence her tooth problem.

Small wonder Gordon was such a mess.

And a mess he was. One of the other things Mrs. Thames was dealing with on this particular visit to San Francisco was Gordon's facelift. (Yes, facelift. At age twenty-six.) And his bills. It seems she was funding the apartment, the car, a credit card, and the charge account at Wilkes Bashford. Gordon wouldn't actually wear clothes that had been dry-cleaned—he would throw out the dirty clothes and go buy some new ones. And Mark would bundle the worn ones into Hefty bags and put them at the curb. Gordon had such wretched taste that Mark knew not to offer them to me.

Anyway it seems that, while she was in town dealing with Gordon's facelift, his bills, and her tooth problem, Mrs. Thames wanted to find a dress to wear to her daughter's wedding. Mark saw an opening and suggested that I could design something for her and got us together. Thankfully he briefed me about all of their combined *meshuggaas* before I met them. I'd like to think I have a poker face and can roll with the punches, but Mark figured that *this* might be a little too far out of my depth to be dropped into without some preparation.

As work proceeded, I did hear about Mrs. Thames' tooth problem as well as Gordon's facelift during fittings (his complaint: he couldn't move his eyebrows, what a surprise). There were other mumblings of having people "dealt with" and such. That all made me nervous that I might not be able to design her a dress that she was happy with. And what might happen to me if I didn't?

To make a long story short, I did the dress, she was happy, I got paid and my car got fixed, and the course of my career changed, all in one little deal.

ACT TWO:

So twice in our friendship, Mark had played midwife (of sorts) for my career and, by extension, my path in life. First by getting me out of OKC and now by showing me (by providing my first customer) that I could earn money by designing clothes.

And happily I never saw Gordon ever again. He eventually moved to Southern California to be with Mark and Vic, and after a time, he up and moved to The Netherlands, go figure.

For my birthday that year, I went to have a tarot reading at this place called Amron Metaphysical Center. The woman who did the reading was named Norma—it was she who founded the place, which was a church of sorts, as well as a bookstore for books on the subject of metaphysics. They also sold crystals, wands, and all of that other kind of thing that the "New Agers" went for.

When I went into her office for the reading, I had a big chip on my shoulder. I had had another reading a while before, and the guy was a total fake. He kept harping on how I wasn't "really gay"—talk about clueless. My friends say that there are two things we can see in those satellite photos from space: the Great Wall of China and that Ken's gay.

Norma began by giving me a running inventory of what was happening in my life, with specific details of times, places, and what people looked like. She floored me by asking, "So what is this about the dress for the wedding?"

She then paused and said, "Have I established my credibility yet? Can we get to work now without the 'attitude'?"

Norma had me there, and I immediately liked and trusted her.

One major question I had was about Mrs. Thames and the dress, and what did all of this mean? Norma told me that this dress was a beginning, that I wouldn't have any more business from Mrs. Thames, but this gig set me on the path I needed to be on.

(As the years passed, Norma was the one to prod me on, urging me to go further on this path and finally to quit my job and start my business. She took on the role of mothering me and called me "Schweetie." One day, years later, when we were out to dinner together, the waiter asked her if I was her son. Without skipping a beat, she smiled to him and said quietly, "Yes he is." I will always be grateful to her and love her forever.)

The two people I remember asking about at that first reading were Matthew and Mark. As for Matthew, she told me that he would be in my life for a while, but we wouldn't grow old together—he wasn't "the one." But it would be fun while it hung together.

Mark, however, was a different story.

"You and Mark knew each other in ancient Rome," Norma said. "You were a page boy, and he was a general. He was really in love with you, but you were just having fun. You've shared some other past lives, but the common theme here was that he was always the older one with the power, and you were always the creative one. That has carried over to this lifetime. This contact with the dress and the lady is part of that karma."

She continued, "Know that there will come a time when this will all change. Now he has the power, and with that power comes a degree of control. But one day he will come to you in a much more humble position, and you will be the one with the power. Once this happens, the karma from the past lives will be dealt with, and your friendship will be on a more equal footing."

ACT TWO:

As I was flying to Los Angeles to kidnap Mark, I reflected on this prediction of Norma's. There was a time that, even a couple weeks earlier, I would have said that she got it wrong. But here I was, heading down to LA. Uncanny.

From that humble beginning with Mrs. Thames, since I had realized that I could actually make money sewing, I started on my journey to create a business for myself.

Being in business for myself appealed to me for a variety of reasons. First, I'm not a "good soldier." If I'm working for someone who I don't respect or who has less knowledge of the job, I'm their worst nightmare. I also make trouble when I'm bored at work. This is an offshoot of the respect issue— generally if I don't respect someone, it's usually because they are stupid or incompetent, or don't challenge me enough in good ways. This pattern of behavior showed up early; that explains how I got fired from Wendy's Old Fashioned Hamburgers. Now I was working for Carmel and realized that if I stayed in display at Macy's, I'd be doomed to working for people like him forever.

Display training, however, was a valuable starting point. Like theater design, display deals in transitory illusions, made to look more expensive and permanent than they really are. In display the more "skill sets" one has, the better-equipped one is to do the job. I learned a tremendous amount working with Donna Louise and Craig, and added to my own abilities, that gave me a range of technical skills to draw from.

What rankled me about working for Macy's was that I was restricted to the "Macy's way"—a stylistic vocabulary of what was and was not to be done in a display. I wanted to be a little more on the edge, a little more quirky; this was always a problem as Macy's had already figured out their formula. So the idea of being a designer was appealing to that side of me as well.

Working for Mrs. Thames showed me what kind of work I liked to do—evening clothes. I liked detail (the beading), I liked working with good fabrics, and I liked rich people. Or more to the point, I liked that rich people could afford expensive clothes.

My shortcomings were in the area of fitting clothing to the body, so I decided to make evening accessories—bags, hats, wraps—that didn't require fit. After conferring with a friend, Julie, who was the accessories buyer at I. Magnin, it was decided that I would focus on cocktail hats. The TV show *Dynasty* was big just then, and Julie said that there wasn't a lot of talent in millinery. I could make a name quickly. So that's what I started making.

And this is where the display training and my sewing came in handy. I didn't have the money to go to school, so I decided to teach myself hat making. Having such a wide range of knowledge to draw from enabled me to come up with ways of constructing them that eventually became my hallmark.

Another hallmark was the black velvet box. I understood, from being in display, that presentation was an integral part of the product. If one had a wonderful product and crummy packaging, one had a crummy product. But if one had a beautiful package for a beautiful product, it would elevate that product to another level. Also, from the technical standpoint, since I worked in display, I understood how to make the actual box.

About the time I was exploring this new direction of being a hat designer, Macy's had bought all the Liberty House stores, and Auntie Bob was looking for display managers for them. He thought he had me tucked away in Pleasanton, champing at the bit to be a manager—all it would take was for him to grant me an audience, bestow the position on me, and I would be sobbing with gratitude. Auntie Bob miscalculated. First of all I realized that nobody in the company cared that Carmel was a nutcase. They had actually shanghaied him to Pleasanton from the downtown store because he was so odious, and Pleasanton was the furthest store east at the time. I figured if the folks downtown were willing to have this person on the payroll even though he really didn't work and just caused grief, their standards weren't as high as they claimed.

Still I was really torn: stay with a "sure thing," or jump off into the unknown? I vacillated for days before my audience with Auntie Bob and drove Matthew crazy with my back-and-forth do I, don't I, do I, don't I, do I, don't I, do I, don't I, do I, don't I . . .?

I finally asked him what he thought.

"You'll never see a display manager for Macy's on the cover of *Vanity Fair*" was his response.

I had my answer.

I, of course, would never tell him this to his face, and it galls me that he gets credit for giving me the best bit of advice I ever got in deciding the course of my career. But Matthew distilled my desires for my career into one sentence, and it changed my life.

Mark was encouraging and felt that I was making the right decision.

On one of my visits to his place, we were talking about me going with Macy's as opposed to having my own business. I remarked that I seemed to be able to achieve a career goal I had set in about six to nine months, and the Macy's goal of being a display manager was happening in just a little over that time frame.

"Perhaps you just needed a higher goal," Mark said quietly.

And with that sentence, Mark confirmed that my decision to break away from the "sure thing" was, indeed, what I needed to do.

ALL GROWN UP NOW

One day in early 1983, Mark announced that he and Vic were moving to Southern California. It was sudden (what a surprise), but Vic had signed on with a Japanese company that had bought into the LA. market and hired Vic to run the company. This was during the time when a lot of companies were being bought up by the Japanese and then spectacularly and expensively run into the ground by crazy Americans. (Sony, anyone?)

It seemed to be a good career move for Victor, but I asked Mark why he had to go. He loved San Francisco, and I could see it was breaking his heart to leave. And he had just landed a spot on the arts commission that dealt with the permits for street artists. I don't think it was a paying gig but could have led to one. We had had several conversations about how much he enjoyed walking around, meeting the street artists, and seeing their work.

Again there was a sense of two felons blowing town in a hurry, but there was one complication. Mark had to go back to Boston for some family event. I can't remember what the event was, but I believe it was a bar mitzvah for a nephew or some such thing. So Mark had to make sure the truck was packed and ready, and while Vic was driving to their new place in Long Beach and unloading, Mark would go to Boston. When he flew back, he would then transfer to a plane headed for Long Beach.

Mark asked me to go by their old place and collect the rest of the mail and meet him at the airport when he arrived. He would have a couple of hours between flights; I could drop off his mail, and we could have some time together.

I looked especially fetching that evening. I wore my olive-green Eisenhower jacket over a black turtleneck and (tilted at a very becoming angle over my right eye) this really cute matching hat that looked like a wool pie plate stuck onto a matching hatband. Great shoes, good gloves, and a pair of high-waisted battleship gray wool trousers completed the look. I met his flight, and we went to one of the restaurants at the airport. Then he told me about his trip.

"Ken, the entire family treated me like I had leprosy," he sighed. "They heard that I might have GRID (they were still calling it that back then) and believed that they could catch it if I coughed on them. I'm sure they broke all of the dishes I used and threw out any silverware and probably even burned the linens."

(Just for the record, Mark wasn't HIV positive; he was misdiagnosed early on, before there was the test.)

Later, as we were walking towards the gate, I decided to make my pitch.

"Mark, why are you moving?" I asked. "You always loved San Francisco! You know you want to stay here! This would be the perfect time to just jump ship and leave Victor, if you want to do that. I know that he's been unfaithful to you and that you don't like it. Now's your chance! Just don't get on that plane!"

With tears in his eyes, he moved towards the gate to get on the plane.

"You just don't understand" were his parting words.

And I didn't. There was this desolate feeling in the pit of my stomach as I watched him walk through the gate and disappear down the gangway. And disappear was the right word.

There came a time when I started noticing (but still choosing not to see) that Matthew's red flags were appearing with more frequency. It started after Matthew quit his job at Bullock and Jones.

Greyhound closed out its offices, and Matthew was scrambling for a job. I informed him that I didn't want to support him, so he better get off the dime and go find new work. He applied at Bullock and Jones, one of the old-San Francisco stores on Union square—our version of Brooks Brothers. They needed a computer person, as computers were trickling down to the smaller retail stores in the mid-eighties. Since Matthew had computer training from his years in the service, he got the job, and I heaved a sigh of relief.

About this time Matthew also decided to pursue his lifelong dream of getting a BA in music—music composition. He wanted to compose Serious Music. I of course was all encouragement, as I was traveling down my own path of getting-out-of-retail-by-being-a-designer, and I wanted to encourage him to do the same. We both would follow our bliss, and all would be wonderful!

This worked out for a while because Matthew could take night classes and work days at Bullock and Jones. I, of course was still working at Macy's and designing at nights and on weekends.

There came a time, however, that the only classes Matthew could take were day classes. He made the case to me that he could swing it with his GI Bill and his savings, as it was enough to cover his half of the expenses and classes. So I consented.

What a fathead I was!

The first thing Matthew did after he quit his job was to petition the court to have his child support payments *lowered* because he was unemployed. The judge said something like, "Uh, NO! If you lose a job it's one thing, but you quit work. NO."

So Matthew said, "Fuck all of them then, I'll just stop paying it!"

That was a big red flag. I really had my eyes squeezed shut on *that* one.

ACT TWO:

When someone shows you who they are, *believe them*. I was soon to discover—much to my dismay—that I was next. I would be hung out to dry in increasing degrees over the next two years, as Matthew contributed less and less to the household expenses and eventually stopped paying entirely. Whenever I would bring up the subject, Matthew would go into either the "I'm a great artist and you are a commercial hack, so you should support me to absolve yourself of the guilt of hackdom" spiel or the "All you think about is money, you have the heart of a cash register" spiel. (He never went into the "I'm a lazy sack of shit who should be grateful for not being tossed out on my ass" spiel.)

During this period, I would subject myself to Matthew's student concerts. Sometimes I could convince Susan into coming with me. One time Matthew was singing in a concert at Old First Church on Van Ness. I wanted Susan to go with me (misery loves company), but she objected to going because it was a Christian house of worship, and she's Jewish. The night before when we were ushering at the Opera House, I made my big pitch:

"If you go to this, I have a gift I've made for you that I'll bring. BUT you have to promise you'll wear it."

"What is it?"

"I can't say, but you'll love it. It's a surprise, so promise?"

She did. Suspiciously, but she did.

I showed up to the church with a waist-length, black point-d'esprit lace veil, somewhat like Jackie Kennedy wore to The Funeral. When I was riding on the bus to the concert, this very old-San Francisco lady (complete with hat, gloves, and a handbag that looked like fender skirts off a beige 1959 Cadillac) sitting next to me inquired about the veil by asking sympathetically, "Did somebody die?"

"No, one of my friends is being forced to go into a Christian house of worship, and this will screen out the Christianity."

"I see," she said weakly and turned to look out the window.

You should have heard Susan when *she* saw it!

"You want me to WEAR that?" she shrieked.

"You promised!"

"Would your mother wear this?!?" Susan was desperately grasping at straws.

"If my mother PROMISED me she would wear it, SHE. WOULD. WEAR. IT," I said, pounding my chest for emphasis.

Knowing she'd been had, Susan "took the veil." Laughing, she decided that it could be good training for another supernumerary role on the Opera House stage. While she was adjusting it, I explained the Christianity-filtering properties of the black point d'esprit veiling. As we walked into the sanctuary, Susan pulled a lace hankie out of her bag. (I was impressed. How many people just happen to have lace hankies in their handbags?) She daintily dabbed her eyes and during the performance behaved like the grieving widow, sighing and dabbing. (It helped that she happened to be wearing black.) It really grieved her to be in a Christian house of worship—that was her "motivation" for this particular role.

Later Matthew told me that Susan was the talk of the evening. People remarked that it was rare to see that type of mourning these days.

ACT TWO:

Then there was the time that I prevailed upon Susan *and* George to go with me to an "experimental" musical performance at a dingy place on Divisadero called The Lab.

Matthew was going to wear white body paint and sing (even though he couldn't remember lyrics nor carry a tune in a Gucci bag), and it was all going to be very avant-garde and "on the edge." Susan was always up for avant-garde—that's how I convinced her to go. This performance turned out not to be avant-garde but more like what Susan would refer to as "Shakespeare-in-the-nude-on-roller-skates."

Well,! What a disaster! First of all, I got separated from Susan and George (it was bleacher seating), and the whole performance was the theater equivalent of a root canal with no novocaine. Having one's fingernails pulled out with pliers would have been less painful, and coincidentally, that's what it sounded like they were doing to all the singers. I didn't hear the end of it from Susan for weeks!

The student composition concerts at the college were even worse. I remember Matthew premiering a piece called Sonata for Cello and Ice Cubes or something to that effect. It was very atonal and experimental, the type of piece that would-be intellectuals would *adore* because it "lacked linearity" (read: had no melody).

Melody seemed to have no place in any of these concerts. The pieces performed usually induced a migraine in either Susan or me. In one case we both had Simultaneous Migraine from a concerto performed on an out-of-tune piano, a (recorded) wailing cat (it was really done by synthesizer, so as not to piss off the People for the Ethical Treatment of Animals—this was in the program notes) and a trash can played with a violin bow. Playing a trashcan is not as melodious as playing the saw, which sounds too close to actual "music." The combination of sounds in this composition also made the fillings in my teeth hurt.

I do have to hand it to her, though; through all of this Susan was a really good sport.

I kept in contact with Mark over the phone, since he was now determinedly making the best of things in Southern California. I was busy with my career, working, and trying to get a design business off the ground. I had decided to start making cocktail hats. (Inspired by those dust masks.) So I undertook to create my first collection and made it my official second job. Every evening at seven o'clock, I would go into my room and work for a few hours.

Between Matthew and work and my hat collection, I didn't have much time to travel south, and Mark didn't travel north. So our friendship became what I call a "telephone friendship." Mark and Vic never seemed really happy from what I could see or hear the entire time I knew them. There came a time in our telephone friendship when the bulk of my phone conversations with Mark seemed to consist of him talking about Victor, and me saying, "Poor, poor dear."

The proportion was three to one: three calls complaining of horrible treatment to one call bragging about "improvement" in behavior. It was something I took as a matter of course, irritating as it was. He didn't seem to hear anything I was saying, but I was used to that.

I didn't worry about it much, as I was working on getting my little business going. Toward this end I had left Macy's in Pleasanton to work for The Emporium in Stonestown in San Francisco. The Emporium paid more than Macy's, which was a prestige job. The increase in pay, combined with the lack of commuting expenses, gave me more money to put toward my new business.

The Emporium was built on an ancient Indian burial ground, and the land was cursed because of it. There were so many strange occurrences there to back my theory.

The first encounter I had with The Curse was when I was working at Roos Bros. all those years ago. The Stonestown Roos Bros. store was directly across the breezeway from The Emporium. I was installing Christmas windows one sunny fall afternoon when I heard an enormous crash and felt the ground shake. I had my back to the glass and thought we were having an earthquake—I got out of the window in a hurry.

The crash I had just heard was caused by a 50-by-50-foot section of brick facing that just let loose and dropped off the façade of The Emporium, with no warning whatsoever. Thankfully nobody was underneath at the time, which was a miracle—this breezeway led to the bus stop. The window I was trimming was destroyed a few hours later when the fire department started chipping away at the remnants of the brick façade; a big chunk of brick facing hit the ground, bounced up, and crashed right through the window, destroying the window and my new display. There wasn't a word of it in the press. I heard The Emporium paid a lot to hush it up. Mark was smart enough to blackmail The Emporium into completely remodeling both banks of our display windows, complete with new props, lighting, and such.

This incident did hit the press in OKC, where Mom asked me about it. I decided not to tell her how close I was to the scene of the crash. She was so nervous that something dreadful would happen to me, being so far away and all, that she would have had a conniption.

I saw more weird things happen when I started working at The Emporium, like the old (operative word: OLD) woman who went to the cosmetics department for a facial and makeover—AND DIDN'T WAKE UP WHEN IT WAS OVER!!! (The clerk at the counter never thought she'd lose a customer *that* way.) The old gal looked soooo natural, like she was sleeping!

Another example: There were three or four employees who announced their retirements and then died from cancer within a few weeks shy of collecting their pension.

After I left there, I had friends working there who would keep me apprised of the latest bizarre goings-on. The weirdest one I heard from my friend Eric. He called me one day, sounding really freaked out.

"You know your theory of The Emporium Curse?" he started.

"Yeah."

"I think you're right!"

"Why do you say that?" I asked.

The story tumbled out. A car had blown up in the parking lot, taking out a car on either side—like in the movies, a big, fiery blast. Everyone thought that was, well, really, really unusual.

Then, as Eric was going to the employee exit (which was through the furniture department), he passed a guy going the opposite way. The guy sat down on a sofa on one of the main traffic aisles—

And took out a gun.

And blew his brains out.

Still hardened from the experience of working there, I commented, "Well, you know he wasn't gay, or he would have done it at Macy's! No self-respecting queen would be caught *DEAD* at The Emporium!

It seems the car that blew up was the suicide guy's, and he had a small arsenal in the trunk. He apparently was one of those radical, militant militia types we were starting to hear of.

The Emporium paid dearly to keep that story out of the papers as well. The one thing they didn't do, however, was to paint the wall. It was splattered with blood and bits of brains for months.

The job at The Emporium was amusing, to say the least. Since I wasn't attached to the idea of continuing to make my career in display, and The Emporium wasn't known for its stellar displays, I could relax. The standards there were so lax that I felt I could phone in my displays. As long as there was *something* on the platform (no matter what it looked like), they were happy. It was like shooting rabbits with a big-game gun.

ACT TWO:

My first boss at The Emporium was a guy named Mikie. He was really good-looking (a cross between Tom Cruise and Dennis Quaid, with a hairy chest), and *really* stupid. A deadly combination in my book. I'm such a vicious queen that if someone is good-looking and stupid, God Help Them! I just can't resist.

And I had quite a bit of sport shooting down Mikie!

Since I had worked for Macy's (and was a candidate for display manager at that), Mikie regarded me as somewhat of a rock star, display-wise. Anything I did was regarded as the absolute standard for him, so I got to thinking one day: just how far could I go into Tacky Territory before being called on it?

I started small with little gaffes in good taste. Then I escalated things to where my co-workers (who didn't like Mikie either) started asking what I was up to. During all this Mikie didn't raise even one objection.

So I had to get his attention.

My big chance was the Prom Shop in the juniors department—could I come up with an idea?

COULD I?!?

"Mikie," I began. "You know the Julie Brown song "The Homecoming Queen's got A Gun?"

"Yeah," he said, eyeing me warily.

"That's it!"

"Waddaya mean?"

"Well, Mikie, we could have musical notes and stars cut out of Foamcore, along with little pink revolvers, and then we could dress the mannequin in that cool turquoise Jessica McClintock "fifties" number they have down there, with hair to death, elbow-length gloves, loads of bangle bracelets, Wayfarer sunglasses (this was the eighties you remember), and a gun!"

"Well . . . I don't know," he drawled, eyeing me.

I had to clinch this. So with eyes downcast, I said dejectedly, "Well, we would have done it at Macy's!"

It took all of fifteen minutes after I installed that display for the angry calls to begin, and an hour later there were petitions circulating, calling for, among other things, my head on a platter. Mikie defended his decision to the store manager, arguing that "Macy's would have done it!"

After Mikie was sent to the Fremont (Gulag-in-Siberia) store, we got Davie. Davie wasn't as good-looking as Mikie but just as smart. One day soon after he started working there, Davie asked me about the prom mannequin with the gun. (Apparently word had spread like wildfire throughout the company.)

"Why'd you do it?" he asked.

In my best Bette Davis imitation, I waved my "cigarette" and said, " 'Cause I'm *bored*, Davie, I'm BORED!"

"If you ever pull something like that on *me*, you'll be in serious trouble!" he barked back.

Casually I leaned in close, looked him in the eye, and coolly said, "You won't know what I'm up to until it blows up in your face!"

And I never had to do anything. I just played deadpan, and it nearly drove him crazy. He was always waiting for the other shoe to drop.

ACT TWO:

Creatively I was making headway, developing a collection of really extravagant evening hats. Inspired by Faberge, I built the black velvet boxes, lined with black taffeta, to house each of these creations, which were wrapped in black tissue. As I said earlier, working in display gave me the ability to build the box and also the understanding of the cachet that good packaging could do to enhance a product. I understood that the sigh of the lid coming off the box, along with the rustle of black tissue, created dramatic anticipation, which was rewarded by seeing the beautiful hat.

Believe it or not, the boxes got press before the contents did. But the hats got press soon thereafter, being singled out in an article on a new boutique called Telaio that just opened on Brady Street across from the Zuni Café. I was selling. Not paying the bills but selling.

As part of building my business, it was suggested that I start making regular visits to Los Angeles to scope out the kinds of boutiques I would be selling in. Susan gave me my first plane ticket there as a birthday gift with the admonition, "Go get 'em, Darling Angel!"

So during this first visit to LA, I sandwiched in a visit to Mark in his new house in Long Beach. Now I'd never been to Long Beach, but it sounded really nice—a long beach! Coming over the hill on the 405 was my first clue.

On the phone Mark had described his new place glowingly as this "cottage down the path behind the main house"; when I got there it turned out to be a shitty little shack cheaply built in the backyard of a tract house. There was, at best, ten feet between his front door and the back door of the "main house," but yes, there *was* a path. It went from the chain link fence gate to the front door. There was no porch.

This was a really depressing-looking house, but I'm sure it was the proper setting for the life lived within. Inside I recognized some of the furniture, sadly diminished, from quite some time with no maintenance. The sofa looked so soiled that I didn't want to sit on it. Some of the good pieces that I remembered weren't there. Other of the good stuff that was still there, looked patched together, chipped, or otherwise damaged. The doorframe to their bedroom was splintered, as if someone had broken the door down at one point. Everything had a patina of stale cigarette smoke and regret all over it. Mark and I sat at the kitchen table and talked.

The topic of discussion was—surprise!—Victor. It seemed that Vic was being sued for sexual harassment by one of the employees at the burglar alarm company he worked for. Actually blackmail was a more accurate word. This guy told Vic that if he didn't fork over a large sum of money, the guy would rat him out to his bosses and sue the company. The Japanese bosses had no use for these types of shenanigans and would have fired Victor's ass if they had heard about this. So Mark had sold most of his art collection, including some museum-quality Coptic textiles, at a garage sale (!!!) to come up with the blackmail money.

"Why?" I asked. "Let him get fired! Maybe he'll learn a lesson and behave himself!"

"You don't understand."

"No, I don't."

"He's the only one working, so we need this job!"

"Why don't you leave and get a job? You can go anywhere you want then!"

"You just don't understand."

Thus ended the visit. I felt confused and a bit disgusted and was glad I wasn't *him*. At least Matthew, my unrepentantly-unemployed-but-still-good-looking-in-white-briefs spouse, didn't get into situations where blackmail money had to be paid. Even if he had, I sure wouldn't pay it! Sell *my* stuff to get *him* out of a jam? Hell no!

Yes, Matthew was good-looking, and I wasn't paying blackmail to get him out of a jam, but he was getting expensive. Comparing him to Victor set the bar really low, but at the time, I didn't see that very clearly.

ACT TWO:

Or more importantly I wasn't ready to see it. In that way, I was just like Mark.

Summers were not my favorite time while I was married to Matthew. This was because we got a visit from Peter, Matthew's son, for at least six weeks every summer. Somehow The Ex overlooked the unpaid child support to let Peter come visit—I'm sure it was a relief for her to get him out of her hair for a while.

I don't really like kids, but Peter was a nice kid, and I did like him. He liked me as well, so things went more smoothly than if he hadn't. We did do things like have water fights while washing the car, and I tried to treat him as I would want to be treated in such a situation. But the whole thing was really wearing.

Particularly worrying was the issue of Peter's mother. I didn't know what she thought of me or of Matthew having Peter living with him and me, namely what kind of scenario she might cook up in her head. I was conscious of the possibility that she might be afraid that I would molest Peter (or more to the point, accuse me of that), as that's what many people still believed gay boys did. Because of this I made sure I was always fully clothed around him (he only saw my bare feet), so as not to have even a hint of anything that could be misinterpreted as unseemly. This I had to endure for six weeks every summer.

My only respite was the trip they would take to Yosemite every year. Matthew had this fantasy (operative word: *fantasy*) that I would go camp out with Peter and him and sleep outdoors in the weather! He kept at it, asking me every year, but I would always say that if God had meant for me to camp out, he wouldn't have made the Ahwahnee Hotel. Really, though, I just wanted to have the place to myself. I looked forward to it.

Even though Matthew became increasingly dependent on my income (read: was mooching more), I would *gladly* pay for the trip, just to get them the hell out of the house!

So you can see why I didn't look forward to Peter's visits—they were too damned expensive. *That* I did see.

The last summer we were together (1987), when Matthew said that Peter was coming out, I didn't get all excited. He got a little put out about this, as I "should" be glad because he was glad.

He had to be told.

"I'm not looking forward to this because it's damn expensive," I said. "During the year I have one extra mouth to feed, but in the summer I have TWO! I don't look forward to having to come up with the money for all of this. Remember, I regard one of the positive by-products of being gay as not having children. I wasn't there when Peter was conceived—*you were*. Therefore, I don't feel I should have to support him."

"You're so selfish! All you think about is money!" he shouted. (It was his standard response whenever I would point out that he wasn't holding up his end of the finances.)

Right then I was reminded of what Harry told me all those years ago—when someone uses the word "selfish," it usually means that you aren't doing (or thinking) what *they* want you to.

The summer of 1987 was when everything really started unraveling between Matthew and me.

To back up a bit, my business was starting to gather steam. In the fall of 1986, I had gotten an agent, and by the holidays, I was selling in a Very Posh Store in L.A. That's where the first rich-and-famous customers came from. They saw my work at this store and went mad for it. So I had started selling.

I couldn't quit the job yet, but things were going in the right direction.

ACT TWO:

What I noticed was that the more momentum my business picked up, the more money Matthew seemed to need.

Besides having a much shorter commute now that I worked in The City, (and eliminating the related expenses), I was actually making more money by taking a step down in prestige—no matter. The extra money was planned for expanding my business, a fact I explained to Matthew as I set out my new budget.

Strangely Matthew seemed to be soaking up the extra money I was netting by the change in job. He stopped paying rent completely, so on payday I would find myself rent-poor and without enough pocket money to buy coffee. Then after working all day I would come home to a perfectly tanned Matthew, who would fill me in on how many cute boys were at the beach.

During this time I still maintained my telephone friendship with Mark. It felt a little sad, as I had seen where he lived and, therefore, could imagine the sad little shack with the battered and soiled furniture. During these phone conversations, Mark would talk about the taps on the phone ("We're being recorded," he would say dramatically), and he would tell me about the video cameras Victor set up to watch him when Vic wasn't around. This didn't seem too far-fetched to me, since Vic *did* work for a burglar alarm company and had access to this stuff. (And he had an inordinate fondness, or one could say a fetish, for stun guns and such like.)

Hearing all of this made me sad, but I still tried to give some good advice and raise Mark's spirits during these phone conversations.

I bumped along at the Emporium, making my designs in the evenings and on the weekends, treating my little business like a second job. Somehow I got enough money together to keep up the momentum and start selling at the Very Posh Store in Los Angeles. This generated some cash flow but not yet enough to quit the day job.

In the spring of '87 Matthew graduated with a BA in music composition. I hinted that he should start thinking about a job, as he would soon be out of school and have more time on his hands. He went ballistic.

"Remember we agreed that you would put me through school, *then* I would help you get your business off the ground!" he shouted.

"Wait a minute! I don't remember anything of the sort! Besides I've seen too many Movies-of-the-Week! They all end the same, where the long-suffering wife puts her man through school and gets traded in for a younger model."

"I'm going to get my doctorate and WON'T be getting a job, so YOU'RE JUST GOING TO HAVE TO GET USED TO IT!"

"You make it sound as if I have no say in this," I said.

"You don't," he shot back.

Right then I decided to open my eyes. I still didn't want to see what this situation was, but something deep inside let me know that it was really tired of walking around with its eyes closed.

During this time I asked Davie if I could go on part-time. He insisted that I was hired on full-time, and full-time I would always be.

"Fine," I thought. "I asked."

So I started calling in sick twenty hours a week.

Quite to my amazement, this worked out for several months. I used a lesson that I learned from Crazy Carmel at Macy's: if you do it big enough, brazenly enough, and long enough, people will just leave you alone and let you do whatever you want.

Aside from calling in sick twenty hours a week, there were other things I got away with when I was actually "working." If I needed to, on my

ACT TWO:

fifteen-minute "coffee break" I would walk out the door right under the time clock, not punching out, to take a delivery to UPS. When I returned I would walk right in, not punching back in, and go back to work. All under the watchful eye of the "security" guard. This way I didn't have to lose my lunch hour.

Word went around the store about my plans, and many people were excited for me and wanted to help out. Helene, the executive assistant to the store manager, volunteered to do all my typing and resumes—on company time. When called on it by her boss, she just said to him, "So what are you going to do, fire me?" Which he didn't do.

Then there was Miss Coke, who worked in the linens department. I didn't know her first name—she was Miss Coke to everyone. She had worked at The Emporium since they had broken ground for the shopping center in 1952 and had that lilac-white-colored skin that one gets from spending years under fluorescent lights.

She liked me. When I would return from a delivery, if I had been paged, Miss Coke would give me a heads-up as to what time and who it was so I could concoct a preemptive story.

One day, though, as I passed by the linen department, Miss Coke grabbed me by the collar and dragged me into the linens stockroom.

Pointing to a chair, she said, "Sit down!"

I was puzzled—had I done something to offend her? She looked upset.

"GET OUT!" she shouted.

"What!?" I asked, confused and incredulous.

"Look at me! Do you want to end up like me? You've got something! You have a chance. There's no place for me to go! I stayed here too long. But you have a future and a talent. SO GET OUT! I mean it! Before it's too late!" She was shaking.

And with that she ran out of the stockroom. I felt like I had just been in a scene from a women's prison film.

My departure from The Emporium was rather sudden.

It was a couple of weeks before the Oscars, and the Very Posh Store had called to order lots of vests. I had a short deadline, so I had to make a choice: work at The Emporium, or further my design business. Hmmm, which would I choose?

There was one complication though. The personnel policies at The Emporium were reminiscent of high school—one needed a "late pass" if one were late (at Macy's we just got our pay docked), and one needed a "leave the building" pass if one needed to leave before the scheduled quitting time (at Macy's we just clocked out). Also if one were sick more than two days in a row, one had to get a doctor's note to come back to work.

So, this particular week I called in sick Monday, came to work Tuesday, and needed to call in sick Wednesday, Thursday, and Friday—three days in a row. This took some thinking, but I figured it out. I would come to work Friday morning and have a relapse (I had a particularly ghastly eye shadow I used on those occasions), so I could go home about, oh, ten. That would give me the better part of the day to finish my vests.

As I was standing at the personnel window to get my "leave the building pass," I noticed a particular vibe coming from the lady there. Not a sympathetic vibe, I might add.

It was the next day, Saturday, when Marshall first called about the studio space she had for rent. As I said, I was looking around for a space to rent

ACT TWO:

and let the word out with everyone I knew. That Saturday morning I got a phone call from Marshall Crossman—she knew my friend Candace Kling and my agent, Brenda—and had heard from them that I was looking for a space. Marshall had just rented a painting studio on Eighth Street between Howard and Folsom, south of Market, and was looking to share it with someone. Was I interested? Of course I was and immediately went over to see the space. Later that day I called her back and rented it. And that's how I met Marshall.

All day Sunday I ruminated: Do I quit, don't I quit, do I quit, don't I quit, do I quit, don't I quit, do I quit, don't I quit . . . ?

Monday morning as I was walking up to the building, I was still going through the chant: Do I quit, don't I quit, do I quit, don't I quit, do I quit, don't I quit . . . ?

I clocked in and walked into the elevator: Do I quit, don't I quit, do I quit, don't I quit, do I quit, don't I quit, do I quit, don't I quit . . . ?

And then in jumped Davie.

The doors closed.

He looked at me with a look of *complete pleasure* on his face, and I had my answer.

"Davie, before you say anything, I'm giving my two weeks' notice."

Davie's face fell (it didn't have far to go). He had wanted to fire my ass right there, and the look on his face confirmed it!

"Well, Ken, I expect regular attendance for the next two weeks!" Davie spat sarcastically, hand on hip.

"That's going to be inconvenient, because I'm doing a photo shoot of my hats for *Image* magazine on Wednesday and will be in just long enough to borrow a mannequin, and then I'll be gone the rest of the day."

What could he do, fire me?

So I launched myself into self-employment in March of 1987.

When I rented the studio, Marshall said that the building owner would put in a skylight for me. It would be a small one (about the size of a hankie), unless I wanted to put in an extra hundred dollars—then he would install something larger. I opted for the smaller one; I don't like spending money I can't carry out with me when I leave.

Matthew was furious.

"Why didn't you ask ME for the money?" he demanded. "You could have had a larger skylight if only you had asked me!"

"Well I assumed you didn't *have* any money, which is always a safe bet! If you have money, then why exactly am I still paying all the rent?!? Besides, would you *give* me the money to put in the skylight?"

"No, you'd have to pay it back. I can't afford to give you money."

That sent me ballistic.

"What about all the money I've given *you* over the last few years?"

"You're treating me like a housewife!" he whined. "I don't get any say in your business!"

"Well, sir, if the shoe fits!" I shouted. "If you act like a housewife, you should expect to be treated like one. Remember, I'M not the one sponging money here! And besides, this is MY business. I don't remember you investing in it, so you really don't have anything to say about how I spend my money to run it! And I don't choose to spend my money on this skylight. It's a business decision—MY business decision!"

ACT TWO:

The sex ended a few months earlier. Matthew's complaint was that we didn't have it enough. (A contrast from our early days when he refused it.) He wanted it every night—which was hunky-dory for him— because he didn't have to get up and go to work the next day.

He had too much time on his hands.

The last time I tried to initiate sex, Matthew looked at his watch and said, "Oh, has it been a month already?"

Furious, I responded, "You know, since I'm paying for it, I'll use it or not as I see fit!"

My eyes were open. And that's what I was seeing.

The final countdown to my divorce started in September of '87.

Matthew was (yet again) complaining bitterly one day that I wasn't spending enough time with him. It was a common rant—that and we didn't have sex any more. (I've said it before; it was because he had too much time on his hands, being unemployed and all.) He wanted to go to the museum, and Thursdays were free; I could at least do that for him? So we went.

We were walking down one of the hallways at the DeYoung, when coming toward us was this blond kid. As he passed he locked eyes with Matthew, and I thought, "Hmmm." (Matthew always had a taste for tubercular-looking blond boys with spines like cooked asparagus. I'm a brunet with good posture.)

After we had walked on a ways, Matthew was seized with a strong desire to look at the art of the Middle Ages. Again. Glad to be rid of him, I walked on to the Asian art, to look at the jades on display. We agreed to meet up later in front of the building.

So we met up, and as we were leaving, the kid came up (or slunk up, to be more accurate), and Matthew gave him our phone number. He explained that Phillippe was visiting from France, and he offered to show the boy around.

Right about then a car drove by, stereo blasting. The song I heard through the open window was "Your Cheatin' Heart".

I came home from jewelry class that night to find the two of them in Matthew's bedroom. They were still fully clothed, but Matthew was looking at Phillippe like a thirsty man looks at water. After a bit of uncomfortable conversation, I went to my room.

A few minutes later, Matthew came in, wanting "to talk." He started and I interrupted:

"Just go ahead and do what you want to do. That's what you've been doing all along. You don't need my permission."

I had my "out."

Four days later they emerged from Matthew's room. Phillippe left and Matthew sat down at the kitchen table.

"We need to talk," I said.

"I'VE BEEN MISERABLE! I WOULD HAVE LEFT YOU MONTHS AGO IF I'D HAD A JOB!" he shouted.

"Well, then, guess what? This bank is closed!" I stated. "If you're so fucking miserable, you'll GET a job!"

ACT TWO:

And I left for work. But not before taking my change jar with me. I also stopped bringing food into the house and started sleeping with my wallet under my pillow. If he was so fucking miserable, then he would also be hungry as well. The meal ticket had expired.

It was over for me.

Now I *couldn't avoid* looking at, or seeing, the obvious—it had slapped me in the face. Matthew was hanging around because I was the meal ticket. It was something I had been able to avoid looking at (*in that way I was like Mark*), but secretly I knew it all along. Allowing Phillippe to "happen" gave me both the motivation to finally look at the issue and also the way out of the situation.

Even so, it felt like I'd been punched in the stomach. It brought back all of the insecurities I felt—about how Matthew was so beautiful, and because he was so beautiful, why was he with *me*? It was hard to swallow this confession that I was just a meal ticket. In my mind it was a slap at my attractiveness, my desirability, my *self*. That's why he stayed around—for the support, not because he found me compelling, desirable, or lovable.

So, as I did the day I was dumped by Brock all those years ago, I left the apartment with my head held high, not showing a bit of emotion. He had taken so much while I chose to look the other way, I'd be damned to let him have this part of me. Besides, as I've said, I prefer to do my crying offstage, thank you.

So, I went to the studio. And had a really good cry there. Off-stage.

This all happened on Labor Day. I called Susan to tell her what was happening, and she insisted we go out for chocolate.

"Darling Angel, it's the only way to deal with such things," she chirped on the phone. "But Heaven knows where we will find good chocolate on Labor Day!"

We ended up at McDonalds, eating the cheapie hot fudge sundaes.

"Well, Darling Angel," Susan exclaimed, after we got settled in. "Thank God we don't have to go to any more of those *excruciating* student concerts! Let this be a lesson to you—marry *UP*. Don't marry someone whose parents bought silver plate."

Words of wisdom there—trust her to have the right take on things. She was right though. When I look back, I was so glamoured by his looks that I ignored the red flags. But now that had changed.

I now call that period in my life, "My-Life-as-a-Fellini-Film."

When I'm furious with someone or something, I get really quiet. As long as I'm talking, there's nothing to worry about; but when I go silent, that means *trouble*. People accuse me of being unfeeling, having no emotions. Having the ability to set them aside until I can deal with them in private isn't the same as not having them; to me, it's a seemlier way of dealing with them. And again it's that thing of casting pearls before swine. So, because of this trouble with Matthew, I went completely silent.

And boy, oh boy, there was, indeed, trouble in my house. I was done with him. It takes me quite a while to make up my mind that I am done with someone, but when my mind is made up, it's made up. For all of September and most of October, I said not a word to Matthew. If he and I were in the apartment (which I avoided by staying at the studio very late), I would act like he didn't exist. That's the way I am when I'm done with someone—I withdraw completely. No screaming or harsh words here—*just ice*. It drove him crazy.

But he drove *me* crazy in other ways. There was Andie, the twenty-two-year-old coed from San Francisco State. She was one of those girls who fall for fags. Andie would show up at our apartment, and the next morning I would find groceries in the fridge. They would also spend lots of time in Matthew's room, knocking boots. (The bisexual issue raised its ugly head again.) I spent longer hours at the studio.

In the meantime, the stock market crashed.

I remember sitting at my worktable, listening to the reports every fifteen minutes or so that October day, telling of the latest drop. I was screwed. There was a sinking feeling in my stomach as well—not yet a year in business, no savings, credit stretched to the limit, leaving my husband, and now this!

It wreaked havoc with my finances. The Very Posh Store got nervous and stopped ordering, and this left me high and dry financially. Another store that Brenda, my agent, had sold to stiffed me and returned ordered merchandise (damaged at that, so I couldn't resell it), which only exacerbated the situation.

One day in late October, Matthew came into my room early in the morning (*really* early—the only way he could catch me) to tell me that Phillippe was coming back for a week's stay, and I had nothing to say about it, so I had better get used to the idea.

Phillippe arrived two weeks later. They immediately disappeared into Matthew's bedroom for a reunion fuck. I went to the studio.

The next day I had an appointment to get publicity photos taken at my photographer friend David's and came home in the afternoon to shower, shave, and dress—only to find the young lovers fucking in the bathtub, something Matthew never wanted to do with me! Somehow I managed to shave in the kitchen sink and get it together to go get those photos taken.

Poor David—he tried and tried his best to make me look "POWERFUL! AND SEXY!" But it didn't work. (I hate those photos, and almost never look at them—for all the good lighting and camera angles, you can plainly see the pain in my eyes.)

Two days later I had to go look at proofs. That day it started to rain, and the roof of my studio was leaking a twenty-gallon trashcan of water an hour. I ran over to David's during a break in the rain, wearing a shapeless black coat, jeans, baggy sweater, and two days' stubble. He brought out the contact sheets, then the buzzer rang.

In walked this guy, who no doubt was genetically the model for the Master Race—Hitler's wet dream in the flesh. David explained that the guy was on a "go-see," so I should just look over the proofs, and he would be done in a few minutes.

In my weakened state, the Hitler Youth was even more intimidating than he normally would be. I was acutely aware of my unshaven, unkempt appearance and wanted to crawl in a hole. Then it happened:

David told the Hitler Youth to mess up his hair, which the kid did. The hair, as if by magic, "sproinged" back into place, leaving him flawless, still. I could take no more.

"I have to go!" I said as I hurried out.

Puzzled, David started to ask what was wrong, but I just held up a hand and mumbled something about I'll explain later and stumbled out onto the street. My only thought was to get to the studio. I would be safe in the studio. And that's where I headed. I would be safe there.

The phone was ringing when I got there. Warily I answered it; it turned out to be Brenda, my agent. My relief was only momentary, as she "needed to talk."

ACT TWO:

As it was, Brenda was pregnant and having a hormone surge. During this surge she started ruminating on whether or not she would be able to represent me after the baby was born and felt she needed to make the call and talk to me about it RIGHT THEN.

After a while Brenda noticed I wasn't saying anything—wasn't even making a sound. As it was, I was trying to stave off a full-blown panic:

Stock market crashed.

Sales of merchandise nonexistent.

Flat-ass broke.

Husband screwing his new boyfriend back at the apartment.

Leaving the husband.

The prospect of no representation and, hence, no income.

I was doing all I could to keep from going insane *RIGHT THEN*!

Yes, Brenda realized that I was unnaturally quiet and started asking if I was all right, did I need someone to come by, should she call 911 or someone to stay with me. She insisted that she was just thinking aloud and probably would keep representing me, blah blah blah, hah hah hah, and not to worry (!!!). But the damage had been done. I got off the phone in a panic and didn't feel safe in the studio any more.

Where to go? I couldn't go home—the happy couple was there, no doubt fucking their brains out. I couldn't stay in the studio—Brenda might call and start in again. So I wandered the streets, ending up at Church Street Station.

Church Street Station was sort of like the gay Denny's, back in the day. It was on the corner of Market and Church, and was one of those classic dive diners, open twenty-four hours, with a counter and tables. In my younger days I used to end up there after a night of dancing.

On this particular night, the only place I felt safe was at Church Street Station. I spent quite a while there, crying into my coffee. The waiter would creep up and refill occasionally, but otherwise he left me alone.

Then came the Susan Hayward moment.

Looking down into the coffee cup, I saw my reflection—unshaven, swollen, puffy eyes—and looked down at my shapeless black coat.

"WHAT THE HELL AM I DOING!?!" I thought to myself. "I need to pull myself together!"

At which point I looked up and out the window just in time to see Matthew and Phillippe walking by, arm in arm, the picture of new love.

"God, take me now!" I thought.

Needless to say, I'm still here.

After that bad night, I went home and posted a note on Matthew's bedroom door that read:

"I DON'T HAVE THE MONEY FOR THIS MONTH'S RENT. YOU'RE GOING TO HAVE TO COME UP WITH RENT THIS MONTH, LIKE I'VE HAD TO DO FOR LONG ENOUGH. I CAN'T LIVE HERE IN PEACE, SO I'M NOT PAYING ANOTHER CENT."

The next morning, I got a note: "I'll be moving out on December 13."

It was over, finally. Or so I thought.

ACT TWO:

Mark was no help whatsoever during this period. After a couple of phone calls, I realized that he didn't want to hear about my divorce—for whatever reason. This was really infuriating. I had listened to him chewing my ear with years and years of "bad-Victor" bitching, so the least he could do was to be a little sympathetic. But he wasn't. He'd just change the conversation to "Victor blah blah blah . . ."

Thanksgiving that year promised to be a sad and gloomy one for me. No money, business in the toilet, divorce pending—I was feeling a little sorry for myself. So my friend Laurel Fenenga invited me out to dinner on Thanksgiving eve to cheer me up.

Laurel is someone who I regard as a brilliant artist. She and I *were* the millinery industry in the Bay Area in the mid-eighties. Where my hats were extravagant, hers were minimal. What we both had in common was a love of quality and a love of the process. In our own ways we developed our respective visions (diverse as they were) based on a similar philosophy—that of doing one's own work, doing it really well, and not copying from others.

So on Thanksgiving Eve, Laurel felt sorry for me, and we ended up going to The Castro for dinner. Parking in that neighborhood being what it is, Laurel had to park the car at Twentieth and Diamond, way up the hill from The Castro. When I got out of the car, it sounded like water running; I listened and heard that the sound was coming from under Laurel's car. I looked under the car and saw a leak in the gas line, leaking gasoline at an alarming rate.

"Laurel, are you aware of this leak?" I asked.

"No, but let's go get dinner and deal with this later" was her very sensible response. After dinner we went back to the car. It wasn't too hard to find—we just followed the rivulet of gasoline in the gutter from Eighteenth Street up the hill.

Looking under the car, it looked like the join between the line from the gas tank to the fuel line going to the engine had popped loose. I proposed going down to the local service station, getting a length of rubber hose and two screw clamps, and bridging the gap. So off we went to the Chevron station.

We returned with the necessary parts, got under the car and, at one point, needed to pull the gas line from the tank loose to get the hose on—this no doubt would produce a shower of gasoline. I gave a count of three, then we pulled and, under the shower of gasoline, quickly got the hose on and secured.

"You know, someone could destroy the millinery industry in the Bay Area with one lit match, just like that scene in the movie *The Birds*," Laurel commented as we lay in the puddle of gasoline, tightening the screw clamps. "You're the only person I know who would do something like this. I'm impressed!"

The millinery industry survived, but my Perry Ellis shirt did not. The gasoline smell never left it.

It was during this crazy period that I learned an important lesson: Don't ask, "What else?" You'll get an answer, and you won't like it.

My life had taken on the quality of "dances with land mines" again. There seemed to be one exploding at my feet every day, and after the detonation, I would ask, "What else can go wrong!?" Then another land mine would detonate. This is something I had been determined never to repeat—I lived with this when I was a teenager, and I'd be damned if I would let it go on much longer, now that I had a choice. This is why I forced Matthew's hand by leaving the note on the door.

ACT TWO:

In early December I had finally gotten an order, for one of my evening vests, and was glad of it. There was one problem: I needed bulk silver to melt down to make the signature sterling buttons and hardware.

Darrell (remember him from my OKC days?) never knew this, but he took care of me by remote control. As I had no cash reserves, my solution was to go to my jewelry box. Darrell had been very good to me. As I sat there, picking stones out of the many heavy silver pieces he gave me, I silently thanked him and hoped he wouldn't find out or, if he did, would understand why. I was able to melt down the silver to finish the order for the vest, which was white.

When I finished this white vest, I left it on my worktable, thinking that was the safest place for it, and went home for the night.

We had an unusual amount of rain during that fall and winter. This particular rainstorm, which started soon after I got home that night, made it into the record books, flooding the storm drains and streets and jamming traffic. When I pulled the big front door to the studio building open the following morning, I wasn't too surprised to see a puddle of water emerging from under the door to our studio space.

"Oh, God, please don't let that be what it looks like!" I implored as I opened the door.

It was. My side of the studio was under three inches of standing water.

It was quite beautiful, actually. The reflection of the studio in the water was perfect, unblemished by any ripples—just like a mirror. The boxes with all my fabric, which were sitting on the floor under my worktable, were expanding noticeably, soaking up as much water as they could.

To top it off, the vest that I just finished—the *white* vest that someone had ordered and would soon pay for, the one I melted my silver jewelry down to get the hardware made for—was soaked, ruined. It was as if someone had found the direct center of it, taken a plumb line up to the ceiling, and poked a hole in the roof exactly over it. Muddy water had been pouring over it for quite a while.

Suddenly an incredible calm came over me.

I didn't feel the need to ask what else could happen. I wasn't upset. *Just calm.*

Marshall came in right then, saw the mess (which didn't extend to her studio), and looked at me to assess my state of mind. I calmly walked over to the phone (splosh, splosh, splosh…) and made a lunch date with a friend.

Eyeing me suspiciously, Marshall asked after the call, "Are you OK?"

"Sure."

"Really?" She was waiting for the meltdown, followed by a call to 911.

"Yeah, I'm OK," I said calmly. "Let's mop up the water, and I'll hang up the fabric to see what dries out. Then I'm going to lunch."

And that's when I knew I'd be OK. It was over.

I was talking on the phone to Mark one evening the first week in December, when Matthew started hectoring me about wanting to open the phone bill. I got off the phone and reminded him that the phone bill was in my name and also that *I had been the one paying it*. For the life of me, I couldn't fathom his concern about the phone bill all of a sudden.

Until he told me about the transatlantic phone calls. *Calls*. Plural.

Needless to say I had a few words on *that* subject. He feigned concern—wanted to reimburse me for them, didn't want to take advantage of me, that's why he wanted to open the bill. (He eventually stiffed me for that as well.) Then he got on his high horse and wanted to "have a talk."

I sat down on the sofa and calmly said, "OK, Matthew, this relationship is over, and you're leaving in a few days, so say what you have to say. Go ahead. I'm listening."

"I HAVE SOME THINGS I WANT TO SAY!" he shouted.

"I realize that. Go ahead. I said I'm listening."

"All I wanted was to be your lover!" he whimpered. Matthew could always do the puppy eyes and the quivering lower lip really well. He was putting on an Oscar-worthy performance now.

"No, Matthew," I said. "All you wanted were the rights and privileges. You didn't want the responsibilities. I never asked you to change your friends, or the way you dress, or who you are, or how you behave. I took you as you were. All I ever asked of you was to support yourself, but that was the one thing consistently denied me."

"What's the other thing you wish to say?" I asked calmly.

"When did you decide you didn't want me any more?"

"The moment you said that you were miserable and would have left me if you had had a job," I answered. "I suspected that you were sticking around because I was the meal ticket—you just put it into words, something I never really wanted to admit to myself."

"Well I was just trying to make you mad!"

"Well, YOU SUCCEEDED! I'm *STILL* mad!"

A long silence.

Then Matthew asked, "What is the future of this relationship?"

I couldn't fucking *believe* this question and was glad I was sitting down.

Obviously he didn't understand that I had made up my mind already. I'm sure he was expecting me to back down—God knows I did it all the time with him—but, although it takes me a while to make up my mind, once my mind is made up, *IT'S MADE UP*.

I had to make myself perfectly clear.

"Matthew, if I see you on the street, I'll say "hello." That's it. If you have any fantasies of us "being friends," or going out to dinner, or getting back together—FORGET THEM NOW! It's *not* going to happen!"

Then I went to bed feeling much lighter.

December 13 couldn't come fast enough for me. It was a Sunday, and I was going to a Christmas party that evening with my friend Laurel Fenenga—you remember, of the pool of gasoline?

ACT TWO:

Matthew showed up that morning with a woman, whose name escapes me, but she had a British accent. I'll call her "Britt." Britt was a friend of Phillippe (which she pronounced "Phillip"), and since Phillippe was back in France tying up loose ends, Britt was pressed into service to help find Matthew and Phillippe a room and help move him in, as I had vetoed his request to use *my* car. I certainly wasn't going to help. I had done my part already.

So I sat on the sofa, drinking coffee and eating croissants, and watching to see that nothing of mine walked out the door. (He did get away with my dove-gray Trimline phone though.)

Not that there was much Matthew had to move. Matthew owned the rotten Herculon sofa that lived in the dining room, a ratty kitchen table and chair that lived in his bedroom, his books and records, a very expensive (and large) stereo (purchased in Japan), and a shabby mattress. There would have also been the piano, but he gave that to the Salvation Army the week before, as there would be no space for it in his new digs. Pity.

(While he was packing, I had a little revenge. Matthew fancied himself a gourmet cook, so I swiped his spice rack and his dildo—I knew he would miss them both terribly, but he wouldn't have the money to replace either of them any time soon. I could tell he was looking all over for them, but he never asked me where they were. I just sat on the sofa looking wide-eyed and innocent.)

After he loaded the first load into Britt's car, Matthew started out. Britt said she'd stay behind to keep me company. As if I wanted company.

The front door closed, leaving me face-to-face with Britt.

"So, are you sleeping with him too?" I demanded, just for fun. "Because, you know, he has another girl named Andie."

"Oh, my goodness, NO!" she stated indignantly in her British accent. "I'm a friend of Phillip, not Matthew."

"So how did you get mixed up in this mess?"

"Believe me, I'm doing it for Phillip," she responded. "I quite frankly don't see what he sees in Matthew."

"It's probably the sex. Well, know that one day Matthew will do to him what he's doing to me. Also know that I supported Matthew for the last three years and am now in debt because of it. That's what Phillippe has to look forward to."

We chatted a little more, and then Matthew came back for the other load. After he took down the last of his things, he came back for a last good-bye. After looking around the apartment, he said,

"It doesn't look like I was even here."

That was true. All the furniture was mine—the good stuff anyway. I hoped Phillippe wasn't counting on having spiffy furniture—if he was, well, *nyah, nyah, nyah!*

"Ummm" was my response.

Then came the big eyes and quivering lip. "Good-bye," Matthew said.

"Good-bye!" I chirped cheerily.

"I'm going now . . ." More quivering lip and big eyes, and a slow walk to the door.

"Good-bye!" I said again, a little more pointedly.

He walked out the door, and closed it slowly. I did a little happy dance— .
. .

And the door opened!

"Take care of yourself," he said, bigger eyes and really quivering lip and a heavy sigh.

ACT TWO:

I walked over to the door, pushed him out, shouted "GOOD-BYE," slammed the door, locked it, and put on the chain.

He was gone.

Then I thoroughly cleaned the house and burned lots of sage.

And went to that party with Laurel.

As I said earlier, Mark wasn't much help during all of this. He seemed not to hear that I was going through a big mess in my life. When I'd start to tell him what was going on, he'd interrupt with a harangue about Victor's misdeeds/or improvements. Looking back, as I was telling him that I was leaving Matthew, perhaps if he had really listened to what I was saying, he might then have had to look at his own situation. It was really irritating, feeling like I wasn't being heard. But I was used to it.

At the end of 1987, after Matthew and I split, I let go of the apartment that we had shared. I never really liked it and couldn't afford it on my own. Then as now, I had a rule: *if I'm not sleeping with 'em, I'm not living with 'em.* So no roommates. Instead I moved into the studio and slept on my broken-down sofa, listening to the mousetraps clacking like castanets at night. (I discovered that mice like Skippy Peanut Butter best. Go know.)

These were primitive digs. For a shower I had a dishpan, a tin can for water, and a quartz heater. After business hours I'd stand there in the dishpan naked, pouring water over myself, feeling all the time as if I were basting a turkey. For food, I had a hot plate that I'd boil water on for ramen noodles and frozen vegetables—a combination that I still refer to as "Austerity Rations." (Breakfast was peanut butter on apples.) Friends would occasionally allow me to house-sit so I could use a proper shower and sleep on a proper bed. This lasted for the first half of 1988. Not ideal, but there you have it. I did what I had to do.

Ditching the apartment and the expensive trophy husband allowed me to focus my resources on my business. I developed a line of jewelry from marbles (as in losing your . . .) that was "popularly priced" and generated increasing cash flow. I was able to hire a (very) part-time assistant to help me make parts and pieces. By mid-1988 I had enough money to rent myself a tiny apartment in a bad end of town—things were looking up!

In the meantime The Very Posh Store was ordering again and with some regularity. Elton John saw my work there and began purchasing things, which progressed to commissioning pieces for him. These commissions, which I was thrilled with, were usually ordered with the instructions: a certain number (of hats, vests, whatever) in two weeks at whatever price I put on them.

I must say that he has all the best pieces. Having someone who I idolized growing up buying *my* work was *too good*. My intention was to top myself every time for him, stretching my work in the process.

It was in August of '88 that I got the order for hats for his concert tour. This was one of those good-news-bad-news things. My agent, Brenda, called me one Saturday afternoon, frantic.

"I just got a call from Tommy, and he told me that the person making the clothes for Elton's concert tour told him she was going to order hats directly from you," she said breathlessly. "He's furious and right now venting on your home answering machine. I had him call there so I'd have time enough to call you to give you a heads-up. I've gotta go; let me know how it comes out!"

ACT TWO:

(In other words, the good news: Elton's concert tour. The bad news: I had to tame a dragon first.)

Fuck! *Shit!* This was serious, and I had to sit there at my desk, waiting for the phone to ring, when what I really wanted to do was bolt for the door. Right then I couldn't afford to piss him off, so I had to sit tight and deal with this.

The phone rang, a stream of invectives from the other end followed, and eventually I got a few comforting words in edgewise, assuring him that I would, indeed, run the transaction through his store. I hung up the phone, which rang immediately. It was the woman who was doing the costuming.

"Goddamn, woman, you almost killed my main account," I said. "Why the hell did you tell him you were ordering from me!?"

"I was concerned that he might not give you all the swatches and information to make the hats match," she stammered, surprised. She was probably expecting a gleeful, grateful voice.

I calmed down, apologized (I didn't want to piss *her* off either or have her decide to use someone else), and told her how to proceed. This involved her telling The Very Posh Store that she had told me to expect swatches and fabrics from her—this way I'd also ask for them, ensuring that I'd actually get them in a timely manner. On my end I'd have my agent pressing for the store to get them to us pronto, so I could get cracking.

Once I hung up the phone, after the adrenaline rush wore off, I realized— *holy shit! I was doing hats for Elton's concert tour!* I did what any gay man would do—I called my mother!

I was excitedly telling Miss Ann about all of this, when the operator broke in with an emergency call for Mr. King from his agent. (No kidding. That was back in the day when they still did that, long before "call waiting.") Now, *that* –not my making Elton's hats—impressed her. Mom thought I *must* be somebody important enough to get an operator to break in on a long-distance call.

During the conversations Mark and I had over these months, I'd keep him posted on my progress. When things were really starting to jump career-wise, I got pulled up short by Mark's reaction. One day while I was working on these hats (and the drama behind it), I was talking to him on the phone. Out of the blue, he blurted out, "YOU JUST GOT LUCKY! I've tried to be an artist, but I just can't get a break, and you just got lucky!"

As an aside, it's interesting the impression some people have that gay men are somehow more supportive and less competitive than straight men. I've heard that misconception from straight people and seen it fostered in all of the PR about "the gay community." Especially during the gay pride celebrations, you see all of the posters with smiling gay faces, hugging, and looking accepting.

But really, gay men are men first—it's that testosterone thing. (I don't hear about this issue so much from the lesbian community. Perhaps it's another one of those dispensations that Saint Sappho gives out, like she does for wearing Birkenstocks and having potluck dinners, things gay men tend not to do.) The testosterone thing is what gives us that competitive drive to have the better career, date the cuter guy, lift more weights, drive the spiffier car.

There was always a certain competitive undercurrent between Mark and me, but I didn't really want to see it. I wanted to buy into the PR about how we gay men were more supportive of each other and all. But this conversation brought this issue right up and slapped my face with it.

ACT TWO:

His outburst said something to me—it said that he realized that I was somehow getting ahead of him, and he was uncomfortable with it.

So he felt he needed to devalue it by saying that it was just dumb luck.

This was really galling to me, especially when I was still financially recovering from the shocks of the recent past. I had to remind him that, indeed, I was fortunate to be having some success, but I did indeed work, take risks, and put in time towards my lucky break. I didn't wait until everything was perfect, like he appeared to be doing, before going forward. It wasn't handed to me on a platter. Perhaps he might have a little more luck if, instead of bitching about Victor, he spent that time making art and trying to put it out there. Then I hung up.

After that Mark and I would talk occasionally, keeping up the telephone friendship. But there was a tension there. I understood that I could never again talk about my successes—I didn't want to have to defend something I was proud of.

During one of our telephone conversations after "my divorce," Mark announced that he got a job working in display for J.C. Penney's (I was appalled). He also told me of a bout of hysterical blindness he had experienced one day while driving home from work. He was driving down the freeway when his sight grew dark, then disappeared completely. Luckily he was able to get the car off the freeway onto the shoulder, and eventually the State Troopers stopped and helped him to get home.

The doctors could find nothing physically wrong with him, which had him frustrated. So he was bitching to me about them.

"Mark," I ventured. "Don't you think this is a sign of something?"

"What?" he asked.

"Well, hysterical blindness is something psychological. When your eyes refuse to see, perhaps there's something you are refusing to see. This is the way your body is telling you to look at something."

"I don't get it."

"Well, think about it. Is there something in your life that you're refusing to look at? Perhaps your relationship with Victor? You know, I didn't feel I could say anything as long as I was tolerating what Matthew was doing, but now I've dumped him, so I feel I can talk. Why do you stay with Victor? Dump his ass! This is what you aren't seeing, and now your eyes are refusing to see!"

After a long silence, he said, "You just don't know what you're talking about. Oh, by the way, now Victor has you recorded, saying to dump me. He taps the phones—I've told you that."

"Mark, this is crazy. I'm hanging up now."

Beyond this point I really kept up the telephone friendship, more out of respect for what Mark had done for me in the past than for anything emotionally I might be getting in the present. My friend had disappeared into some weird sort of relationship. He was gone.

In 1989, my studio mate, Marshall, and I were getting rumblings that the Catholic Church, which owned the building where we rented studio space, wanted everyone out. The guy who held the master lease on this building was this oily lawyer, known around town as "the bad-boy lawyer," because he hung around with bicycle messengers and started one of the South-of-Market clubs that contributed to the gentrification of that area. (Which, by the way, for a while in the late '80's was known as "SOMA-you-know-like-Soho-in-New-York" said all in one breath, even though South-of-Market bears no resemblance to Soho in New York. It's yet another example of that galling mind-set I call San Francisco's "New York Envy.")

I really wanted to continue sharing space with Marshall because, aside from really enjoying her company, I was learning a lot. Marshall is an abstract painter, and from her, I learned a lot about abstract art—its appreciation as well as the process. Our space was really one big room with an L-shaped divider, so when I sat at my desk, I could watch her paint. I learned that, in her case at least, every move she made with the paint was totally thought out and intentional but looked totally spontaneous.

This is the exact opposite of what I thought the process of abstract painting would be.

We both loved color, and it was interesting to observe, over time, that color combinations she would use, would show up in my work (and vice versa). I found it quite interesting to see color in a different context other than fashion.

Another thing Marshall and I shared was an appreciation for discipline. Where people sometimes thought that Marshall and I were in our workspaces "having fun!" (as it was usually put), we really were there for the fun parts but endured the tedious parts as well. That's the less-than-glamorous part of the creative process and the part that weeds out the less-than-serious. It was this appreciation of discipline that we shared that bonded us as friends.

Anyway, Marshall and I received one too many three-day notices nailed to the front door of our studio, even though the bad-boy-lawyer was fighting the Catholic Church to hang onto his lucrative master lease. We started looking for a new space, which we found the day before the '89 quake, and signed papers for on the day of the quake—actually about fifteen minutes before the quake!

This location, which I still refer to as the Howard Street studio, was the former business address of a publication called *Inches*. When my assistant, Shelley, asked what kind of magazine that *Inches* was, I told her that it *wasn't* the trade publication for the yardstick industry. We found out this was their previous address because of the mail we received—for a number of years, actually. If there was no return address where I could mail it back to, I considered the mail from *Inches* fair game and opened it. (*I'm sure I just admitted to some mail felony or something.*)

This made for some rather amusing—and sometimes disgusting—reading and viewing. Especially one particularly gruesome series of Polaroids of a very fat guy, shot from the neck down. (He had apparently confused *Inches* with the publication called *Bulk Male*.) I put on my rubber gloves, picked up these photos with a pair of tongs, and carried them out to the trash bin next to the bus stop on the corner of Eighth and Howard. They were really *that* gross.

1989 was the first good year I had in business, and I had a lot of money saved up, anticipating the move. Since this was the first time I was signing on the dotted line for five years for anything (I held the master lease and Marshall sublet), I decided to have a big studio-warming party. Part of the budget was to buy a plane ticket for Mom, so she could attend the party. I called her and gave her the news.

The next day Mom called back to tell me to put the ticket in Kathy's name. Mom didn't want to travel alone and would buy her own ticket, so she and Kathy would both be there. I got two for the price of one. (Laurie, of course, wasn't invited—whenever she's around, it's All About Her. This was MY party.)

And then, the *next* day, Kathy called me to tell me that Mom wasn't coming.

I was immediately pissed off. She wasn't going to weasel out of this that easily! I was furious. I immediately got on the phone.

ACT TWO:

"So what is it I hear from Kathy that you're not coming to San Francisco for the party!?" I demanded.

"Well", Mom started weakly, "I really can't afford the ticket, and so I thought Kathy should go, and . . ." She trailed off.

"Didn't you think you should do me the courtesy of asking ME what I thought about this? Let's remember just WHO is paying for that ticket!"

I thought that was a good strategy—Mom employed that one many times while we were growing up.

"Well . . ."

"I'm going to say something I've never said to you. You know, when I graduated from college with a 3.94 average, summa cum laude, top two percent of my class, I was taken to Taco Bell to celebrate afterwards! At the time I said it was OK—IT WASN'T! I regard this like a graduation. It's a big step, and those who care about me will *BE THERE*. If you want to be counted among them, you know what to do! I'm going to hang up now because I'm so upset with you!"

"I don't want you to be mad at me!" Mom whined.

"Well, I AM mad! I'm hanging up now!"

And I did.

I sat there at my desk, shocked at what I had just done. I really hadn't drawn such a hard line with Mom since moving to California, and I rarely talked to her like that. It was easier to just give in. I especially had never really come out and heavy-handedly fought for something like this—acknowledgment of an important milestone in my life by my only living parent.

This was something I expected from her. When I was younger, I'd bring home straight A's to no real reaction. When I'd make her something to wear that she requested, she'd never wear it. When I graduated from college summa cum laude, when I moved to San Francisco, when I started my own business, when I got my first Important Press, when I got the gig to make the hats for Elton John's concert tour in 1988, all of these passed by her without much enthusiasm, much less any commemorative activity.

I never called her on this, because that would have drawn attention to how I felt about something she did, which was never allowed. Any criticism of her, perceived or actual, was forbidden. Calling her on something like this would also tell her that I did want some positive recognition, which would make it more likely that she'd withhold it. Miss Ann could weigh in on how she felt about anything I was doing with my life (which she did frequently and with relish), but I knew not to express my feelings about anything she had done. It wasn't allowed, unless it was glowingly positive and majorly ego stroking.

But somehow I needed to make a point here—that I wanted my mother to be there for a big day that represented a huge step and be happy for me like the rest of the people in my life were. It would be a first. *And I wanted it.*

Kathy later called me and said that Mom had called her right after speaking to me, crying and whining that I was mad at her and that she wished I would understand, blah blah blah.

"Ken, I just said to her the same thing she would have said to us: that she made her bed, now she has to lie in it," she stated. "You know, that's just what she would have said!"

Mom *came* to the party, which was in early December.

The day of the party, Mom and Kathy slept in at my place, while I was at the studio, answering messages and getting things ready. One of the messages on the machine was from a florist. When I called him back, he asked when he could deliver a rather large bouquet. After we set the time, he asked, "Don't you want to know who it's from?"

ACT TWO:

Trying to sound blasé, I replied, "Oh, that's probably from Elton." (*Wild guess.*) He was crestfallen—he wanted to tell me himself.

(As an aside, after the earthquake, he had his people call to see if I was all right or if I needed anything. I was so impressed. As a courtesy I sent an invitation to this party, never expecting even a response—he kindly had his people send his regrets. And now flowers! No one can talk against him to me, ever. A truly wonderful man.)

Later I brought Mom and Kathy over to the studio, just about the time the flowers were to arrive. The florist arrived and heaved this very heavy bouquet up the stairs—it looked like the horse came in second at the Kentucky Derby it was so big—so I casually said, "Mom, why don't you read the card?"

It said, "Dear Kenny, (*By the way, he's one of only two people I allow to call me Kenny*) Congratulations on your new studio! Sorry I couldn't be there—thanks for everything. Love, Elton."

I thought Mom would plotz!

The "look" Mon wore that evening is how I will remember her forever. It was a variation of her signature look, sort of inspired by Kim Novak in the film *Vertigo*. Mom was always short (five foot one), and in later years thin (ninety-eight pounds), had lively brown eyes with full lashes, fine cheekbones, slightly olive complexion, and an aquiline nose (which I wish I'd inherited). Her white-blonde hair (it covered the gray) was always done up in a French twist. The suit was gray flannel, with straight skirt and short, six-button collarless jacket, under which was an off-white silk blouse. Low-heeled black patent shoes and wire-rimmed bifocals on an "old lady" chain around her neck. She had arrived at this look about ten years before and stuck with it for the rest of her life.

At the party Mom was a hit playing the Queen Mother. Everyone somehow knew who she was, and she enjoyed giving guided tours to the bouquet and pointing out that rock stars send her son flowers. She went over big, regaling people with stories of the Baby Genius and How She Recognized That Her Son

Had Talent. I overheard her telling a small group how she really encouraged her children to do what they loved and never tried to impose her choice of career on them.

"WHAT HAVE YOU DONE WITH MY MOTHER?!?" I shouted. "SHE wanted me to be a pharmacist! You're an alien! I just KNOW it!"

Later I was able to tease out the reason for Mom's resistance, and it all had to do with fear. Mom was afraid that the high-tone people I associated with would laugh at the small-town gal, and she wouldn't know what to say to them. To her surprise, my friends are really nice people from a variety of backgrounds and not stuck-up at all.

In the final analysis, though, Mom was more afraid that I would be angry with her (and stay angry—the apple doesn't fall far from the tree) than she was afraid of being ridiculed by some high-tone people. In my mind it wasn't the ideal reason to come, but at least she was there.

Mark was invited and agreed to attend, but guess what? True to form, there was some lame excuse or another, but the end result was that he—*again*—didn't show, and I was disappointed but not surprised. He did at least send flowers. As I generally did with Mom, I didn't say anything, just to spare his feelings. Besides what good would it do?

Really Mark was looking a lot like Mom. Not acknowledging my successes, bailing out on the invitation to this important milestone. Looking back, I can see the connection. But I didn't then. Because, no doubt, I didn't want to see it. Like Mark.

Telephone friendships enable one to get out of all sorts of social situations, and the flimsiest of excuses will work. I can't remember what excuse he gave, and it didn't matter. I wasn't surprised. By the time of this party, I had already accepted that he had disappeared, and the telephone friendship was really just me going through the motions, trying to hold onto someone who wasn't there any more.

ACT TWO:

I went back to OKC that Christmas, and I felt like talking. Mom had had a near-death experience the year before at Christmas (*long story*), and I was feeling like I wanted to have some conversation more serious than "Look at this story in *People* magazine!" Since we had almost lost her, I didn't want to regret a missed opportunity to ask her some Important Questions, like: Was She Happy, or: What Were Her Dreams And Desires, or: What Was She Thinking When She Married Don White, or: Could I Have Her Alligator Handbag? So over the course of the visit I tried to get these conversations going, to no avail. Mom was having none of it, and I got very frustrated about it.

Mom did, however, come through with a nice gesture.

It was one evening, and she was dressed in one of her pastel-paisley, quilted, satin hostess gowns for lounging around the house before bedtime. Even at home Miss Ann looked good—when she got home from work, she'd change from her work clothes into one of these pastel, quilted, satin lounging outfits. Later, the French twist would get wrapped in the pink silk scarf she wore to sleep in. Mom had trained herself long ago, like the Japanese geishas do, to sleep in one position so as not to spoil a hairdo. She never even turned over or mussed the covers—the hairdo was *that* important.

We were in her bedroom, sitting on her bed and going through her jewelry box, looking at her jewelry and things. In the bottom of the jewelry box lived a gold compact, stored in its little black grosgrain slipcase.

The compact was a wedding gift from my dad. They were married in 1955, and "their song" was "Stardust". So, as a wedding present, Dad bought Mom this heavily engraved gold compact that, when opened, played "Stardust." (He had really good taste.) I was always enchanted with this compact and sometimes would go into Mom's jewelry box when she wasn't home to play it.

I don't remember her ever carrying it. She was always "saving it for a special occasion." It still had the sticker on the mirror, saying "Stardust."

I took the compact out of its slipcase, wound it up, and listened to it play for a few minutes.

"Mom, ever since I can remember, I've always loved this," I said. "I want it."

So right then, she gave it to me.

As a bonus she also gave me another of the "Holy Grail" jewelry pieces— Dad's fraternity pin, which was a tiny but exquisite piece— rose gold and enamel, studded with tiny emeralds, rubies, and opals. She told me the story of the pin again that evening:

"When your father's mother died of cancer, back in '49, he was still in college," she began. "Before she was buried, he pinned his fraternity pin, which was important to him, on her suit. When you get 'pinned,' you get only one. So all of his fraternity brothers felt bad for him, chipped in, and bought him this one. It's a lot fancier than the one he had, but they thought so highly of him that this is the one they got."

"Ken, I want you to have these now, while I can see you enjoy them," she said softly, looking down into her lap. "I know you'll use them and not shut them up in a box somewhere."

I didn't give any thought at the time about how she phrased that comment.

They were my favorite Christmas presents that year, especially the compact. I have them both to this day.

ACT TWO:

Back home in San Francisco, I should have busied myself with settling in to the new studio. There were walls to build and organizing to do. But I couldn't make myself do it—I was angry and didn't know why. All I wanted to do was to throw chairs through walls, which scared me. So I decided to get into therapy to figure out what was going on.

Now this was a big step for me, as I was wary of therapy and therapists. Living in California all those years, I had met people for whom therapy was a lifestyle choice, seeing the same therapist for years and years and not making any decisions without the weekly consult. They seemed not to actually get any better. So I decided that, to be comfortable with the idea of engaging in the process, I wanted to give it a time limit—one year. With that limit I began my search.

Happily I got lucky on the first shot and found a guy named Dennis, who really nailed what I was after on the first visit. He understood that I was not looking to become a permanent fixture in his practice but wanted to do my work and eventually go on my way. (I didn't tell him of my time limit though.) I liked him a lot. He was gay and, thankfully, not incredibly good-looking, which meant I wouldn't spend time lusting after him or trying to make him like me. Better still, he was a good listener who made insightful comments and also laughed at my jokes.

For anyone in therapy, you all know the way one feels when embarking on that particular journey. What I was looking at was the denial I had gotten into, especially about Mom and growing up. Although I remembered what had gone on during my childhood and adolescence, somehow I didn't want to actually face some of the underlying reasons for Mom's behavior, i.e. she was a little crazy and liked being cruel at times. Not stupid, but cruel and crazy and thoughtless and self-absorbed. I also realized that, if she thought she might have had a choice, she might not have had children. In my mind, I had built up a romanticized picture of her so I didn't have to face this.

For a few weeks I felt like they had doubled the force of gravity and nobody told me. This alternated with some tremendous anger directed at Miss Ann. I didn't want to talk to her on the phone and was able to keep her at arm's length for a time, because of the time difference and distance. There came a point when Mom noticed and started Asking Questions, so I decided to write her a short note, telling her that I was in therapy right then and, for a time, didn't want to have contact. I would let her know when I was ready.

Next therapy session:

"What do you think will happen?" Dennis asked at the session after I mailed the note.

"Oh, she'll call."

"Really?"

"Yes, that's her style."

And she did.

It was a Friday, and I looked at the clock—12:00 noon, which meant two o'clock in OKC. She would be at work and, therefore, wouldn't be calling, so it was safe to answer. I picked up the phone only to hear her voice. I made an excuse and got off the phone.

Next therapy session:

"So what do you think will happen now?" Dennis asked.

"If she called me at noon on Friday, she wasn't at work—she would never call from work. So that meant she was at home, sick, and I made her sick with that note. All my fault."

"So what next?" he asked.

"She'll be in the hospital by Monday."

"Really?"

"Yeah. That's a family trait—Grandma used to do that too."

ACT TWO:

Kathy called me that evening. Mom was in the hospital. She went in with a terrible back pain, which was the result of a fractured vertebra. This was the result of cancer from her lungs and liver, which had metastasized throughout her body. They gave her three to six months. This was March 3, 1990.

Mark called one day that first week, when I was dealing with Mom's imminent death. I was on my hands and knees scrubbing the studio floor; it was a way to get the floor clean and physically work through some of my sadness and confusion about Mom's upcoming demise. That's what I do when I need to sort through things—I clean or organize. Somehow it helps.

After the hellos, Mark asked me what was new. I told him about Mom's cancer, expecting him to be sympathetic; his own mother, Sophie, had died of it.

Foolish me.

In my weakened state, I had forgotten that Mark had disappeared into his relationship with Victor and wouldn't be able to get past his own concerns, even for me. Instead of sympathy I got another earful of Victor's latest misdeeds. Leaning against my desk while listening to this diatribe, I looked longingly at the bucket and scrub brush, and thought how I'd much prefer scrubbing the floor to listening to this again. I got off the phone in a hurry.

I was losing my mother and had already lost a friend. Mark's voice was still there on the telephone, but the person was gone. He couldn't be there for me anymore—his world and awareness had disappeared into this relationship with Victor.

Next therapy session:

"She's in the hospital. Wow! Boy, you really know how to call it!" Dennis said. "Where does it go from here?"

"She's going to fuckin' DIE before I get these issues resolved!" I shouted.

And eventually she did.

I was a churchgoer during this time, but it wasn't a normal church. It was called Amron Metaphysical Center, and it was housed in this big, blue Victorian house on the corner of Van Ness and Vallejo. Norma was the founder (and the very charismatic driving force) of this church, and she had taken me under her wing several years before. Susan was my glamorous Jewish Mother, and Norma was my beautiful Guru Mother. In many ways Norma was really more "mother" than Mom was. That happens sometimes.

I went to church at Amron the Sunday after I heard about Mom's cancer and told Norma what was up. She was a bit surprised because she had met Mom at the party in December. Then she looked at me and said, "Get there within the next ten days."

After I came home from church and made travel arrangements, I decided to call Grandma to see how she was taking the news. Grandma didn't seem to be too upset—I assumed that it was because she had lost one child, my Uncle Herb, to cancer already.

"So, are you going to go see her?" I asked. "Kathy tells me Mom's asking for you."

"Well, you know, I can't ride in a car for very long, what with my arthritis."

"WHAT?!?"

"Here's your Aunt Helen." Grandma passed the phone to Aunt Helen.

"So are *you* going to see her?" I asked.

ACT TWO:

"Well, I'm short of help at the liquor store," Helen replied.

I let a few beats skip.

"What I'm hearing here is that it's INCONVENIENT. You own the store—you could close your doors." I stated evenly. "She doesn't have a case of the flu; she's going to die. She's asking for you."

My reaction confused them. The standard reaction in the Yockers family would have been to say something like, "Oh, I understand, and that's OK," but I was living in California and doing therapy now! I wasn't in the mood to play this game. The change of script threw both of them.

Grandma grabbed the phone. "Listen, buster, we don't have to take this! We're your family, and we're all you've got! You have to just be OK with this! You shouldn't be questioning your elders!"

That was a side of Grandma that I had never seen, only heard of from Mom. Telling me that I had no say here and shouldn't have been questioning them—how dare I do that—on something like this made me furious.

"There's a right thing and a wrong thing to do! You know the difference!" I shouted and then hung up.

And for myself I also knew there was a right thing and a wrong thing to do.

On the one hand, I was furious with Mom for her gratuitous cruelty (we were looking at that in therapy), and part of me wanted revenge. This was the ultimate revenge—being mean to Mom, denying my presence and comfort, when she was deathly ill.

But on the other hand, I didn't want to be like her. Venting my anger or, worse yet, not going to see her was, well, *cruel*. No two ways to look at it. And I didn't want to be cruel, just because she was.

But again I had drawn a line in the sand, where I wanted no contact until I was ready, and now look where I was. I didn't want this to be yet one more manipulation to get me back in line.

Next therapy session:

"Your plane reservations are for the day after tomorrow," Dennis said. "What are you going to do?"

We talked and talked, and I came to a solution that I could live with: I would go, and in my mind it wasn't my mother I was going to see, but this scared, lonely old woman who was dying.

She needed comforting, and that's what I would do.

I realized that, eventually (since I was obviously going to outlive her), I would get my issues resolved with Mom and would grow to regret behaving cruelly if I were to do so.

So I would go and do what was necessary to make her feel comfortable and comforted, to ease her transition as best I could.

Kathy and I talked over the phone several times before I went back, and we both came to the conclusion that we could learn something valuable from this experience, if we paid attention. We were already seeing how Mom's family was reacting to her illness and imminent death.

Kathy picked me up at the airport, and we went immediately up to the hospital to see Mom.

ACT TWO:

On the drive to the hospital, Kathy told me of an experience she had with Mom the night before that sounded like a past-life flashback.

It seems Mom was sitting up in bed and told Kathy that they were serving lobster on the lower deck, and could Kathy go get her some. Kathy played along, asking all sorts of questions, which Mom answered. It seemed Mom was in her stateroom on a luxury liner. She even pointed out where the closet was and the vanity table. She was traveling in a stateroom on one of the upper decks, and they were serving lobster, could Kathy go get her some?

Mom was deathly afraid of water and *NEVER* would have entertained the idea of setting foot onto a boat. She was even skittish about driving over a bridge and had no more than a few inches of bathwater in the tub—water made her that nervous.

Besides, she was raised during the Depression in Kansas and didn't even know anyone who had ever been on a luxury liner.

"Did you ask what the name of the ship was?" I asked.

"It so freaked me out, I didn't but wish I had," Kathy replied.

When I walked into the hospital room, there Mom lay on the hospital bed, her breathing labored, her body already skeletal. But what really hit me: *Mom's hair was down!* This was only the third time in my life that I remember seeing that. That the hairdresser hadn't been called, this signaled the end.

Kathy stood on the opposite side of the bed, and we made small talk, while Mom struggled to breathe. She was hooked up to a machine that went "BEEP . . . BEEP . . . BEEP" every so often.

"Oh, by the way, Laurie's pregnant," Kathy said offhandedly.

"Is it her husband's?" I asked, without thinking.

BEEP BEEP BEEP BEEP BEEP BEEP BEEP BEEP BEEP BEEP!

I looked over at Mom, who was left wide-eyed and gasping at that last question.

"It's a legitimate question!" I said to her as the nurse ran in.

Later we left the hospital, because we had an appointment with the funeral home, to make arrangements. Strangely enough it was the same funeral home where, years earlier, I had dated someone (*very briefly*) who worked for this same mortuary. (*NOT* Darrell—another guy. I seemed to be going through a period of dating mortuary workers. Go figure.)

This guy's job was to drive to the hospitals and pick up the bodies that were going to be handled by this mortuary. He (I can't remember his name) lived in the apartment on the premises that was accessed through the garage. This meant that caskets with dead folks in 'em were usually parked in front of his front door, waiting for the next day's funeral.

(As an aside, the thing I most remember about this apartment was the pair of standing torchiere lamps on either side of his bed, with rose-colored bulbs in them. The funeral home used these very same lamps in the "viewing rooms," at the head and foot of the casket. Created a certain, er, *ambience*, so to speak.)

I learned two things during this brief affair: *One*, that I absolutely *cannot* get it up when there's a dead person parked outside the front door, and *two*, If someone asks you to take a cold bath and then lie very still, go home immediately.

I was pondering all of this as we went into the funeral home to make Mom's arrangements.

We needed to make them anyway, what with how things were going—better sooner than later. Laurie, Don, and my niece, Anna, were there, waiting. When we were called in, Laurie brought Anna, who was ten at the time.

ACT TWO:

"Do you think it's a good thing to be bringing her in here like this?" I asked.

"Yeah," Laurie said a little belligerently. "She's old enough!"

It was a bone of contention between Laurie and Mom, after Dad died, that Laurie wasn't asked to be in on Dad's funeral arrangements. Never mind that she was only twelve at the time—Laurie felt that she herself was the widow and the rightful person to be making the decisions, and it always rankled her that Mom didn't take her along. This was her way of getting back—and Anna played the part well, being a carbon copy of her mother.

The "counselor" (as he was called) reeked of the used-car lot and cheap cologne. I remember his very shiny, gray polyester suit, with some big gold-nugget jewelry and lots of oil—in his hair and in his manner. He kept suggesting things "for your beloved mother" that would run the price of this service into the five figures at least, one item being the metal casket.

(I was thinking that my sofa needed reupholstering, and so I was going to do my damnedest to keep from putting more money than necessary into the ground. Mind you, I wanted to do the right thing and give Mom a dignified send-off, but there are limits, you know? Being a practical gal where money was concerned, she would have understood.)

We were shown to the casket room, where they were all set out under the spotlights, just like new cars (and priced similarly). Mr. Counselor kept steering us to the metal ones, because "they have a watertight seal to ensure a dry grave." Laurie was eating this up.

Kathy and I were looking at a nice, dignified wooden casket lined in white satin. It had a fruitwood finish, just like Mom's favorite furniture. It was also considerably less money.

"But we can't guarantee a watertight seal because it's wood!" Mr. Counselor implored.

"We'll take this one," I said firmly. Laurie cringed but knew that Kathy would back me up, so she was outvoted. We had to take Laurie aside and remind her that Mom wasn't going to be living there—she would be somewhere else, so comfort wasn't an issue.

We were then led to the "vaults." It seems there is legislation that says that a casket needs to be put in some sort of concrete box, so "the grave doesn't settle," as it was put to us. (Meaning the ground doesn't sink down and crush the casket.) There was the minimum standard by law, a concrete box that cost about a hundred dollars.

Mr. Counselor whisked us past that to show us the vault (ten thousand dollars) which was, as he put it, "lined with the same type of material they use for the nose cones of missiles." (A direct quote.)

"If you have a wooden casket, you *have* to have this vault to ensure a dry grave!" he exclaimed. Laurie again was all over this.

"I have a question," I said.

"Yes?"

"You keep using the phrase 'to ensure a dry grave.' Why is that an issue?"

The look on Mr. Counselor's face told me he'd never heard THAT question before. He turned and looked at my brother-in-law.

"Ken has some religious beliefs regarding burial," Don said.

"What!?" Mr. Counselor asked.

"I believe the body should return to the earth as they say in the Bible," I replied. (The gay boy, evoking the Bible.) "How can that happen if you have it sealed up and practically shrink-wrapped?"

ACT TWO:

"I BELIEVE IN JESUS CHRIST, AND I BELIEVE YOU CAN GO TO HEAVEN WHEN YOU'RE BURIED IN ONE OF THESE VAULTS!" Mr. Counselor thundered.

Holding my hand up to stop him talking, I calmly said, "Your beliefs are not under discussion here. We'll take the concrete box and the wooden casket. Write it up."

I managed to take some time away to visit with friends, but the main thing was to go to the hospital and spend time with Mom. When I went to see her the next morning, Mom seemed confused and upset. She was wide-eyed and trembling. I asked her what was wrong.

"Where's Mama?" she asked. "Where's Mama?" Her voice was small and scared, almost like a child's voice. Her eyes were wide and scared when she looked at me. But it was her choice of words that hit me like a hammer—never in my life had I heard Mom refer to Grandma as "Mama." It was either "Your Grandmother" or "Mother," but never "Mama."

This was the question of a child, one who was feeling abandoned and scared, and it absolutely *broke my heart*. I looked down on this woman who, like a child, *just wanted her mama to be there to comfort her*. The look in her eyes said it all to me—all she wanted was comfort from her mama, but she never got it. Especially now, when she most needed it.

I burned with fury that nobody in the family came!

Especially Grandma. Grandma couldn't get out of herself and her narrow little world long enough to come comfort her dying daughter. Mom's favorite sister felt her liquor store, where she'd sat on her fat ass for the last thirty years, couldn't be left closed for a few days, so she could visit a dying sister.

Since I had escaped that narrow little world, it was strange to me that people could react this way. It certainly explained a lot. How could Mom be "present for us kids" as Dennis-the-therapist would say, if she had never experienced it in her own childhood?

It would be nice to say that I totally forgave her and was healed and all in that moment. That didn't happen right then. But I learned an important thing about how she grew up, and this made it possible later, when I was able, to forgive her. She did the best she knew how.

The doctors said that she wasn't going to last as long as they thought. No surprise to me as Mom was ninety-five pounds dripping wet when she was healthy, and she was now down to literally skin and bones.

Holding her in a sitting position once to help the nurse, I could feel all her vertebrae and ribs, like there was only a thin piece of leather covering them. That said, Mom was struggling to take every breath, struggling to keep going.

The evening before I was to fly back home, I went to see Mom. She was watching the TV. I stood at the door and watched her for a time before I went into the room. What I saw was a woman who was too scared to live but now at the end, was *scared out of her wits* to die. It was heartbreaking, and I had to get myself under control before I went in—otherwise, I wouldn't be any comfort to her. And, rightly so, it really *was* all about her right then.

She looked up as I entered and smiled weakly. I turned off the TV. I tried to smile, but the tears came anyway. I wiped them away.

"Will you brush my hair?" she asked. "You used to like brushing my hair when you were real little—I'd like my hair brushed."

ACT TWO:

So, for a while, I brushed her hair and pulled it all back in a braid, and fussed around about how beautiful she looked now.

Then we sat there, quiet, looking at each other.

"Mom, this is really hard for me, and I know it's hard for you. I know we're at the end of the line. Know that you did a good job in this life, and you raised three kids who are all healthy and able to make it on their own. You did a good job, and now your job is done."

"When you decide it's time, you can go. Don't feel you need to hold on because of us, because we'll be OK. Know that where you're going, there is no anger and there is no fear. Also know that we'll be here praying for you, and that one day you'll be on the other side to greet us."

"Kenny?"

"Yes, Mom?"

"I'm worried that you and Laurie don't get along."

"Mom, that's just what it is and isn't your concern anymore. It's between Laurie and me now."

"Kenny?"

"Yes, Mom?"

"Take care of Kathy."

"I will Mom, I will."

"I love you."

"I love you too, Mom."

I kissed her tenderly on the forehead and sat there with her until she drifted off to sleep.

Mom was sleeping the next morning when I stopped by before going to the airport. Her nurse, a solid, strong blonde lady, gave me a hug and said that she'd take good care of Mom. I thanked her and left.

I got home in the early afternoon and went to bed. I told myself I should have gone to work but somehow didn't feel like doing anything.

The phone woke me up after midnight. It was Kathy.

"She went about one thirty this morning."

It was the first day of Spring.

In my mind, Mom's passing on the first day of spring was a sign from her—a message saying to go forth, like she was going forth, into a new season of life.

Kathy picked me up from the airport and told me of her last experience with Mom.

"They called me at work from the hospital, telling me that Mom was crying and asking for me. So I went up and asked her why she was crying.

ACT TWO:

"She told me that she was crying because I wasn't married. I asked her if she thought that I wasn't going to be happy because I wasn't married, and she nodded. I told her that Keli and I were really happy together and that she should have no worries. She told me she loved me and fell asleep.

"I went back to work and stopped by again on my way home from work. She was still sleeping, so I didn't want to wake her."

"Ken, she's at the funeral home now and surrounded by flowers. It all looks so beautiful, but it still makes me cry . . ."

During the drive Kathy told me that Laurie never went to say her good-byes. She just pretended that Mom would get better, and her visits to the hospital took just that tone, obliviously chattering on while ignoring the inevitable.

That evening Aunt Helen and Uncle Bob and wife Betty came down from Kansas. (Grandma still couldn't ride in a car for very long, and her attitude was, "Well, she's dead so what would be the point?") It seems the folks in Kansas couldn't rearrange their schedules while she was alive but were able to for the funeral.

There was the public viewing that evening, and at first I was torn as to whether to go or not. But again, to show the proper respect to Mom and the people who came to pay their respects, I did.

Mom was laid out in her favorite gray suit and ivory silk blouse—the one she wore to my studio party to be exact. Her hair done as she always had it. Her hands were folded across her chest, and her nails were lacquered with her favorite shade of dark red polish. But something was missing—it was her glasses. Kathy brought them later, and Mom was buried with them.

I had some time alone with her and had a good cry. So this is how it would end. I felt like I had lost her twice in a short period of time—first losing the illusion I had in therapy, now losing the actual person.

We all ended up back at Mom's house. Neighbors had started bringing food by, lots of cakes and casseroles, which the relatives were tearing into. I didn't feel like talking and went to sit on the stairs and look out the front door.

Here I was in that haunted house. In the mental state I was in, I could hear all the years of screaming, the slamming and yelling that Mom's psychotic second husband did, the fighting, the screeching, all the years of unhappiness. (To this day I can't summon up even one happy memory of that place.) Finally I could take no more of the ghosts and went out to sit in the front yard, where it was quiet.

The limousine picked us up the next morning to take us to the church for the funeral. This was a church we had gone to a time or two when we first moved to OKC, and lately Mom had been attending. It was one of those dirt-gray, concrete brick, "Danish-modern" Methodist churches, with fake pipes behind the altar to make believe there was a grand pipe organ. When we walked in, all the other mourners were there. I looked around and saw quite a few of Kathy's friends, and one or two people from Mom's place of work. That and the folks from Kansas made up the small group there.

It was a stark contrast to Dad's funeral, where it was standing room only.

The preacher, who I didn't know, gave the eulogy, if you could call it that. What he said essentially was that he didn't really know Ann King but just was *sure* she was a really nice lady. It seemed that, even though she attended the church, fear prevented her from interacting with the other parishioners. She came, listened, and went home, without talking to or being talked to by any of the other parishioners.

The burial was to be in Kansas, next to Dad. There would be a graveside service there as well, for those who didn't come to OKC for the funeral. After the service, we drove up to Kansas, and landed at Grandma's.

There was a discussion as to whether or not there would be an open casket at this service; it was closed at the funeral. Laurie, of course, was for the open casket—it would afford her a dramatic opportunity, denied her at the funeral, to publicly and dramatically show her grief.

(Also to show her new jewelry. She hadn't waited until Mom was buried to grab Mom's big diamond pendant, which she wore to the funeral.)

ACT TWO:

Kathy and I, however, were against it. I thought it barbaric, especially at the graveside service, to have people who hadn't laid eyes on Mom in years—in some cases decades—gawping at her now. My reasoning was that there was a time and place where, if one wanted to pay respects that way, they could have done so.

Grandma was in a state about this. She was in such a state that she refused to go to the service. Her excuse: she didn't want to get out in the ice and snow, as she might fall and break a hip or something. Other family members supplied the expected response: "Oh, that's OK, I understand."

After the funeral Uncle Bob hosted a gathering in his big new house at the edge of town. Grandma, of course, was there, braving the very same ice and snow—apparently she was no longer worried about slipping and falling.

She was standing next to me in line at the buffet, when she turned and asked me The Question: *"How did she look?"*

This immediately infuriated me.

If you want to clear a room after a funeral, this is what you say:

I turned to her, fixed her with The Eyes That Weld Steel, and said, "SHE LOOKED DEAD!"

All movement in the room stopped, and Grandma turned white. I moved in for the kill.

"She didn't look like she was sleeping, she didn't look peaceful, SHE LOOKED DEAD!!!"

I looked around, and everyone had vanished, like cockroaches when you turn the light on. Except for Grandma, who stood rooted to the spot with a look of horror on her face.

For the rest of the evening, nobody would get within fifteen feet of me.

The next morning at Grandma's house, it sounded more like a party than the aftermath of a funeral. All the family was going through old family albums, laughing, and commenting on how they all should do this more often. Grandma started grilling us on who was left what in the will, another family tradition.

Usually the will was brought out at times like these so everybody would know what their "take" would be. I announced that we hadn't actually read the will yet because we were still grieving the loss of our mother, and really it was none of their business, as for sure none of them were mentioned anyway.

We went back to OKC and began the task of sorting through the house, which Kathy stood to inherit. Mom had said many times that she wanted Kathy to get the house, and God knows Kathy earned it! She was Mom's handler for the last ten years and was primarily responsible for maintaining the place, because Mom wasn't suited for hard manual labor.

Happily everyone (especially Laurie) behaved themselves, and there were none of the ugly squabbles that sometimes erupt when breaking up an estate. We all went through the house to decide who would get what, what would be sent to charity, and what would be sold. Kathy made arrangements for an estate sale for the stuff that nobody wanted. With all that taken care of, I flew back to San Francisco and back to therapy.

The rest of that year was taken up with work, therapy, more work, and more therapy. I finally came to peace with Mom, realizing that she was, indeed, crazy but not stupid, and more importantly, she wasn't a monster all the time. (Just human.)

There was a certain liberation I felt when I got to the point where I forgave her. I realized, starting with what I observed when Mom was dying, that she did the best she could. Miss Ann was operating from a position of fear and anger her entire life, and this came from being raised in a situation where she

ACT TWO:

never felt safe or loved. I got to see this clearly by how her family behaved. Consequently, she couldn't provide that feeling of safety and love for us, simply because she had no experience of it. But she did the best she could.

She did the best she could, and as a result, she didn't do too badly. Mom taught me how to work hard, how to spend judiciously, and serving as a negative example, how not to get taken advantage of. I came out OK, and in a strange sort of way, my upbringing is my source of strength. It gave me a certain sense of the absurd, and made me tough, and gave me the knowledge that, whenever I got knocked down, I would always have the strength to get back up, dust myself off, and move on.

Another thing Mom did before she died was to give me to Norma. Norma told me about this a few weeks later. I knew that she had called Mom in the hospital because I asked her to (actually Mom asked me to ask her to call).

"We talked for over an hour," Norma said. "She talked about being scared and angry her whole life, and asked if this was the result—that it was eating her insides out. I didn't answer her; I think she already knew what the answer was."

"Then she said, 'Norma, he's your son now. Take care of him for me?' And I said that I would."

Mom is now in a place where there is, indeed, no anger or fear, and my wish for her is that she enjoy this and truly own and experience it. As I am enjoying the freedom and responsibility of leaving the past behind and being an adult.

And it seemed to me, that having both parents dead definitely made me a grown-up, if I'd had any doubts beforehand.

After dealing with all of the estate issues after Mom's death, I returned to San Francisco to take up life again. When I arrived back home, there was a message on my answering machine from Susan.

"Darling Angel! We need to go to Max's Opera Plaza to have a big fat dessert! You need it, and I have something to celebrate!" she said.

So one Saturday evening, before going to the Opera House, Susan and I settled into a banquette at Max's and ordered up something big, fattening, and chocolate. Then she turned and looked at me.

"So, what are we celebrating?" I asked.

"I don't have lung cancer!"

I guess Susan saw that I might have gone pale (*I was certainly feeling a little wobbly!*), so she quickly said, "I know what you've just gone through with your mother and all, and so I didn't want to say anything before. But I got the news a few days ago that this was all a false alarm."

"Well, thank God that it was!" I exclaimed. "Let's look forward to years of good health for you!"

We sat there for a few moments, quiet.

"You know, dying isn't something I'm really afraid of," Susan continued quietly. "Because, Darling Angel, if I had to go tomorrow, I can truly say, *wasn't it great!* I've done everything I wanted to do, been to many of the places I had hoped to travel to, and even played Lady Capulet on the stage of the Opera House—quite well, I might add. If I went tomorrow, I wouldn't have any regrets."

This hit me like a ton of bricks.

Susan has had a wonderful life to be sure, which she has fearlessly created. She's had more than her share of troubles, health-wise and otherwise. I had seen her through some of these issues over the years, and watched how she always ended up back on her feet with her delightful outlook intact. Susan lived through all of the bad times but chose to embrace the good times, which she actively sought by being such an adventurous spirit.

I contrasted that with Mom, who was too scared to live and, then on her deathbed, was too scared to die. Seeing these two examples in such rapid succession made a real impression on me.

When I go, I want to go like Susan!

It was definitely a celebration of life that evening.

The following Sunday I went to church at Amron and discovered that Matthew was there, along with Phillippe. *Of all people!* At first I wanted to leave, I was so furious; but I stayed as it was *my* church, and I would be damned if I would let Matthew run me off. I sought out Norma to say something like "Can you fucking believe this?!?" She told me he had been there the week before and had asked after me.

After the service Matthew tried to engage me in conversation, but I didn't respond. I just walked out. At home I sent him a short note, telling him that I couldn't stop him from going there (it was a public place) but to leave me alone. He was part of my past, and that's where he needed to stay.

The letter I got back was quite a doozie! The only thing I really remember from the letter was him saying something like "you have to get to a place where you can accept me as your friend before you can dismiss me from your life."

Needless to say, this was fodder for therapy. When I read the letter to Dennis, he asked me what I thought.

"Well, when I was with him he talked that way a lot. I just thought that, with an IQ of 140, he was talking over my head."

"What do you think now?"

"I think it's bullshit. Why would I dismiss someone who I've accepted as a friend?" I replied.

"Exactly. Now what do you want to do?"

"I want to tell him how I feel." And that was my homework.

So I wrote another letter. In it I said:

"Matthew, I said you are part of my past and need to stay there. No reply was requested. So, again, I will state for clarity: You are part of my past, and you need to stay there. Leave me alone, don't contact me, or talk to me if you see me. No reply is requested, just in case you're not sure."

Later I heard through members of the church that Phillippe was threatened with deportation (no green card). Matthew had the idea that a successful businessman who went to Amron (that would be *me*) could sponsor Phillippe for a green card, and then he could stay. Indeed.

As for Andie, the girl he was boffing for food while waiting for Phillippe to come back to San Francisco, I ran into *her* in church as well. When our eyes met, it must have looked like two angry cats, fur standing on end, ready for a fight. But, I, for one, decided that church was not the appropriate venue for that kind of scene.

"I would like to ask you out for coffee," Andie said.

"Why?" I asked icily.

"Because I want to apologize."

Who could refuse that?

ACT TWO:

I got some good dish with that coffee. Andie told me that during the time she was "with" Matthew, he was telling her that he loved her, but she was temporary until his boyfriend came back. But he also thought that he and I would eventually get our problems resolved and stay together. Talk about covering all bases! She said that Matthew was really hurt and surprised when I said that I would only just say "hello" to him. He was doubly surprised that I actually didn't stop him from leaving.

And then she gave me a really heartfelt apology for any misery she caused during that time.

———

As for Matthew's family, they all still liked me (I made them feel welcome in my home), and we've kept in touch. That's how I learned that Matthew eventually moved to LA and became a "dial-a-psychic" for one of those "976" numbers we were seeing in advertisements around that time. This job came to an unceremonious end when Matthew went to work one day, found the doors padlocked, and the furniture gone.

He must not have been a very good psychic.

So he and Phillippe moved to Palm Springs, where the career trajectory of a dial-a-psychic leads to "body worker," more commonly known as "massage therapy."

When Joseph (Matthew's brother) and George started the process to become Joseph and Georgette, I was the first one they called. George was going to become Georgette—what did I think of that?

My response was something like "Well, duh." Remember I always referred to George as my "sister-in-law." Now it was going to be made official.

There was a flurry of phone calls to me from the family after this news hit the wires. Sister Frances called one day, all in a state, asking me what I thought of the whole thing.

"Now I've heard from all of you! Damn it, Frances, YOU'RE divorced. Your sister Mary's divorced. Your brother Tom's divorced. Your brother Matthew's TWICE divorced. Your sister Rebecca's divorced. Joseph and George, uh, Georgette, have been together twenty-eight years. I think they know something WE don't know, so we should just wish them well and *GET OVER IT*! So, tell everyone else in the family just that!"

Georgette made the transition, and she and Joseph married. I have their wedding photo—Georgette made a beautiful bride. They've been together now about forty years, I think, and both are very happy.

A prologue here: Georgette still likes to call with the latest gossip, and this is what led to the phone call recently, telling me of Matthew's new paramour and Phillippe's disposal. Matthew had given up the Dial-a-Psychic work and embraced bodywork. (This is the career trajectory for a Dial-a-Psychic.)

What I learned was that he was working for a posh spa in Palm Springs; that's where he met The Woman.

Then he *wasn't* working for the posh spa. And was with the woman. Coincidence?

I guess this is what they call the "Dial-a-Psychic Retirement Plan."

Georgette told me that Phillippe was surprised by all of this and was really hurt that he got ditched for someone else. *Did he think he was special? Wasn't he paying attention?* I wanted to be catty and call Phillippe to ask what he did that put Matthew off men. At least when Matthew left me, he went to another man. But actually I know what it was—Matthew could always spot a sucker.

ACT TWO:

Instead I told Georgette to thank Phillippe for me. He was my excuse to take that monkey off my back, which freed me to move onward and upward.

While I was dealing with all of this family stuff in therapy, the topic of Dad came up. Dennis asked me about him, and my first response was:

"The most vivid memory I have of him is the day after he died. He came into my room and sat down on the bed. I said to him that I thought he had died yesterday, and he replied that yes, he did, but he wanted to come back to tell me everything was going to be OK.

"I blinked and he was gone, along with my childhood." That was the first time I put it into words.

As I may have mentioned before, Dad died five days after Christmas on December 30, 1968—I was ten years old. It was a Monday; he had a heart attack while driving to work at a power plant somewhere in western Kansas. He stopped at the hospital in Ellsworth, thinking he had indigestion, and was a goner before they got his boots off.

I don't know how everyone did it, but the word got out quick. There was a standing-room-only funeral at Trinity Methodist Church (the funeral home was too small), with people coming in from all fifty states and a few foreign countries. The place was packed! From what I heard tell over the years, Dad was a really popular guy and knew many different people from his different lives—The War, college, life before he married Mom, the National Guard, the Shriners—they all came. The entire Air National Guard unit Dad belonged to showed up in uniform to give tribute. I've never seen anything like it to this day.

It was a real shock for everyone, especially Mom who, I think, really didn't realize how good she had it until he was gone. Dad's death threw her into a long period of mourning, which I remember mainly because she really "wasn't there"— not to eat, not to comfort us kids, not even to shriek at us occasionally, the activity she most enjoyed.

She was blank with grief.

Since Dad traveled quite a bit during the week when he was alive, the weekends would find Mom standing at the front door, watching and waiting. It was as if he might magically drive up the street, and this episode would all have been a bad dream.

Life eventually went on though—Mom started shrieking again, got remarried, we moved to Oklahoma, blah blah blah.

During my adolescence, Dad was really just a shadowy memory, one that Laurie especially would try to resurrect every Christmas—she always wanted to "make it like it was when Daddy was alive." One year, under the tree, I found a gift labeled "To Our Father" from Laurie, written in her very large, dramatic-but-fatuous hand. The "gift" was one of those plastic memorial wreaths to put on graves for Memorial Day that were sold in the grocery stores, the ones that were in the cardboard boxes with the cellophane windows. I was mortified and threw it in the garbage so Mom wouldn't see it and get upset.

I think of this shadowy memory as "Saint Daddy." Saint Daddy was a mythic figure who could do no wrong, and his passing divided life into two distinct periods (especially for Laurie—she's never recovered from his death). These periods were: Before Daddy Died, and After Daddy Died. B.D.D. was a golden age, where life was just one stream of happiness and contentment and Kodak moments, whereas A.D.D. was a vale of tears, a grim life with no glimmers of happiness. (I actually couldn't distinguish between the two; to me they were both grim periods to be endured until I became a grown-up.)

Saint Daddy was a font of knowledge (he graduated with honors, straight A's actually, in college, you know), had "perfect pitch" (usually told to me when I was practicing the violin—and badly), and a talented mathematician (I remember him patiently trying to explain fractions to Laurie; I understood him long before she did). Saint Daddy was a pillar of self-discipline (he quit drinking JUST LIKE THAT! and smoking too! after the doctor told him to, and *never* took it up again), and he was a high standard of all that was manly, the one that I personally was held to (you run and throw a ball like a GIRL! What would your father say!).

Saint Daddy was also a talented woodworker. He had a little shop in the basement, where he made furniture and worked on his other projects. In this he was like Grandpa Yockers, Mom's dad, whose tools he used. Grandpa Yockers used to hide out in the back of the garage where his workshop was, Mom used to say, to get away from Grandma.

Mom only compared me favorably to Dad once, and that was when she was discussing my temper. She told me that I had Dad's temper. When asked what she meant by that, Mom told me that she had seen Dad mad only twice in their marriage, and neither time was at her (he *knew* better!), and she was really glad of that. Apparently he had a very long fuse, but when he had had enough, RUN FOR COVER!

Saint Daddy was just a concept to me. Since I was only ten when he died, and he traveled so much, I never really had a memory of what he was like as a person. My memories are more of history, incidents, and occasions.

Perhaps a little information about the man himself is in order here. I'm just relying on what I remember being told for some of this, but that's the way these things work sometimes.

Dad was born Wilbur Dean King on May 19, 1923, in Heyburn, Idaho, to Kenneth Francis King and wife Gertie. He was an only child because Gertie almost died in childbirth, so the legend has it that Dad was cherished and spoiled.

Gertie kept scrapbooks of little Wilbur all through his growing-up years. I remember these, as they were stored in our basement in a blond-wood bookcase that Dad had made in his workshop. I would pull them out to look at from time to time. Little Wilbur was quite creative with his watercolors and loved his mother. There were quite a few pictures he made for her in the scrapbooks, telling her how wonderful and beautiful she was and how he loved her ("I LOVE YOU MOMMY! I LOVE YOU MOMMY! I LOVE YOU MOMMY! I LOVE YOU MOMMY! I LOVE YOU MOMMY!" they screamed), with lots of purple flowers. Little Wilbur also had an early love of photography (well, posing at first, but later he took pictures himself), so Gertie documented family life in photo albums as well. Grandpa was in some of the photos but didn't seem to be a dominant presence.

Wilbur graduated from Heyburn High School in 1941. He was class president his senior year, class vice president the year before. Wilbur also made the honor roll in 1940 and '41, as well as being in theater and music. I still have his class pin awards to prove it, still pinned to the scrap of dark blue velveteen that Gertie attached them to all those years ago. When I was a child this scrap of fabric lived in Mom's jewelry box. She gave it to me a year or so before she died.

After high school the scrapbooks show Wilbur went to college for a year or so, before going off to war. Wilbur's yearbooks from this time had him in the orchestra (piano), the band (trumpet), president of the student council, and, I believe, in theater as well. There was definitely a pattern here. The scrapbooks ended when Gertie died of cancer.

One snapshot about Grandpa: Soon after I moved to San Francisco in 1981, Laurie drove cross-country to visit (in July, in a VW bug with a husband and an eighteen-month-old daughter and no air conditioning). Laurie intended to stop in Twin Falls, Idaho, on the way to visit Uncle Waldo. Uncle Waldo was

ACT TWO:

really Dad's cousin by Grandpa's sister Aunt Inez, but he was close in age to Dad and they were like brothers, hence the term "Uncle."

When Laurie got to Uncle Waldo's house, there was a note on the door, saying, "Gone to San Francisco." (I should have put one up, saying "Gone to Twin Falls.") I got a call about that time, at work of all places, from Uncle Waldo (whom I hadn't spoken to since we visited them when I was four in 1962), telling me he and his daughter were coming to town and could we all meet. We all did, at his son's house. (In The Castro. Son was just leaving with his "friend." Wearing leather. And handcuffs on his belt. You get the picture.)

Anyway, during this visit, I started asking questions along the lines of "what kind of person was Grandpa? What was he like as a person?"

After some uncomfortable hemming and hawing, Waldo's daughter blurted out, "Oh, out with it! He was a mouse! Say it! Gertie wore the pants in the family, and after she died, Mary took over the pants-wearing."

After Gertie died, Grandpa married this vile woman named Mary, a hypocritical Mormon who drank coffee, dyed her hair Superman-blue-black, had gaps between her teeth, blue-white skin, and played around on her husband, which is how she met Grandpa. Dad HATED her and wouldn't allow us to call her "grandma"—we had to call her *MARY*. (He was very clear on that.)

On the very rare occasions when Grandpa and Mary would visit, they were made to stay in a hotel because Mary was so odious. Mary would tell Mom that she planned to be buried in a black lace negligee, so Grandpa would choose her over Gertie on the "other side." Mary was one hateful piece of work. On the night before Dad's funeral, she asked Mom to alter a coat she got for Christmas so she could wear it to the funeral. (Mom said she would cut it up the back with a pair of pinking shears—*that* was her idea of altering it!)

Years later when Laurie was on her genealogy kick, she discovered that, after Grandpa died, Mary had baptized Dad "by proxy" after his death, to the

Mormon Church. I don't know the particulars on just how they do this peculiar thing, or why, except perhaps they have too much spare time on their hands—but Mom was apoplectic when she heard. Dad was a Mason and *hated* Mary *and* the Mormon Church, and was no doubt at that very moment spinning in his grave because of all of this.

Mom called Harry, who informed her that churches could do whatever they want, and suing them won't change things. Besides, the Mormons had more money for litigation than she did.

Laurie, in her clueless way, thought it was "cool" that Dad showed up in the Mormon records. She never understood what the fuss was all about.

During the war, Wilbur flew bombing missions over Europe and, once back from the war, continued his passion for airplanes and flight. On the walls of his office at "the shop," there were photos of different airplanes he either had flown or wanted to fly. He even had his silk flight maps from the war mounted on large boards, hanging on a wall in the basement. I eventually took them off the boards and now have them carefully stored away.

After the war Wilbur went back to college and studied electrical engineering—there was no trace of his previous artistic threads of study. I remember looking through some slides of his from that decade. The ones before the war (judging by the dates printed on them) were very artistic/bohemian, with one series shot in this hunter-green living room, filled with Noguchi-inspired furniture of black lacquer and salmon-pink boucle upholstery. There was a gal who had the whole black-turtleneck-red-lipstick-hair-cut-with-nail-scissors thing going, and my guess was that they were listening to jazz. It looked very avant-garde for the time.

The slides from the post-war period were of power plants and electrical installations. And airplanes. Lots of airplanes.

After college Will (or "W.D.", as he was ever after known) went to work for General Electric in Cincinnati, where he met his future business partners, Bill Horton and "A.V." Gardner. I still have the sterling silver GE electric motor cufflinks he got as an award while working there.

ACT TWO:

The three partners eventually bought a bankrupt electric motor-winding concern in Salina, Kansas, called Mid-States Armature Works. (It lasted until 1999.) They turned it into a business that made switchboards and such for power plants, airports, and other industrial applications. This was before Dad met Mom.

Dad met Mom through Ruth Wilke. Mom and Ruth were best friends, who met because they looked so similar that they were very often mistaken for one another. Ruth and Mom both worked in banks as well—Mom for Bank of America, Ruth for First Savings. Ruth was from Germany, one of the refugees from Berlin who made it to the US. She ended up in Salina because the only sponsors she could find lived there.

One afternoon Ruth and Mom were trying out Ruth's new Polaroid camera by taking pictures of each other in the cemetery, posing on the monuments (why did they do that?). Later they had a double date—Ruth with Will, Annie with Bob—for dinner at The Plantation on North Broadway. (Mom and Dad used to take us there as well, where we would order "jumbo shrimp" and ponder the knotty-pine paneling and the red, button-tufted vinyl banquettes. I don't remember it looking like a plantation, just a large square building with a peaked shingle roof.)

At the end of dinner, they had all changed places—Mom with Dad, and Ruth with Bob. Mom married Dad, and Ruth married Bob. (Twice. But I have no information on what that was all about.) Ruth had her camera along on the date.

For years Mom kept in her wallet a Polaroid photo of that night, with the four of them in a round, corner banquette, looking young and stylish and smiling for the camera.

This is how the legend goes. There's nobody alive who can confirm or deny it.

Mom and Dad were engaged in April of 1955 and married in September 1955. Laurie was born in February of 1956. This explains the enormous bridal bouquet Mom carried. Years later I would hear Grandma and Mom argue whether or not it was 1954 (Grandma) or 1955 (Mom). By that time I knew what was what and could count to nine. Their argument just drew attention to the fact.

I remember Mom telling me that Dad was really hung over on their wedding day—you can see it in the photos. He had been drinking heavily the day before and all through the rehearsal and dinner. She got really angry with him and told him that he had to choose between the bottle and her, and she wasn't going to marry him the next day. He waited all night on the steps of the church, and when she arrived, Grandma told her in no uncertain terms that She. Was. Getting. Married! (Goddamn, that cake cost a hundred dollars!). And he went to get ready for the wedding. But the drinking went on, though we kids never saw him drunk. Mom made sure of it.

"Their song" was Stardust. For a wedding present, Dad got Mom the gold compact that plays Stardust—the one she gave me that last Christmas. (Couldn't you just DIE?)

This established a pattern: He got her really nice, stylish gifts, which she never used. Good handbags and gloves, and expensive perfume (this is where I first saw the word "Balenciaga"), none of which Mom would use.

The newlyweds moved into a new house Dad had bought before they married at 906 Willow. It was one of those post-war "ticky-tacky" boxes, built on a concrete slab with no basement. (Basements were really useful in "tornado country", and only the most lowly of housing went without. This was certainly a starter home. Judging from the home movies, the kitchen was painted chartreuse.)

Laurie was born on February 16, 1956, as I said, and judging from the home movies, she was treated like a little princess. Legend goes that Dad had the mumps and it supposedly rendered him sterile, so Laurie (who looked exactly like him) was regarded as a little miracle.

I came along on February 18, 1958 (after we had moved to the larger house on Wesley Street), and Kathy arrived on February 12, 1959. (You remember, Dad's birthday was May 19. For our slower readers, that's nine months. Probably the only time he got it and had to make it count.)

ACT TWO:

If you were to ask what I remember most about Dad, I would say "his smell." It was a combination of sweat and machine shop, with faint whiffs of nicotine and occasionally alcohol. He worked in "the shop," as he called it, wearing gray uniform shirts and pants and leatherwork boots (his "work clothes"), his pants held up with a thin brown leather belt with a "University of Idaho" buckle (I myself now wear that belt on occasion). Dad would come home from work smelling like sweat and "the shop."

Every now and then Dad would bring me home old gauges and such from the shop for me to play with and take apart. I never seemed to get them back together, but somehow it proved to be an education, as I have a way with mechanical things to this day.

Dad traveled to the various power plants and other installations throughout the region, either in his car or by a small plane. When I was young, he took the training and tests to get a pilot's license; I remember going to the airport with Mom to sit in the car and watch Dad practice his "flybys" and "touch-and-goes" so he could get in the hours to keep his license current. He kept his pilot's license all his life.

Bill Horton had his own plane, but Dad would rent a Cessna or Piper from the local airport when he wanted to fly somewhere. There were times that Dad would take me with him to go to a site where some work was being done. We would go there in the plane, and he would let me "fly" it with the other steering wheel, by watching the "wings" in the gauge on the instrument panel and keeping them level with the horizon. I thought this really grand. The most exciting time I remember was almost crashing into another plane—I just thought it was fun, little did I know.

Airplanes were his one passion. He made models of them and, as I mentioned earlier, had photos of all types of planes in his office at the shop. Frequently he would say that the perfect way to die was in an airplane.

Once he had to crash land an airplane in a field, which stopped the talk of dying in an airplane. (It came too close to reality.) The plane threw a rod in the motor, and the motor conked out. Afterwards Dad got the damaged piston from the motor and had it mounted and framed, with a little plaque that said, "Lest I forget." It didn't stop him from going up again though.

In 1967 Dad took a commission to build a power plant in St. Croix, Virgin Islands. He traveled there periodically as the work progressed, but as they neared completion, he had to be gone a month. It was decided that Mom would go stay with him in the apartment the company had rented there; we three kids would stay home, and Grandma would stay with us.

Other people would look on this trip to the Virgin Islands as a golden opportunity, but Mom just complained a lot when they returned. The comment I remember most about the whole experience is that she hated the apartment because it had a terrazzo floor. And, since she got a really good suntan before she left, the natives thought she was one of them and continually hit on her, so she stayed indoors most of the time.

Dad was a member of the Air National Guard, eventually becoming a lieutenant colonel, which meant he got the "farts and darts" on the brim of his hat, much to his delight. This was one outlet for his love of flying (he was a navigator), and it also got him away from Mom. He would be away at "camp" for a weekend or so a month and two weeks in the summer. It was during one of those camps, in 1968, that he contracted hepatitis.

Thinking it was the flu, Dad didn't know that the hepatitis had already set in by the time he came home from camp. But, as we had planned to go to the Ozarks for vacation (and he didn't want to disappoint us), we went. During the vacation he turned a bright yellow, and when we came back, we all had to get the shots. It was at this time that the doctor told him to quit drinking (bad for the liver), and he decided to quit smoking as well.

So he quit both, cold turkey. Or this is how the legend goes.

It was many years later when I found out the truth. Grandma took in ironing to make a little extra money. She did ironing for some of the guys who worked at the shop. They told her that, since Mom had cut off Dad's pocket money (she controlled the purse strings and hence the booze intake, she thought), he would just take money out of petty cash at work to buy the booze. He drank early and often, and quit early enough so he didn't smell when he got home. Since Dad drank at work, the concern was that he might electrocute himself or someone else. Mom was never told.

Dad didn't argue with Mom in front of us, and she told us many times that he wouldn't argue with her—PERIOD. (Again, he knew better.) When she would try to start an argument, Dad would take us kids out for ice cream, leaving her to fume in private. (I remember the ice cream trips—my favorite was mint chocolate chip at the Peter Pan ice cream store. This didn't help my weight problem.)

As I mentioned, Dad was also a Shriner. (He was an Elk as well, whatever THAT is—the Elks had the best restaurant in Salina.) He went to the Isis Temple, this big, neo-Grecian pile on Santa Fe Avenue across from Asbury Hospital. I was unclear about what the Masons actually did, but knew that I was expected to join the DeMolays, whatever that meant, when I was old enough. Dad was a member of the Isis Oriental Band, which was the Shriners' parade band in Salina. The Oriental band would dress up in these very colorful, satin, "Persian" bloomer costumes complete with gold hoop earrings, fezzes that had "Isis Oriental Band" embroidered in rhinestones on them, and shoes with the turned-up pointy toes. Dad's bloomers were magenta and topped with a chrome yellow tunic.

They would paint their faces dark, glue on crepe-hair beards, dress up, and go out and parade around while playing these funny-looking horns. Dad's being a member of the band was good because he was the only one who knew how to read music—everyone else played by number. They were able to add more to their repertoire because now they had someone who could transliterate new music into numbers for the musically illiterate. It was said that their performances improved dramatically—Dad knew how to keep time as well.

The Oriental Band had its own room in the basement of the Isis Temple (no doubt because of the racket caused by rehearsals), and Mom was engaged to help redecorate (it looked like a rundown dive bar as I remember it). We kids were brought along to watch. That was the only time any of us got to go in there. There was a bit of a stir in the temple about Mom doing the job, as she wasn't in the Eastern Star (she was never the joining type). But she worked for free, so everybody looked the other way and let her decorate.

Some fond memories I have of Dad center around Christmas. I remember him behind the windup movie camera with the blinding spotlights while we opened packages. He never showed up in any of these films, much to my regret.

Other memories center around gifts Dad got for Mom. I remember the year she got him his Rolex watch. I was in the jewelry store with her, and remember her telling the salesman, "THIS one. If he wants to buy me something, *THIS* ring."

The box that appeared under the tree was huge and clanked when she shook it (which she did, being home all day). The Christmas season was gloomy, and I know Dad went to heaven when he died, because—Mom said she made his life hell because she thought he had gotten her another appliance. The big box was the last to be opened and without much enthusiasm on Mom's part. Inside was another box.

And another.

And another.

And another.

And another.

And another.

And another.

And another.

The final box was a box from the jeweler, and inside was The Ring.

"Which made me feel *this small*," Mom would say when telling this story. As well she should have.

ACT TWO:

The next year Mom coveted a particular dining room set and went to visit it regularly at the furniture store. Close to Christmas there appeared "Sold" tags on it, but the "Sold to:" on the tags was left blank. Dad's life was hell for the rest of the season.

On Christmas morning there was a tiny package under the tree for Mom. Thinking that he had bought her another piece of jewelry (imagine being chagrined about *that*, but she was), she unwrapped it to find a piece of paper—the sales slip for the dining room set. The doorbell rang just about then, and the deliverymen brought it in and set it up. Imagine how much he paid to have that happen? Remember, this was in 1963.

My other memories of Dad are diffuse and not really coherent. They are more impressions, really, and hearsay. I don't know for a fact that he had just subcontracted with a big firm back east to do all of their production (which meant we would be rich), nor do I know for a fact that he kept all the blueprints for the switchboards for the new Kansas City Airport in his head, and they went with him when he died. But this is what I remember being told.

Dad was away quite a bit, that I remember. And he also used to say, "Someday, we'll (fill in the blank)." In his case, someday never came.

So, once he was gone, Dad receded into memory, not a real presence in my life.

Which leads me to the experience that changed me in a profound way.

It was December 30, anniversary date of Dad's death. Through a chain of circumstances, I found myself at a séance led by Norma at Amron Metaphysical Center—someone had canceled at the last minute, so she asked me to be a guest. I had no particular agenda in going, really, as it was all so unexpected.

Norma was channeling an entity who was saying to me that I would be successful and blah blah blah, which I was only half-listening to. Then she said, "This isn't what you came here for. There's someone you want to contact. Who is it?"

"My father." It came out unexpectedly—he really wasn't a presence in my life and not really an issue.

Norma had some trouble bringing him forward, as he was somewhat reluctant, but eventually there he was.

"Do you have any questions for me?" he asked.

"Yeah. Did you die just to get away from Mom?" It was a joke I still use—he had had enough, so he just died. It was easier than divorcing Miss Ann.

"Yes, I did" was his answer.

Then there tumbled out the story of his childhood and his marriage with Mom. Gertie, it seems, went off her head when she almost died in childbirth and beat Dad mercilessly when he was a child. Grandpa was too weak to do anything about it, so he just let her go. This damaged Dad's spirit, which is why he made the choices he did.

While he was speaking, I saw in front of me a photo of Gertie I remember from our family album and, next to it, one I have of Mom in high school. The similarity of appearance is something I never noticed before.

Dad had married his mother. It was a match made, if not in heaven, in Freud's office. He had a weak father, who worked in his workshop to hide out from his wife, and a mother who wore the pants. Mom also came from a weak father, who worked in his workshop to hide out from his wife, and a mother who wore the pants. Dad had a workshop to hide out in when he wasn't traveling, and Mom wore the pants.

"So you see, Ken, I couldn't take it anymore. Imagine the hell she put you through, but then imagine being a grown-up man who wasn't strong enough to fight back," he said.

"But why around Christmas? Your timing really sucked, you know!"

ACT TWO:

"I know, but I had to go. It was time, and I had to go. I thought she was angry with me, so if I went she would be easier on you, but I was wrong. For that, I'm sorry. Please don't be mad at me!"

Then he was gone.

I was really stunned by this. It made all the bits and pieces make sense—the scrapbooks that Gertie made, filled with his drawings saying "I LOVE YOU, MOMMY! I LOVE YOU, MOMMY! I LOVE YOU, MOMMY! I LOVE YOU, MOMMY! I LOVE YOU, MOMMY!" screaming all over them, seeming to plead something deeper (like "DON'T BEAT ME, MOMMY! DON'T BEAT ME, MOMMY! DON'T BEAT ME, MOMMY! DON'T BEAT ME, MOMMY! DON'T BEAT ME, MOMMY!"); the mouse of a father as a role model; the change of direction after the war; the drinking problem nobody talked about—it made sense that he would repeat the pattern with a woman who looked like Gertie and, more importantly, behaved like her.

To say I was blown back would not put too fine a point on it! It took me some time to digest this. Strangely I felt Dad's presence around me all the next day. That evening when I was in bed, I decided to talk to him.

"Dad, you know, I'm not mad at you. Everything worked out OK in the end; I ended up OK. If you hadn't died, my life would be extremely different now, and I can't imagine that I would be happy living in Salina, being an electrical engineer and running your business."

"Besides, you said you were sorry. Somehow, in the vast scheme of things, that is what I have wanted to hear from someone in that situation, and it satisfies something deep inside. So, no, I'm not angry with you. Go with God."

There's something liberating about not being angry with one's parents anymore. Mom's death helped me confront my issues with her, and come to some resolution about her and her particular situation. Even though I didn't realize it, I needed this resolution with Dad, and was fortunate enough to have the experience I did. When it is all said and done, they did the best they could with the information and upbringings they had. It wasn't ideal, *they* weren't ideal, but I'm not perfect either. I did turn out pretty well, all things considered.

The one thing that *was* hard to put into words was that this experience, for the first time in my life, made me feel, for lack of any better way to phrase it, "more male." Until then I didn't feel a connection with Dad and that whole energy, and after the séance I did. It is only in retrospect that I realized what I had missed—that connection with the male half of the equation that was my parents.

It was only after this experience that I recognized that I had more in common with Dad than Mom. Dad was the world traveler. Dad started his own business. Dad had all the friends. Dad was the college-educated one. Dad was the one who left his hometown to strike out on his own. And strangely, as time goes on, I look more like him and less like Mom.

Sometimes therapy needs some helping hands from other planes or places—I know one therapist and his client who were grateful for just that help.

Mark came up in my therapy as well. The first time we broached the topic was soon after I came back from Mom's funeral. I started the session by complaining that Mark hadn't seemed to register what I had gone through. During our last phone call, he paused long enough for me to tell about the funeral but then soldiered ahead with yet another stream of complaints about Victor.

"What do you say to him when he does this?" Dennis asked. "Do you take care of yourself in this situation?"

"Well, no, I usually try to suggest solutions to his problems, and ways he could either get out of the situation or get Victor to behave better. Or I'll say something like 'poor, poor dear'."

ACT TWO:

"Do these phone calls seem similar to other phone calls you've told me about?"

That stopped me dead. Just then I saw it clearly for the first time and recognized a pattern.

Mark and Mom. Mom and Mark. They both had gotten confused in my mind, because they both dealt with things the same way. They both liked being victims. And they both treated me the same way. So I reacted to them both in the same way. That same mixture of loyalty confused with affection and annoyance.

"Your mother used to do the same thing on the phone, if I remember," Dennis continued. "And you always suggested ways to try to fix things. Then she'd play the 'Yes, but…' game. You used to get really frustrated about it, I remember you telling me."

That was so true. Looking back, I think Mom suffered from a severe depression the last years of her life. She would go to work, come home from work, lock herself in, watch TV, take her bath, and go to bed by 10:00 p.m. She did this from the middle of my college years until she died—twelve years, all told. Mom never went to the movies (the last movie she saw was "Patton" in 1970) and only started going to church the year before she died. The rest of her time was spent reading *People* magazine and rattling around her big house.

Mom had no friends—friends had proven to be so disappointing, because she chose unwisely and had no boundaries. The only people she interacted with, were the folks at the bank where she worked. And her kids.

She would complain bitterly to me on the phone that she was lonely and didn't know what to do about it. I remember hearing her say repeatedly, "They don't tell you what to do once you have your kids raised and educated!"

My response would usually be along the lines of "Why would you want 'them' to tell you what do to anyway? You can decide what you want to do yourself!"

Then I would make suggestions (night school, church, hobbies, reading groups) and hear "Yes, but...." And then I'd hear some sort of "reason" that she couldn't do whatever I just had suggested.

I was doing the same thing to Mark—somewhere in my mind, he had become Mom to me. There were certainly parallels, but I hadn't chosen to see them until Dennis brought them up.

He floated the idea that Mark and Miss Ann were both depressed, because depression can immobilize people and narrow their worlds. This certainly made sense in Miss Ann's case and, I think, Mark's as well.

I would say that this depression of Mom's started about the beginning of my second year in college. It stemmed from a long chain of events that started when she changed jobs from Guaranty Bank to working at the Chevrolet dealer.

While I was finishing up high school, Mom went from working at Guaranty Bank and Trust to being the cashier at Boyd Chevrolet. Why the change, I don't know. Money, perhaps, or not enough respect. She felt that she should have been head teller, even though she hadn't been at Guaranty all that long.

One day soon after she started her new job, she came home from work at the dealership all-aflutter. It seems there was a certain used-car salesman who was paying her a lot of attention.

His name was Gary Jones. He took her out to dinner about two months or so after she started working there, so we got to meet him when he came by the house to pick her up. Operative phrase here being "used-car salesman" (this was before the days of "pre-owned cars"). About my height with dark hair; obviously capped teeth; "western-style," tan, bulletproof, polyester leisure suit with the brown topstitching on the yoke, and a belt buckle the size of a hubcap on one of those used cars. Later outfits usually included tight Wrangler or Lee jeans (never Levi's), beige plaid western shirts, and cowboy boots (which he called "shit kickers"). I also remember a cowboy hat on the shelf behind the backseat of his car (a '76 Chevy Monte Carlo loaner from the dealership with a CB radio—remember those?), the hat, of course, being visible through the rear window. Sort of a primitive form of window display, I guess.

Gary was a puzzlement to us kids. Mom had finally, fully and thoroughly, embraced her Nancy Reagan phase (she kept to it until she died), so it was a curious mix—the used-car salesman dating Nancy Reagan.

And he took her to COUNTRY AND WESTERN BARS! And she WENT! Willingly! Too bizarre for words!

It only took a few months before Gary moved in. Now, I remember Mom getting all righteous and sanctimonious about other of her acquaintances who were "shacking up"—she ragged on and on about how low that was, and they were no better than they should be. Somehow, though, this wasn't the same thing. Or at least *she* didn't regard it as shacking up—this was a far more noble relationship. We kids knew not to call it shacking up; we knew not to say anything at all.

All in all, though, this was an unusual situation. Remember, this was Nazarene country in the mid-seventies, and such things were still frowned upon, but having him living there gave us kids some relief from Mom's tantrums and torture. As it was I was still in high school when all this started, so I had the distractions of a job, school, persecution for being a fag, and homework to keep me busy. That's why, to this day, I'm a little fuzzy about dates. I know all this started while I was a senior but can't remember if it started the summer before senior year or during—not important anyway.

When Gary had been living with us for a few weeks, he started in on Mom about an idea he had: a business proposal. It was, as I remember, a type of insurance for auto breakdowns, sort of like Triple-A but not really. He began with a folksy, "Just a little idea I had" approach.

Over the next weeks, he stepped up the pressure, playing on Mom's dissatisfaction with her job by selling this as a way for her to be her own boss.

All she had to do was finance the operation, which *had* to be launched in, are you ready?—ATLANTA!

ATLANTA! I remember thinking, "Atlanta? Why not here?" I never really had a good grasp of geography, (I still get it confused with geometry) but even I knew that Atlanta was not the financial center of the country. *WHY ATLANTA?* It didn't make sense!

Of course, Gary would have to live in Atlanta to get things going, so he would need an apartment and a car to commute back and forth in. Since he wouldn't be working for Boyd Chevrolet anymore, he wouldn't have the demo car he got to drive. (This is where the Cadillac came in. Mom leased a '76 Coupe de Ville for this venture.) Also he would need some sort of income while he was setting things in motion.

Of course.

Papers were drawn up. Or more to the point, Gary drew papers up. Mom sent me, with papers in hand, to see Harry one Friday afternoon to have him look them over before she signed them. As he was reading, I watched the color drain from his face, then come back a brilliant red. "Oh, man!" I thought. "This doesn't look good."

Harry leaned over his desk, took off the George Burns Glasses, fixed me with his most serious look, and shouted, "TELL HER, QUOTE, DO NOT SIGN ANYTHING UNTIL SHE TALKS TO ME, UNQUOTE, EXCLAMATION POINT, EXCLAMATION POINT!"

"That bad, huh?"

"I WILL REPEAT FOR EMPHASIS! QUOTE, DO NOT SIGN ANYTHING UNTIL SHE TALKS TO ME, UNQUOTE, EXCLAMATION POINT, EXCLAMATION POINT! Got it?"

"Yes, sir."

ACT TWO:

"Now get home as fast as you can. That jackass might beat you there and talk her into it."

So I got home as fast as I could. When I came in, Mom asked, "Well, what did Harry say?"

"He said, 'QUOTE DO NOT SIGN ANYTHING UNTIL SHE TALKS TO ME .UNQUOTE. EXCLAMATION POINT. EXCLAMATION POINT.' He repeated it for emphasis."

"Oh, I thought he would say that. He just doesn't want me to be happy!"

Quite the response I expected.

That weekend went on as usual. Mom and Gary went out for the afternoon, came home, changed for dinner, went out again, and stayed out quite late both days. Monday came, and he had her signature on those papers. I found out later that he had used the "If you really loved me, you would sign these" gambit.

When Harry found out, he hit the ceiling. I hope he sent her a whopping bill for that consultation.

There was much excitement as Gary and Mom both went to Atlanta (ATLANTA!) to find him a place to live and an office. The place and the office both had to be nice, so potential customers would think he was legit. They had leased the Cadillac before they left, but it was tagged in Georgia, so he would look less transient. There were trips back and forth for both of them, and Mom was really excited about the future of not working, as she was *sure* her investment would pay off handsomely—Gary promised it would! She was actually bearable to live with during this time.

As the months wore on, however, and the money kept going out with none coming in, Mom became increasingly nervous. Gary knew how to dodge and get her to stop nagging, but it was becoming apparent to all of us (except Mom) that the man was having a really good time in Atlanta (ATLANTA!) on her dime.

In the meantime Laurie and Kathy both talked to me about how Gary had tried to get into their pants. This was most perplexing—he was very vocal about how much he loved Mom but was hitting on both sisters. This was too oogy for words, way too close to incest for me! They certainly couldn't go to Mom about it; Mom would just blame them for somehow enticing him. I wanted to not believe any of this, but one day, denial was not enough.

I was sitting in the family room, watching TV after school. Gary was back from Atlanta (ATLANTA!) for a short visit. Mom was still at work, and it was just the two of us in the house.

He came over, sat down on the sofa, and started rubbing my back (!). Then he started rubbing my back under my shirt (!!). Then he stood up, and undid his fly (!!!!!).

(Years later, when trying to ascertain just why Mark stayed so long with Victor, I asked, "Since he wasn't good-looking, was he at least good in bed? Or did he have a big dick? You can forgive two out of three." That day I found out which two Mom forgave.)

There was some cliché porno dialogue like "you want this, don't you" or words to that effect, but I was totally grossed out. It was big—no doubt about it—uncut (uncircumcised, for you straight folks) and the ugliest penis I have ever laid eyes on, even to this day—and I've done lots of field research. I ran to my room, slammed the door, and put a chair under the doorknob. I didn't come out of there until he left the next morning.

As the situation unraveled, Mom's mood swings kicked in with a vengeance. (This was when the tranquilizers first appeared.) It was becoming obvious, depending on the point of view, that the money would run out before the business got going (to her), or that Gary was pissing the money away without even trying to get anything started (to us kids and Harry). As it was, checks for back payment of alimony to a heretofore, unknown ex-wife (*SURPRISE!*) cleared the bank, plus other disbursements for obviously non-business expenditures. Even in the face of all this, Mom doggedly refused to face facts. Gary was still the hard worker who would make this business go and get her out of working for other people. After all, he *promised*! And he *loved* her!

⌒

Not all bad came from Mom's misbegotten liaison with Gary Jones. Gary had a large family, some of who became Mom's friends (or at least friends until everything blew up). One of Gary's sisters was named Kay. Kay lived in Clinton, Oklahoma. She had blue-black died hair and looked like Jo Anne Worley of the TV show *Laugh-In*, with thick false eyelashes and blue eye shadow (not worn ironically). Kay also had a succession of ex-husbands, a fondness for large gold hoop earrings, and a job as a cashier at the local Safeway. If you were to call Central Casting to cast the tough-broad-with-a-heart-of-gold, you would get Kay.

Kay had only one son, Terry. We kids had never met Terry until one summer day when Mom came home from work with an odd request for Kathy and me.

"Kay's son, Terry, was in a real bad motorcycle accident," she said. "He's at the hospital here because the surgeries they had to perform were too advanced for that rinky-dink hospital in Clinton. He doesn't know anyone here, so I think it would be a nice thing if you two would go visit him and keep him company."

Kathy and I weren't real enthusiastic about this—a redneck from Clinton, Oklahoma, whom we didn't know or have anything in common with? I mean, really! We were city kids! What could we possibly talk about? Tractor pulls? But we did it because Mom was still in the "love him" stage with Gary (this was before the money went), and if we didn't, there was sure to be a screeching fit that would jam the radar at the local airport.

So the next evening we went up to the hospital, found Terry's room, and knocked on the door. We didn't hear anything, so we quietly opened it and found him in a lip-lock with a girl, presumably a girlfriend. We knocked again, and they abruptly stopped and guiltily straightened themselves up.

I was smitten. This was a corn-fed, weight-lifting, strawberry-blond country boy with blue eyes and a dimple in his chin. Yes, he had two broken legs and one broken arm, but damn! he was cute. And immobile. (The rapidly deflating tent in the sheets also caught my attention.)

If this had been a few years later, knowing a thing or two, I would have looked upon the situation as one rife with possibilities. As it was, though, I was so repressed that I didn't even admit to myself that I was smitten. Kathy and I managed to get through some small talk and stayed just the polite length of time, so we could say we did our duty, and left. I couldn't sleep that night.

Since Terry was really alone in the hospital (Kay had to work and couldn't make the trip very often), and since he was PRACTICALLY a cousin (as Mom and Gary were shacking up and, therefore, sort of married), I volunteered to visit him daily. It was summer, school was out, and I had a flexible schedule, so I could visit daily so as to ease Kay's mind—so she didn't have to worry, you understand. Really, no trouble at all!

I so looked forward to those daily visits. Terry and I would talk about not much of anything, just passing the time, but it gave me the opportunity to look at him a lot. After leaving I always would feel an ache that I couldn't define and impatience for the next day, so I could go back to visit again. This went on for weeks—Terry was a badly injured boy, and boy was I glad of it!

The day before he was released from the hospital, I brought him a St. Christopher's medal and explained that St. Christopher was the patron saint of travelers, and he should wear it whenever he got back on the bike. He seemed touched by the gift.

After Terry went home, there was a big hole in my day, and I missed him terribly. I couldn't talk about it, because I suspected that if I did I would be called queer and harassed even more than I already was. I didn't hear from him, because he was back in his life with all his friends; and I was just this guy who would visit him in the hospital because his mom asked me to. But I ached and couldn't express why.

A month or so later, Kay asked me to come visit and stay overnight. I could hardly contain my excitement! I would get to see Terry again! And see him I did!

Straight boys, when they aren't clued in, can be very exhibitionistic. Terry did a lot of weight lifting in gym shorts (as much weight lifting as he could manage in twin leg casts) and sitting around in his underwear—boxers, my favorites, because of the tantalizing glimpses one gets.

I, of course, being the shy type, kept fully clothed at all times.

He still couldn't walk without crutches, so Kay let me drive him around in her car—a Chrysler Cordoba with the Corinthian leather interior, just like Ricardo Montalban said. We cruised the main drag in Clinton, Oklahoma, repeatedly, and Terry introduced me to all his friends as his friend Ken from the Big City. When I think back, it seemed a bit like he was showing me off. Or I would like to imagine he was.

At one point during one of these drives, he looked at me and said, "You know, you look really cool driving this car! You're really classy!"

Music to my ears!

But events took their turns, and Mom was soon embroiled in the unpleasantness at the end of her time with Gary. Sister Kay screwed Mom as well, by borrowing money for new clothes so she could land a better job and then not paying up. True to form Mom expected all of us to shift into blind-hatred mode, so all of this conspired to keep me from meeting up with Terry again. I felt a void but knew that this would have to be the way it was.

But it didn't really occur to me until I came out (much later) that this was my first love. I wish I had known then, because I might have done things a little differently. Or not. But I would have paid a lot more attention to my feelings and allowed myself emotions that, even to this day, I have yet to experience.

One incident that happened during this time takes the "Stand-By-Your-Man" award for 1976. As you may remember, Mom had this thing about her hair. She had a standing appointment with her hairdresser that would not be denied nor missed for any reason. We kids had strict instructions not to disturb her there, unless a nuclear warhead fell on the house. As a result I never saw her during a comb-out-into-the-French-twist. I always timed it so, if I had to go there, I arrived just as the final coat of lacquer was being applied.

Well.

Mom was at the hairdresser's, curlers out, hair ratted up, and ready for the comb-out (think "Bride of Frankenstein on a Bad Hair Day"). This being Saturday morning, the shop was full, and there was the usual burble of activity of women getting styled-up for Saturday night out. Then suddenly—

WHAM!!!

The shop door flew open, hitting the wall with enough force to leave a dent in the fake wood grain paneling before bouncing back. Standing there was a wild-eyed woman, looking very much like "High-Noon-at-the-OK-Corral" meets "Joan-Crawford-with-the-Coat-Hanger."

"WHICH ONE OF YOU BITCHES IS ANN KING?!?" she demanded, veins popping in her neck.

ACT TWO:

(You're probably wondering how I know all the details since I wasn't allowed to go to the salon while Mom was there. I heard about everything later at work. I worked at the ice cream place down the street from the salon, and two of the ladies who witnessed this spectacle were talking about it as I was cleaning tables. Hearing Mom's name got my attention real fast, and I made sure their table, indeed the whole surrounding area, as sparkling clean.)

Well, everyone turned, looked at Mom, and pointed to her. The interloper stomped over to her, stuck a finger *UNDER. HER. NOSE.* and screamed, "YOU'RE SCREWING AROUND WITH MY MAN!" At which point a very sordid story tumbled out, for all the salon to hear.

(I'm *sure* the ladies dined out on this story for months afterward.)

Her name was Priscilla (why *do* I remember that?), and she was "dating" Gary the entire time he was "dating" Mom—actually before Mom met him. Even while he was living at our house, he was "seeing" this woman. And the kicker? THEY had a child to prove it. A three-year-old named Cara (again, just *why* do I remember this?) Priscilla even brought a photo of the bastard child for Mom to have and threw it in her lap.

After dropping this bomb, Priscilla parted with, "YOU STAY AWAY FROM MY MAN, BITCH!" Another slam of the door and she was gone.

Oh! My! *GOD!!!* When Mom got home, goddamn was she mad! I don't know what irked her more—the fact that Gary was two-timing with this slattern or that she had to endure this confrontation *in front of an audience when her hair was not done!* I'm sure you ladies out there understand; this would, indeed, be a conundrum.

Either way Mom raged on for a few days about how *dare* that slut come into "her" beauty shop and accuse Gary of two-timing! And that photo (which she showed us while raging about that woman later), what did it prove anyway? The child didn't look anything *like* him!

I would just hand Miss Ann her glasses—this was a clear case of the apple not falling far from the tree.

But you know what? He, of course, denied it, talked her down, and she believed him—and stayed with him even after being humiliated in the beauty shop like that.

(Fade out with Tammy Wynett singing, "Stand by your man....")

It was only a matter of time before the Atlanta (ATLANTA!) deal fell through. In four months Gary burned through $28,000 in 1977 dollars. He came back and, since he didn't have a job, he conned Mom into *BUYING HIM A USED CAR LOT* to run! (After all, he *did* quit his job "for her" to start this business and now needed an income!) Now it wasn't a posh lot, just one of those rinky-dink, bare-light-bulb-and-tattered-pennant, ten-car operations at Tenth and May, but really! Hadn't he gotten enough?

After a month or so of Gary running the lot, it was decided that it was time for him to move out. So he did. Then one day, while I was ironing a shirt for work, there came a call from his bank.

"I'm just calling to confirm an address on an order of checks for a new account for Gary Jones," the woman's voice on the other end said. "We like to confirm this before we send new checks out."

"What is the address?" I asked.

"7812 NW 27th Street . . ."

"Hold it right there!" I said. "He doesn't live here, this is not his address, nor is it his phone number. Take that information off his account. And don't call back here again!"

"I see," she said and hung up.

ACT TWO:

The phone rang as I was walking out the door to work. It was Ruby from Harry's office and she said in her beige-tweed-voice,

"It's your mother. She's here and needs for you to pick her up."

"What's wrong?"

"I can't go into it now, but could you please come? Right away."

(I loved the way she said, "Right away." Full stop, without the exclamation point, in that beige-tweed voice of hers. I can still hear it in my head, to this day..)

When I got to Harry's office, Mom looked to have been crying. Harry was standing over her, with a mixture of concern and annoyance on his face.

"What happened?" I asked.

"Come into my office. We need to talk," Harry said. "Ruby, you take care of Annie."

It seems that after I spoke to the woman from the bank, she called Gary at the rinky-dink car lot and told him what I had said. Mom had the bad timing to be sitting in his "office" when he took the call. Gary told the banker that, of course, he lived there, etc., etc., and that I was just causing trouble. The woman told him that, until he could get his affairs straight, they would hold the checks.

From what I remember Harry telling me, this caused a "kiting" operation to collapse. Kiting, as best Harry could explain, was some sort of bank fraud. Since I could never figure out how to balance my checkbook, he didn't go into much detail.

Gary got mad as hell and started slapping Mom around in his office. She escaped and headed to Harry's because it was close by.

"Son, lonely people do very foolish things. Your mother is a very lonely woman," Harry said. "I try to watch out for her, but she *is* a grown woman, even though she makes these foolish choices."

We had another of our conversations, this one centering on Harry's concern about how Mom's stupid decisions impacted on us three kids. In bits and pieces, Harry let escape that one of his concerns had been the contract with the hillbilly mafia that Don White had out on us. Yes, there was a hillbilly mafia in OKC during that time—we had gotten a visit from the Oklahoma State Bureau of Investigation right after the divorce, telling us of just that contract on us.

Yes, contract. Hillbilly mafia—it *does* exist, or at least it did then.

From what I was able to stitch together (he never came out and said anything specific—he was a lawyer, you remember), it was Harry who engineered the solution: "You got a hit man, she's got a hit man. If anything happens to her, you'll be found in a ditch in western Oklahoma with your throat cut." That sort of thing. That's how things were still handled in Oklahoma in the late seventies.

I sort of knew beforehand that we weren't in danger any more but didn't know the whole story. From what Harry said, I don't think even Mom knew. He just took it upon himself to take care of the problem.

"You know, this means you'll have to pay for your own college," Harry said. "This won't ruin your mother, but the money your dad worked hard and paid premiums for to make sure you all got your education—it's all gone."

Later that evening I went to visit my friend Steve and his brother, Tony. You remember Tony, the "redneck gentleman"? Tony had a neck that was good and red (and short and thick, for that matter, and *very* muscular—MMM!) but believed that any man who would hit a woman was lower than pond scum. I told him what happened and how terrible I thought it was.

ACT TWO:

"And cops prob'ly won't do nothin'," he said.

"Especially when she doesn't want to file charges. There's nothing to be done, is there?" I replied, sighing, making myself look every small, helpless, tiny inch of five foot five and one hundred twenty-five.

"Well, there might be if there was a case o' beer involved . . ."

It was the first case of beer I ever bought. Being only eighteen, it was a bit of a trick, and it cost a lot more than if I was "of age," but I managed. I don't know exactly what happened after that, but knowing Tony and his friends, most of whom could lift an engine right out of a car with their bare hands (winches are for sissies), well . . .

In the meantime, I had a pow-wow with Laurie and Kathy. Since Laurie worked in the emergency room of the hospital at Del City, she knew a lot of police officers. (I use the word "knew" in its biblical sense as well, because it is a safe bet to assume she had "known" most, if not all, of the officers she ever met.) Laurie "conferred" with them as to what to do and gave them Gary's license number and description of the car.

Mom started proceedings against Gary, suing for monetary damages as well as punitive damages. Harry filed the lawsuit, and the case hit the newspapers (it was a slow news day), which was really embarrassing. I was thankful that I was known on a first-name-only basis in college, because I did hear some of the other students talking about the case in the student union and how stupid Mom was.

As I sat there at the table that morning, one guy shouted, "Jesus! What an idiot! She gave him all that money! What was she thinking?"

He didn't know the half of it, I thought. He had no idea that the guy was also hitting on her daughters *and her son*. And what of her second husband and all of the drama there? He *didn't* know the half of it—had *no* clue!

Gary lit out for Europe, or so we heard. It seems he had accumulated some black eyes and broken ribs, his sister said. I wonder what happened.

I was secretly relieved that he was out of the country. The appointed day in court arrived, and Gary didn't show. The judge issued a summary judgment, and I didn't have to testify. Naïve as I was, I was terrified that if this went to trial, Gary's hitting on all of us would come out, and it would somehow shatter and devastate Mom and, by extension, the whole family. Even though it was Gary who was doing all the misbehaving, Mom would have never forgiven us kids; she would have blamed us for destroying her happiness and her fortune. In her eyes *we*, not Gary or her foolishness, would have been the reason this whole thing failed, both the business and the relationship. She went to her death not knowing.

Later the judgment ran out, and instead of renewing it, Mom let it lapse. Gary is back in the country, and Kathy saw him at the Oklahoma State Fair just a couple of years ago, with what looked like another widow in tow.

I remember one particular evening during this crazy time, the evening when I got it cemented in my head that one of my functions was to take care of and "fix" Mom. She was really upset that Gary had left and taken her for a lot of money. Here she was, alone, with a whopping legal debt, inheritance mostly gone, no man, and egg on her face.

It was just past sunset, when the air is dark blue. There were no lights on in the house yet, just the fading blue light from outside. Mom had recently started taking tranquilizers frequently; that night she also had a cocktail or two, which she usually didn't do.

We were at the kitchen counter, me on one side, Mom sitting on one of the bar stools opposite. We were talking about all of this business with Gary. Suddenly she began to melt down and lose control, crying uncontrollably and collapsing onto the counter. "Help me, help me, I can't take it any more!" she began shrieking.

I was panicked by this. Here she was, the adult (sort of) in this situation, and she wanted *me* to help HER! And I didn't know what to do! This was one of those *oh fuck* moments; what did I know? I was just a teenager—one who had been through some things, to be sure—but just a teenager. I still remember that feeling of panic, and how helpless I felt in the face of it. *Oh fuck!*

Right then I resolved that I'd make sure I knew what to do, to fix any situation—I'd *never* be in a situation like that again!

This idea of "fixing" things and people was something that we were looking at in therapy. Dennis really called it right when he drew the connection between my behavior with Mom on the phone, and the similarity to my behavior with Mark on the phone. If I could "fix" them, then I wouldn't feel helpless. Something I had resolved never to feel again.

"Somewhere in your mind, Mark and your mother are the same person," Dennis said. "Both seem helpless, and your instinct is to fix the situation, which you learned as a teenager. Both are adults who have chosen to be in a certain situation. But Mark isn't your mother—it's not your job to fix him. And you can't fix him. It's in his power to do that, but it's not in your power. It's his choice, his job."

I'd have to learn how to live with the "helpless" feelings, while allowing Mark to fix his own situation—or not. Easier said than done.

A few weeks after coming back from dealing with Mom's estate in OKC, I got another call from Mark. It was about noon, and Shelley, my assistant, was there working. She was the one who answered the call.

"What's up?" I asked, rolling my eyes at Shelley, knowing where the conversation would lead and wanting to get it over with already. It was going to be another version of "What Victor did to me."

"Victor dented the refrigerator with my head," Mark blurted out.

"What?!?" That got my attention. "What happened?"

The story spooled out that they had had another one of their arguments, and Mark threatened to leave. Victor told Mark that if he left, Vic would kill himself. Not a bad idea, I thought—too bad he didn't do it. It would have saved a lot of trouble.

At that point Mark threw Vic's anti-anxiety pills onto the floor and poured a pitcher of water over them, turning them to chemical sludge. Not strategically a good idea. If you have to tranquilize 'em to keep 'em around, it's not a good idea to destroy the pills.

Whereupon Vic threw Mark against the fridge, and the rest is history.

Well!

That's when I let Mark know exactly how I felt about domestic violence. Once that line is crossed, there's no going back. As an illustration of my point, I reminded Mark about what Mom had gone through with her second husband. This time I did the *long* version of the story, as he claimed not to remember me telling it before (and I *had* done that several times).

ACT TWO:

Mom was left well-fixed, as they would say, after Dad died. After he died there were a number of insurance policies that surfaced, only a few of which she knew about. This meant she wouldn't have to go to work but could, as she said, "stay at home" to make our lives hell uninterrupted. This was said in a virtuous tone with hand held to chest, like she was sacrificing something for the good of her offspring. Great. She gave up sewing and cooking ("Never DID like doing either of them!") just so she could make us do them and complain about the results.

For the first four or five months after Dad died, Mom had an extended ulcer attack and lived on only iced tea and cigarettes. As a result she lost a considerable amount of weight and, I think, for the first time in her life emerged as a beauty. (And she really was—every gay man thinks *his* mom is the most beautiful, but Mom really was.) She was short and tiny framed, with her salt-and-pepper hair, warm brown eyes with full lashes, and a beautiful profile with a German nose and had discovered cheekbones thanks to the weight loss.

Miss Ann always had good clothes, which she generally made for herself. Her major expense was good shoes, and until the day she died, she had at least fifty pairs, all well kept in boxes in her closets.

The weight loss meant new clothes, and Mom went sort of "mod," as mod as a Kansas widow dared do, even going so far as to show her knees in church—in itself a new activity. (After Dad died she sort of "got religion" for a while, but it didn't really stick.)

Then there were the wigs, which were in fashion just then: one real "Ann Miller" number in Superman blue-black, one "shag" in salt and pepper, a really nice ash-blonde short flip in human hair that she looked really good in, and the wiglet with the barrel curls (very Joan-Crawford-meeting-the-board-of-Pepsi).

She also bought records—Booker T and the MGs, late Elvis. Make no mistake, though, life with her was still "dances with land mines," but at least now it had a better sound track.

But all of that aside, Miss Ann was a widow woman in Salina, Kansas, with three kids and no prospects for a husband. Not a good position for a woman to be in, in 1969 in Salina, Kansas.

Life danced along through the minefields of my early adolescence, when one night in March of '71, the phone call came that would change everything.

The call came late at night, so we kids heard about it the next morning at breakfast. Mom was all dreamy and told us that an old boyfriend from years ago had finally found her. It seems he was stationed at the air force base in Salina in the early fifties, and that's how they got to know each other. He tricked a telephone operator into getting Grandma to tell him Mom's married name earlier that evening. It never occurred to me at the time to ask why he had to do that—why didn't he just ASK?

His name was Don White, and he lived in Oklahoma City. They had talked for hours, she told us, and it seemed like "old times," and could he come up to see her next weekend? She said yes, of course! She just knew we would all like each other, which was her way of saying "GODDAMN, YOU KIDS BETTER MAKE NICE OR ELSE!!!"

We never ever knew what "or else" meant, but we knew it wasn't pleasant.

WELL! When her family heard, they were apoplectic! This I did not understand. I was thinking, "Good! This will get her out of our hair for awhile!" It never occurred to me that something was afoot if Grandma had to be tricked into telling Mom's married name. But I was thirteen and thinking of more immediate concerns, like will he take her out for a long dinner so we can have some relief? Maybe we would get to watch *Dark Shadows* and Johnny Carson and the *Late Show* for a change, before she came back to bear down on us again! And will Grandma stay with us (always more fun and better cooking), or will we get Aunt Helen?

Grandma, Aunt Helen, even Uncle Bob, all weighed in on the serious mistake she was making, which only made her more determined to see it through.

"Nobody wants me to be happy!" she shrieked. "Nobody cares about MEEEEEE!"

So Don was invited to come visit the next weekend, just out of spite.

ACT TWO:

Creepy is the adjective that still comes to mind when I think back to him on that first meeting. He was short with bad posture; with small, closely-spaced, rather beady eyes; and a bit too much wavy, salt-and-pepper hair, done a la Bobby Sherman with sideburns treading dangerously close to being late-Elvis. Don also spoke with a mushy Okie accent that automatically deducted ten points from his IQ. I also recall a gray and black, hounds tooth, bulletproof polyester suit (you know, the type with the fake belt in the back?), complete with an enormously wide tie and a pair of very ugly, brown alligator shoes. To complete the package he drove a white Porsche 912. He seemed *very* uncomfortable meeting us kids, and as some people who don't like kids do, he tried too hard to make a good impression. It had the opposite effect.

Just so there was no hint of impropriety, Don got a motel room. That changed as the weeks went on, and he visited more frequently. Once or twice Mom went to visit him in Oklahoma City (Freedom! Grandma stayed with us and cooked . . .), and when they were apart, they talked nightly on the phone. We kids were subjected to the daily play-by-play of the sweet things he said to her and how she yearned to be with him and how he loved her dearly and how her family had got him all wrong.

One weekend I was sent to Oklahoma City with Don to do the male-bonding thing. We didn't call it that in Kansas in 1971—I don't believe there *was* a name for it. I was subjected to it with regularity, this male-bonding thing, being a sissy kid of a widow woman with two daughters. It was believed that prolonged exposure to older males (be they uncles, Dad's old business partners, or neighbor men) and all they represented (body odor, beer-swilling, crotch scratching, sports), and being free from the sissifying presence of too many women, would serve as a proper education in how I was to behave. The only thing it really did was to give me a taste for a certain kind of man in my adolescent and adult fantasies.

What I found when I arrived in Oklahoma City! Don lived in an apartment in a motel he owned—the Sands Motor Hotel on Route 66. This place was ALL the clichés! The buildings were painted flamingo pink with turquoise trim, with trees planted around the mermaid-shaped (no kidding!) swimming pool. This pool had one black tile at the edge for the eyelash, red tiles at the edge for the lips, and *one pink tile* for the nipple—Don thought that really clever. The photo of this pool featured prominently on the postcard promoting the place.

Don's apartment was decorated in early seventies bachelor's pad, with red shag carpet on the floor and walls (this gave me vertigo!), black-vinyl upholstered furniture, and wrought-iron, Mediterranean-style occasional tables and matching swag lamp.

The most notable feature in this apartment, though, was the swarm of cockroaches. I had never seen a cockroach before (really! Mom was one of those white-glove-clean gals who put us through spring-cleaning every weekend), and to be confronted with *SWARMS* of cockroaches was really off-putting, to say the least. Being a real sissy where insects are concerned, I couldn't sit, let alone *sleep,* in that apartment the entire time I was there. It's hard to sleep standing up and not touching anything.

The generations of dead cockroaches lining the drawers and cabinets in the kitchen were an astonishing sight. I imagined it to be the mausoleum to the House of Cockroach, where I supposed the families of cockroaches celebrated Memorial Day by setting up little plastic wreaths and bringing picnic lunches of food scavenged from Don's bed (yes, there were cockroaches and bits of food in his bed as well) and remembering their ancestors. Seeing all this made me ponder what it was that Mom found attractive about him.

I believe it was in May when Don brought the rock of an engagement ring. It looked like he took a headlight out of the car.

"Hey, if you can get a glove over it, it's *too small!*" Mom said one day when showing it to her friend Vivian. "If you have to look for it or feel for it, then it's NOT BIG ENOUGH!" Vivian shot back and roared with laughter. I didn't get the joke.

I *have* to take a little detour here to introduce you to Vivian. She was Mom's best friend from high school and a real original, and I *loved* her.

ACT TWO:

In 1969 Mom reconnected with Vivian, one of her high school friends. It was their twentieth class reunion, and Vivian had moved back to town while her husband, Brad, was stationed in Alaska of all places. Vivian had a round face, short red hair, blue-white skin, and freckles all over her body (as much body as I could see, anyway) She also had a fondness for leopard-print chiffon scarves, cool sunglasses, and big, thick stogies.

Vivian had two cars, one of which was a 1966 Pontiac GTO, which she used to drag race on weekends. It was white with red interior, bucket seats, mag wheels, Thrush pipes, and a Hurst shifter. Oh, baby! And it had a suicide knob on the steering wheel, so she wouldn't have to put the stogie down to drive. We could hear her coming two blocks away, and she would always screech up into the drive, honking and yelling, "Hey Annie! Let's go!"

Vivian was my Auntie Mame before I saw the movie. She taught me how to mix a scotch and water (lots of ice, as the scotch eats it up, she would say), and it was from her I learned about things like how to keep a Tareyton with a long ash stuck to your lip while still smoking it.

"Cheap lipstick," Vivian said conspiratorially. "High wax content." Her preferred color was Mercurochrome orange with matching nail polish.

Vivian also encouraged my creative impulses. At the time I was working on what I called my "house"—it was a dollhouse made of cardboard boxes, and I made all the furniture. Looking back, I did a really good job—we're talking channel-tufted upholstery on a very small scale. Vivian would always look in on the current decorating project (I was always redecorating, what a surprise) and comment favorably.

I also learned about origami through Vivian. One day she brought me two how-to paperback books on origami and a stack of beautiful colored paper to practice with. (And it wasn't even my birthday.) Mom was none too pleased—she didn't want this side of my personality encouraged, as I "couldn't make any money that way" and was already a sissy. As Mom was holding forth with those opinions, Vivian, who had her back to Mom, just looked at me, smiled, and rolled her eyes.

Vivian also told me about all the things she and Mom did when they were teenagers, like stealing toilets to plant in the Catholic Church garden with the statue of the Virgin emerging from the porcelain. Or wrecking cars while ogling the boys.

But you'd never know it by us. Even though she was experimenting with Mod, Mom had Nancy Reagan taste and behavior even before that term was coined. When Vivian would get going after a couple of scotch-and-waters, Mom would get that thin, tight-lipped smile that usually meant "Shut the hell up!" It was fun to ask a few pointed questions of Vivian at these times, because it usually resulted in one of those rare occasions when Mom would tell us that we could go do something we otherwise weren't allowed to do, just to stop the situation before it got out of hand.

Vivian was our source of surprise and adventure, and I looked forward to every visit.

I remember the night I saw my first sports car. It was a balmy summer evening after dinner (in Kansas there is no such thing as dinner after 7:00 p.m., and never as late as 10:00 p.m., as decent people are in bed by then!), and we heard a small "beep-beep" from out front. We all ran to the door and looked out to see Vivian sitting behind the wheel of a shiny, black MGA convertible (top down, of course), with chrome wire wheels and red leather interior. Her sunglasses and leopard-print chiffon scarf were in place, and she was puffing on her ever-present stogy. So this was her other car, the one she kept under a tarp in the back of her driveway!

"Hey, Annie! Let's go for a ride!" Vivian roared, waving her stogy.

Mom, Kathy, and I piled into this two-seater and bounced around the dirt roads on the outskirts of town until way after sunset, dirt in our eyes and bugs in our teeth.

ACT TWO:

Back to Mom and Don. They set the wedding date, June 7 of 1971, not even three months after the first phone call. As the days ran up to the wedding, Grandma, Aunt Helen, and all the rest continued to be upset, apoplectic, and otherwise in a state. Still they brought over what I now call "temporary" wedding gifts—you know, those items like the glass carafe with the candle underneath on the silver-plated stand from Target? These gifts say, "I needed to get something but didn't want to invest too much because this marriage has a snowball's chance in hell." They really compared poorly to the wedding gifts Mom got when she married Dad!

Years later, when we were breaking up Mom's house after her funeral, these wedding presents were the things nobody wanted. Temporary wedding gifts show up consistently at tag sales and thrift shops.

The wedding was in the evening. I remember what Mom wore—it was a dusty-sky-blue, stiff shantung dress, sleeveless, with empire waist and a big box pleat in the center front of the knee-length skirt—not a "wedding" dress but a really nice one. Her hair was pulled up, with the barrel curls in a cluster on the crown of her head. They were married at Trinity Methodist Church, where we had been going to church since Dad died (and where the church elders conned Mom into buying them a set of handbells for the bell choir in Dad's memory).

After we came home from the church, while Mom, Don, and everyone else were in the family room for the reception, I locked myself in my room and had a good, long cry. I wasn't articulate enough at the time to express what I was feeling. Looking back, I realize that they were tears of deep despair. I had a premonition that, even though life was difficult now, it was just going to get worse in a really dramatic way.

Mom's friend Ruth, who was the maid of honor at my parents' wedding (and this one as well), came in and tried to comfort me. She tried to put a positive spin on the situation but, after a few minutes, let her guard down by saying doubtfully, "Well, this *might* work out."

I didn't understand why things were moving so fast or exactly *why* Mom was compelled to marry Don. Still I didn't know at the time that getting married in less than three months to someone you only saw on weekends might be unusual.

But that aside, what I did understand was that we would be moving to a strange city, where we wouldn't know anyone. Life would be turned upside down.

During their honeymoon in Oklahoma City, Mom and Don bought a house in Bethany, one of the many suburbs of OKC. As it was told to me, this suburb was formed from land donated by a devout Nazarene, a good Christian who, in the city charter, forbade blacks to walk the streets. The Civil Rights Act of 1964 overturned this, but that was only seven years earlier, and Jim Crowe was still very much alive in spirit. The sale of alcohol was still prohibited in the city charter, which was no problem because the Oklahoma City limits line (and a liquor store) was only two blocks away from the house.

This was Mom's dream house (she didn't know of the term "wet dream," or of she had she would have been too freaked out about the sexual imagery to use it), colonial style, two stories, red brick-faced, with six bedrooms and two bathrooms, a two-car garage and large lot. "OF COURSE YOU KIDS WILL LIKE IT!" we were told. Of course we would. What were we going to do, live in a tent in the backyard?

Going through the house in Salina to prepare for moving was a month-long exercise in Mom-imposed chaos. She wanted everything done ALL AT ONCE and wasn't really happy that it wasn't happening more quickly. We had lived there thirteen years, with all the accumulation that suggests. So many things of value ended up in the landfill or were passed on to charity that might still be here had she just stopped to listen for *just a moment*.

Speaking of packing, Gwenda got the sack as well. When Mom started dating Don, she explained to Gwenda that she was "still there" for her, but as events accelerated, Gwenda started Asking Questions. Apparently she'd been through this before.

ACT TWO:

Perhaps I should introduce you to Gwenda:

One sign that Mom was coming back to life after Dad died was her desire to get out of the house. As she had no job and had slave labor in the form of three kids to do the housework every day, Mom had time to spare. For a while she took a Bible study course, but that eventually petered out, and she decided that volunteering was going to be more satisfying.

She decided to be a Big Sister. Why, I'll never know, but there you are. For some reason the Big Sisters gave her the most incorrigible girl they had, a thirteen-year-old named Gwenda. Gwenda was a miniature Janis Joplin, down to the frizzy hair, crushed-velvet hippie clothes, and whiskey-and-cigarettes voice. Her mother, a badly bleached blonde, was divorced and worked in a dive bar. She lived on Crawford Street with a man she wasn't married to and Gwenda's other siblings, who all had different last names. Gwenda was astonished that Kathy, Laurie, and I all had the same last name.

Apparently Gwenda had a choice between reform school and Mom. No doubt there were days that she wished she had chosen reform school. Especially the day in home ec when she took a pair of shears up the back of one of the other girls' sewing project. Gwenda said it was because the girl was making fun of her and calling her names (this is the first time I heard the word "slut"), which was probably true, but I wouldn't know.

When Mom got the call (the school called her instead of Gwenda's real mom because *she* couldn't be located), Mom descended on the school (and Gwenda) in a very Old Testament sort of way, bellowing in that Voice-of-God way she could do when chewing out non-relatives. She verbally hammered poor Gwenda about what she had done and hammered the school officials about allowing the sort of harassment that led to this sort of thing. Something she'd never think of doing for me.

Soon after, Gwenda ran away and hooked up with a guy who bought her lots of new clothes. Mom went to find her and eventually did, bringing her back. I thought Gwenda looked cool, as the clothes she got were really high-early-seventies midi- and maxi-skirt outfits, complete with the lace-up, thigh-high boots and fur hats, very Giorgio d'Saint Angelo—my favorite being the black Persian lamb maxi coat. The clothes disappeared when it was discovered that Gwenda also got crabs, along with all the cool new clothes. We kids didn't know what that was, and it wasn't explained to us; but for a long time, there was a can of Lysol spray in the bathroom that we were instructed (with much embarrassment) to spray the seat with after Gwenda would visit.

For a while Gwenda was like a cousin who visited us frequently and lived nearby. Mom spent lots of time with the juvenile authorities, steering her through the system such as it was in that time and place. Looking back, I find it interesting that she could spend all this time on Gwenda, listening to her and helping her sort out her problems. She certainly wasn't doing it with us.

When it looked like Don and Mom would get married, Gwenda started feeling insecure and causing some trouble. Mom, of course, went into her "she's so selfish, she doesn't want *me* to be happy" routine.

I don't know how Gwenda ended up. Events had taken a turn when Mom and Don got engaged, and Gwenda got tossed out when we started packing.

Looking back, what Gwenda experienced was crueler than what we kids had to put up with. We at least had stability (or rather, predictability), but Gwenda had none of that. Our family represented some sort of normalcy for her. Even though Gwenda was far from reformed, she came to believe that we would still be there for her—our situation appeared less transient than what she was used to. Mom held out the potential of having some kind of security and cohesive family experience, only to snatch it back when it became inconvenient for her courtship with Don.

I do remember our last time together. Mom was introducing her to a new Big Sister and trying to put some positive spin on the situation. Gwenda sat silently, looking down at her lap, saying nothing, showing no emotion. The new Big Sister looked like No Fun At All—she looked more like a matron in a women's prison film, what with her gray clothes and Sensible Shoes. She eyed Gwenda suspiciously the whole time, just waiting for the jailbreak. All in all, it went badly.

ACT TWO:

Gwenda had been dumped for a man yet again. Just like she had experienced with her mother. And not too surprisingly, Mom didn't, or wouldn't, see what she had done.

Day in and day out, the torture that is commonly called moving continued. July 2 was the exit date, so we spent the two days before, packing everything the cheapskate wasn't paying to have moved into the U-Haul van—we were having our own "adventure in moving," just like it said on the side of the truck. The caravan to Oklahoma started out in the early morning with Don driving the truck; Mom and Aunt Betty in the car with the dog, the cat (heavily sedated) and us kids; and Uncle Bob (Betty's husband) driving his car with our cousins Brian and Greg. We got to OKC at about rush hour. Pulling up to the house, which we had seen in photos already, was strange. It made the whole move seem real.

As I looked around, I vowed that, at the very first opportunity to escape Oklahoma, I would run like hell. (When it finally came, I just drove real fast—it's the same thing.)

Once we got to OKC, life plugged along, with Mom screaming at us to get everything unpacked. She really never had to break a nail or mess up her hairdo in her life, as she knew that a well-timed screech at the right decibel level required for the job would get us hopping to it.

There was also redecorating to do. This being 1971, Mom anticipated the vogue for Bicentennial-inspired decor. She started with the family room by ordering red-white-and-blue-striped wallpaper. This all coordinated with the oak wainscoting and the Ethan Allen colonial-style furniture. (She called it "Early American," but if any early Americans had color TVs, I hadn't heard about it in history class). This started Mom on a mania for wallpaper that forced Kathy and me to learn to do it well and *fast*.

In the meantime we had moved Don from his bachelor pad. What an experience! The cockroaches I saw on my earlier visit were just the proverbial tip of the iceberg. Not only did he have them swarming all over the kitchen and living room, they were in his bed linens, in his clothes hamper, in his closets, his dresser drawers, his cereal box—you name it.

Once we moved his belongings into the house, the cockroaches moved into the house as well—an infestation that took literally years to be rid of. This was because Mom was so cheap about such things; she thought a spraying or two of Raid would do the trick and would never spring for an exterminator. When Kathy inherited the house after Mom died, the first thing she did was to call in the professionals, who took several visits over the course of a year to finally put to death the descendants of Don's cockroach progeny.

I thought it incomprehensible that someone could live in any degree of comfort with such an infestation and wondered at his sanity as well as Mom's blindness to reality. This was, well, unusual, and I thought it said something about Don the person—or, at the very least, about his standards of hygiene. Mom didn't appear to be bothered by any of this. She had a ponderous capacity for denial.

As you can see, we were very busy kids the first few weeks after we moved in. Which helped us to sleep very soundly at night. I was an especially sound sleeper, needing nothing short of nuclear holocaust to wake me. So imagine how I felt waking up in the middle of the night, about a month and a half after we moved in, to hear Mom screaming and crying!

Disoriented, I ran down the hall to their room (they got the big room, all 15 by 15 feet, freshly wallpapered by Kathy; and I was in a red-and-white Victorian print, furnished with a molded-plastic-made-to-look-like-expensive-wood French provincial bedroom "suit," as it was pronounced in Oklahoma) to see Don holding both of Mom's wrists against the headboard, and her crying and screaming, "LET ME GO!" By this time we three kids were all awake and headed toward him, when he turned to all of us and said, "You better leave me alone, or I'll kill all of you."

ACT TWO:

Kill?!? KILL?!?

In all the screaming and verbal abuse Mom heaped on us (and there was *lots*, make no mistake about it!) we had never heard the word "kill." It was used in reference to bugs or weeds (or in one case Vivian, when she told about a particularly alcohol-sodden adventure that she and Mom had had when they were teenagers), but it was never ever directed at us!

Kill. It was at that moment that life, though difficult up until then, became surreal. I wouldn't have described it as surreal at the time, but that was because I didn't know what the word "surreal" meant, until later. By that time, though, the chaos that our life became seemed normal and unremarkable.

Mom just called them "incidents." And the next day, we were expected to act as if nothing had happened.

It was decreed that I needed to "earn my keep" (my sisters were spared this task somehow) by working at the Sands Motor Hotel. Don was converting the motel to apartments—it seems traffic on Route 66 wasn't as brisk since Interstate 40 went in—and I was sentenced to work from eight to five Monday through Friday. I pretended that it was going to be absolute torture to have to be away from home so much of the day, sort of like Brer Rabbit begging not to be thrown into the briar patch.

To sweeten this deal, Don happened to hire a new manager for the place, named John Bernard, married to wife Sandy. They got an apartment on the property as well as his salary. John was a real babe and my first boy crush. He was tall and lanky with a good tan only to his waist. He also had curly sandy-brown hair, sleepy hazel eyes, a cleft in his chin, and a kind smile. And John had a motorcycle and drove a British-racing-green Triumph convertible.

He always wore long pants, and I only saw his legs when we would go for a swim in the mermaid-shaped pool. He would wear this pair of faded, red boxer shorts with a worn-out jockstrap, leg straps peeking out from underneath the hem. I was fascinated.

What poor John got as his helper was a shy, neurotic, pudgy, short sissy kid with braces on his teeth, who was a little slow on the uptake. God bless him, he was really nice to me and polite, something I didn't experience much at home. I would get there at eight o'clock and we would have coffee.

"You're doing a man's job, you should drink a man's drink!" he declared right away that first morning.

(SO grown-up! I was told that coffee would stunt my growth, but I drank it anyway. I have gotten no taller since then.)

We would then go about the planned work for the day, stopping at noon to have lunch. Sometimes Sandy would come home for lunch, sometimes just the two of us. I thought it was grand! Mind you, I never let on to Mom—I wanted her to think that this was pure hell of the worst kind. If she thought I was enjoying myself, she certainly would have put a stop to it!

Then there was the day the FBI showed up during lunch. The two agents really DID look like Ephram Zimbalist Jr. from the TV show, with the gray suits with the skinny lapels, white shirts, and skinny ties, hair parted on one side and loaded with Brylcreem, and the leather wallets with the ID that had "FBI" in big blue letters. They wanted to chat.

It seems that Don had been hiding out a fugitive from justice—a guy who had knocked over a bank in Jacksonville, Florida—and they wanted any information we could provide. It seems the gent had moved on just days before, leaving no forwarding address.

Now Mom used to work for a bank before she married Dad, and when the show "The FBI" was on TV, she would always tell us that we should always cooperate with the FBI, otherwise they would "get" us. Since I was on the

ACT TWO:

job longer than John (by days actually), I led them into Don's old apartment where all the records were kept. They took what they wanted and left.

That night at dinner, when Mom asked me what I did at work, of course I told them all about the exciting visit.

"You didn't tell them anything, DID YOU?!?" Don demanded, beady eyes narrowing.

"Well, yes, I showed them all the records in the apartment, and they took some," I replied. Seeing his reaction to this was a thrilling mixture of fear and pleasure—he went all purple, and his eyes bulged out, and he started shouting something about you stupid, queer sissy . . . goddamn how could he do a thing like that . . . oh my god, I can't believe it, etc., etc., while jumping over the table to lunge at my throat.

After the visit from the FBI, I started keeping my eyes open a little more, and that summer proved to be a real education. Along with learning to do a mean drywall, repairing the riding lawn mower, and telling time by the shadows, my education included learning about drug dealers, prostitutes, and which mistresses of city councilmen were in which apartments. The Sands Apartments, which it was now dubbed, was not IN the bad end of Bethany, it *was* the bad end of Bethany.

John was really sweet and protective, all the while explaining what everything that was happening meant. One day a blonde (well, it was a wig, bad Dynel that any respectable drag queen could have spotted at fifty yards) came to rent a furnished "efficiency" apartment. Her name was Linda Freeze. When she signed the lease, instead of dotting her "i," she made a circle—you know the type.

She drove a red VW beetle, and I would see her go to her apartment with a man (she never seemed to have moved in), and an hour or so later they would leave. I was puzzled about it and asked John.

"She's a prostitute."

"Prostitute? What's that?"

I got the CliffsNotes explanation of what a prostitute did for her career. There were similar explanations for drug dealing (apartment 36, you stay away from that shit! It's trouble!), mistresses (numbers 19, 25, 38 and 41), and stolen goods (stored in the house on the property by Don). I learned that thirty-days notice to be condemned meant the place was really a falling-down firetrap that we had to make look like a sound building. I also learned not to look up while you're spackling a drywall joint on the ceiling, unless you are wearing safety goggles—drywall compound in your eyes burns like hell and makes it real hard to blink.

I mentioned the house on the property. It was another of the many puzzlements of that place. Don built it to live in, complete with its own pool, apparently with wife number two (Mom was number three). The house was abandoned and left to fall into ruin in favor of the cockroach-infested apartment he lived in (which, by the way, took the exterminators three trips to clear out and was later declared a Superfund site). The house was used to store any stolen goods Don just happened to be fencing at the time. The pool looked like the lair of the Creature of the Black Lagoon.

All good things come to an end. Summer break was over before I knew it, and John and Sandy were moving to another state. I would be going to school, and my summer job was over.

The first couple of wife-beatings were alarming, but after that, we kids began to accept the "incidents" as part of our weekly routine. There was a pattern to these events, which happened with such regularity that, if I had been a little more enterprising, I could have made a fortune by charging the neighbor kids for a show. After a while they became routine and not as remarkable as they were in the beginning. It was usually Thursday, there usually was a fifth of Chivas Regal consumed by Don (I amassed quite a collection of those velvet bags the bottles came in), and the evening would be off and running just about ten thirty, right about the time the neighbors went to bed, so as to keep more than one household awake into the night.

ACT TWO:

There also was to be expected some sort of destruction of the house, from the sliding glass doors that lost out to some flying logs, to a kitchen ceiling that got pockmarked with a broom handle (it looked like gunshot holes), to the upstairs bathroom being denuded of ceramic tile (he had found a hammer). We all eventually took this in stride—didn't everyone's mother's second husband (*I never considered him a stepfather*) break up the house in a drunken rage every Thursday evening? Mom, of course, would be crying and upset, but the next day all was repaired. I'm really good at home repairs now.

There was *one* incident, however, that got Mom mad—REAL MAD—at him. I mentioned before how Miss Ann was about her hair. Sacred territory.

This particular evening, Don was winding up into another one of his sessions and got it into his head to take a gallon of milk out into the garage and splash it all over the new car—a 1970 white Thunderbird, bought because it galled him to see Mom driving the aqua tuna-boat Pontiac that Dad had given her in 1968. It seems the solenoid on the starter was going out on this car, and everyone knew that repairing the solenoid on a rare, exotic 1966 Pontiac Catalina sedan was an expensive—no! *impossible*—proposition! Or so Don said.

Anyway.

Don was splashing milk all over the garage, and Mom came out into the garage to tell him to stop wasting good food. She was hit with a wave of cold, healthful milk.

BUT.

It hit her hair, her *freshly* done hair. And not enough to damage the whole thing but just one side, so she would have to try to repair it and smell like curdled milk until her next appointment.

OH! MY! GOD! was she mad. A baseball bat appeared in her hand out of nowhere, and she chased him all around that garage, beating the hell out of him in the process as the neighbors looked through the garage door windows in astonishment. (There was a party next door, but WE proved to be the entertainment.) It was a wonder that there were no dents or broken windows in the car! Don was black and blue for weeks.

Miss Ann was like that—you could beat the hell out of her, you could destroy her house, you could sell her car, you could threaten to kill her children, you could turn her existence into chaos, but *MESS WITH HER HAIR and DIE!*

There were many more "incidents" that first year, such as the time Mom's friend Ruth came to visit from Salina, only to have the visit cut short when Don beat the shit out of Mom just before the three of them were headed out to dinner.

She was appalled that Mom would sit still for this type of treatment after being married to a nice guy like Dad (remember, she *dated* him) and left late in the evening for home. She explained to Kathy and me as we helped her load the car, that this was *not* normal behavior, and she couldn't stand by and watch Mom accept this. I wanted to die of embarrassment!

One of the worst incidents, though, happened the following spring. It started in the usual way, continuing with the usual beating and destruction of property, and wound up with Don yelling, "YOUR KIDS ARE DRIVING ME AWAY!" before storming out the door and driving off.

I heaved a sigh of relief. I didn't know what I personally had done but wanted to so I could do more of it. I felt elation that perhaps we would finally be rid of him. But no.

"You have to help me get him back!" Mom sobbed.

ACT TWO:

"*WHY?*" I demanded.

As the four of us were kneeling in a big group hug in the dark, the whole sordid story tumbled out. It seems that they not only dated in the early fifties, but he had, indeed, gotten her pregnant! Then he ran his sorry coward's ass back to Oklahoma, leaving her to deal with the consequences. And what consequences they were!

Remember, this was 1952 in Salina, Kansas. A young woman (she was twenty-two at the time) coming up pregnant and unmarried—well, the talk from everyone in town alone would have been enough torture. But then there was her family and the treatment she suffered at their hands.

I heard about another, less kind-and-gentle side to Grandma. Among other indignities, she made Mom sit in a bathtub filled with turpentine to try to induce an abortion. Apparently the entire family made her life hell, extorting sums of money and home furnishings from her in exchange for their "help."

I thought, "Oh, *that's* why they were all upset when he came back on the scene!" Now all of what I thought of as overreaction made absolute sense, given the whole story, which we kids obviously didn't get at the time.

Don, of course, held a grudge about her decision to put the child up for adoption, but what could she do? He didn't step up to the plate and marry her, for chrissakes! What else could she do? So, in his mind, his "bad behavior" was his way of "punishing" her for not keeping the child, and she was sitting still for it.

So we continued to play the whipsaw game. I call it that because our emotions were whipsawed back and forth. If Mom was mad at Don, he was evil incarnate, and if we even looked at or talked to him, we were siding with the enemy. Nothing but *BLIND HATE* would do. BUT if she was not mad at him, we had to love him like a father and be really nice, because if not, we were selfish and would hear her screech, "YOU DON'T CARE ABOUT MY HAPPINESS! YOU'RE JUST SELFISH AND WANT TO DRIVE HIM AWAY!"

But after this "incident," I was really flummoxed. Even at thirteen years old I thought that, if he did you wrong (and thoroughly so) like that twenty years before, *why* would you think it would be a good idea to even speak to him, let alone *MARRY* him?

I already told of Mom's first anniversary and how it ended in her almost losing her life. As you may remember, it was after this that she decided that divorce was the only alternative (and when I met her lawyer, Harry)—otherwise she'd end up dead, and we would end up God-knows-where.

Long-distance relationships can be a recipe for disaster.

This is because of the potential for concealing unpleasant things. Along with the alcohol abuse and propensity for wife beating, Don concealed a drug habit, a tendency toward bestiality (with "Brandy," his male toy poodle, no less), hints of unwholesome interest in kids (I always kept a watchful eye on Kathy), and small-time "hillbilly mafia" connections. He got his drugs by mail (how convenient) from a pharmacy in the Valley View Hospital, a small hospital in some godforsaken hamlet in western Oklahoma. There were times when the package would be late—those were hell-to-pay times, where the rages were more severe because they were complicated by withdrawal. There were a few times that we witnessed these withdrawals, and at first we were told it was a bad case of the flu. But I had never heard of flu making one believe spiders were crawling all over one's body.

I don't know if the drugs created the propensity for violence or just fueled it, but violence it was. The two are forever linked in my mind, and I really have no tolerance for either of them. They both made my life a tornado when I was younger, and I understood the connection between them.

In my life I have been lucky in that, when there is information I need to proceed (whatever that means), it is put in front of me, and IN ITALICS so I won't miss it. The first time I remember experiencing this was after one of the many "incidents," as we took to calling them. This one involved Don's kicking in a door of one of the upstairs bedrooms, for whatever reason. (All the doors in that house now have full-length mirrors on them, as mirrors are usually less expensive to get than replacing oak-veneer doors)

ACT TWO:

Mom and I were standing there looking at the damage. It was sunny. Then for a brief moment, the sun was a little brighter, everything was a little more sharply focused, and Mom had a funny look on her face. She turned to me and said, "You can *CHOOSE* not to live like this."

This all happened in an instant. Then everything was back to normal.

Except for me.

The idea of *choice*, and that *this* was a choice and that I could *choose* not to do this—that life was choices—that idea really rocked my world. I puzzled about why Mom was choosing the situation we were now in but couldn't fathom it. But it gave me something to hold onto—that even though I didn't now, one day when I was a grown-up, I *would* have a choice.

And I certainly wouldn't choose the kind of life I was living then!

When I moved out on my own, I chose not to have any chaos or violence in my life. When Matthew and I got together, I told him in no uncertain terms that, if he ever raised a hand to me, he should either knock me out and be gone before I came to, or he should kill me. If he didn't do either one of those, he would live in a world of hurt for a long time to come. Many things I could (and did) overlook, but violence and chaos were something I did *not* choose to have in my life. Dancing with land mines isn't the way to live.

This is why I couldn't understand or comprehend Mark's choice to stay with Victor.

After I finished with Mom's story, I insisted to Mark, "You need to get out of there! Once this line is crossed, there's no going back!"

"But I don't have any money to move," he said.

"Call one of those places that buys up households of furniture, tell 'em to make a price and be out by 4:00 p.m., and then get on a plane to San Francisco! But you have to get out!"

Mark played the "Yes, but . . ." game for a little bit, so I got him off the phone.

If you want to know what I feel or think about something, unedited and without my "Miss Manners filter" on, wake me out of a sound sleep to ask— the later the hour and sounder the sleep, the better. I'll let you know exactly how I feel, in no uncertain terms.

So imagine, a couple of weeks later, getting a call about one thirty in the morning and hearing Mark's voice. Through the mental fog, I assumed that either he was at the bus station or the airport and mentally revved-up to go to get him.

"Ken, I'm living in fear! Victor's gone right now, and it's the only time I can call. He has taps on the phones and watches me night and . . ."

"WAIT! You mean you're still *there*? You haven't left?"

"No."

"Why not!?"

"I still love him."

That last statement sent me ballistic.

ACT TWO:

"Listen. You woke me out of a SOUND SLEEP just to complain?"

Silence from Mark.

"Since you woke me out of a sound sleep just to complain, you're going to hear what I have to say and have wanted to say for the entire time I've known you two!"

Which got me started on a harangue about how they were not well-matched and never seemed to be happy with each other the entire time they were together. I could never for the life of me figure out just why they were together. And now that Vic was beating him, the situation had lurched from the neurotic and fell solidly into the pathological, and I couldn't listen to it any more—it wasn't helping him and was just making me crazy.

"Mark, I'm going to say one last thing, and then I'm hanging up. I will do anything I can to help you get out of that situation, but I! WILL! NOT! listen to you complain anymore. I can't fix this situation, and from the sound of it, you can't either. You need to leave! When you're ready to leave, call me. Not before."

"Well, I won't bother you again," he said sarcastically.

"You won't!"

With that I slammed down the phone. And couldn't get back to sleep.

Act Three:

I got the call for help in late March of '95. Five years later.

It was a Sunday afternoon, and I came into the studio after the gym to pick up messages. On the machine, in a little-old-man voice, was Mark!

"Hello, Ken, this is Mark," he croaked in this thin, reedy voice. "I'm leaving Victor and wanted to tell you. Call me when you can."

I looked at the machine, astonished. It took five years, and this was the only way he could say it. But I said to him all those years ago, don't call until you're ready to leave. And now he was calling.

For a few minutes I sat, thinking about this—not wanting to call but knowing I had to. Did I want to get hooked back in to this crazy situation? Did Mark indeed want to leave, or was this just a false alarm?

Really, I did tell him not to call unless he was ready to leave, so I needed to assume that he was. What to do?

I dialed his number, and Victor answered the phone. The minute I heard Vic's voice, I got this weird vision of an evil black vortex, accompanied by a wave of nausea. I hung up the phone, my heart pounding and the hair on my arms standing on end.

"What the hell was THAT?" I thought. I was shaking all over; never had I experienced something like this. It scared me—it was like looking into an abyss of pure evil! (I know it sounds dramatic and very New Agey woo-woo, but there you have it. It did scare me. It was very real.)

But I knew I had to call again. So I took a deep breath, dialed again, and made nice to Victor, who eventually handed the phone to Mark.

"So, where are you going?" I asked, after the pleasantries had been dispensed with.

"I don't know," he responded shakily.

"What do you mean you don't know?"

"The group said just to have a bag packed. It's something my family arranged. I don't know where they're taking me."

"Oh, great!" I thought. "My friend is being kidnapped by deprogrammers his homophobic family arranged for."

"Well, let me know where you are and how you're doing!" I said as cheerily as I could. No doubt he couldn't know because Victor would just follow him there.

I was away on business the next week. From time to time I would think about the call and where Mark might be. This was during the time when all of the drama surrounding O. J. Simpson was starting up, and it was on the news day after day—you couldn't ignore it. Hearing about it day after day triggered all of my angst surrounding domestic violence, and my thoughts ran to Mark frequently.

Since that last phone call, I thought about him many times, wondering just how he was doing. There had been an article in *Vanity Fair* that I had read, where the guy beat his child to death—the wife in this story was a former author who turned into a hollowed-out wreck from the abuse he heaped on her—she apparently was unable to stop him from beating his own daughter. And now the O. J. thing. My concern was that this would be the way it would end for Mark—that he would be found dead, with Victor long gone. I would hear it after the fact in lurid headlines in the gay press.

As it was, though, I wanted to know that Mark was, indeed, out of that situation and safe. Finally I decided to write a letter to his brother in Boston.

Mark had two brothers, one in Boston (David, a lawyer), the other in Florida (Robert). His father was also still alive. "The Judge," as Mark used to call him, had had a stroke and was gaga, so he couldn't know much of anything. I couldn't remember where in Florida Robert lived, or which brother was the good cop and which one was the bad cop, so I sent a letter to brother David the lawyer in Boston—his office was listed in the phone book.

In the letter I outlined where Mark and I met and the circumstances when we last talked. I finished up with an offer of any help I could; they only had to ask. Once it was sent off, I felt I couldn't do anything else but wait. Besides I was going to Paris with one of my customers in a few days!

Upon my return from a rather grueling trip to Paris, I found a call on my machine from Mark's brother Robert, the one in Florida. (It turned out he was the good cop.) He asked me to call him back as soon as possible as it was urgent. He left a number, so I called.

"I'm glad you called back," he began. "David got your letter and sent it along to me. He asked me what this shit was all about and let me know he didn't want to get involved in Mark's drama."

"How is Mark? Where is he?"

"Ken, he's still there. He didn't have the courage to meet the man from the group, Victor has him so scared. He tells me that Victor has guns and has threatened him with them if he tries to leave. So he's still there."

Robert outlined the attempts he had made to try to find some sort of safe haven where Mark could go, to no avail. There were homeless shelters, there were women's shelters, there were shelters for recovering substance abusers, but nowhere for someone in Mark's situation to go. When he called the Los Angeles gay community center, the people there didn't want to hear about it. We were under siege with AIDS, and even *talking* about gay domestic violence . . . well, it was the community's Dirty Little Secret. And that's why Robert called me: I was the last resort.

"So what do we do now?" I asked.

"Well, I asked him if he was well enough to go out for lunch with someone, could he handle that? And he said he could . . . " Robert ventured tentatively.

"OK, Robert. I'll call you back in a few minutes."

My next call was to Mark.

"Hello, Mark! It's Ken!" I said as casually as I could. "Hey, I'm going to be in LA tomorrow on business and wanted to see if you would like to do lunch?"

"Uh, OK." I could hear confusion in his voice.

"I'll pick you up at noon, your place!" I said brightly. "See you then! Bye!"

ACT THREE:

The next call was to my travel agent, ordering a round-trip and a one-way ticket. And a car—Chrysler LeBaron convertible. I figured that, if I got my head blown off, my last ride would have been a helluva lot of fun, and I wouldn't have to pay for it—I'd be dead.

I called Robert back.

"Done. I'm going down tomorrow morning. He thinks it's just lunch, and I didn't say any more, just in case the phones are still tapped."

"Now, what do you want out of this?" Robert said, suddenly suspicious. "You're not family, so . . ."

"So, you think Mark will go from the frying pan into the fire?"

"Well, I don't know you, so . . ."

"And I can understand your suspicion. You're probably thinking that I'm going to want something out of this."

"Yeah."

"Well, sir, not every gay person is like Victor. Mark and I are friends, and he got me my first job in San Francisco. I made a promise to Mark many years ago that, when he decided to leave Victor, I would do all that I could to help. I made a promise. It's the right thing to do. Besides it sounds to me like you have no alternative."

"What can we do to repay you?"

"Now don't get ahead of yourself. I only have limited means, and when he gets here, he's not going to have anything. I'm willing to do what I can to help, but I'm going to need help from you as well. So save the repayment thing to help Mark—he's going to need it! I'll call you tomorrow, once he's here."

After I rang off, the full impact of what was about to happen hit me. Watching Mom and Don and that whole train wreck as previous experience, I knew that this wasn't a situation where I'd snatch Mark away, and then God would be in her heaven and all would be right with the world. This was going to be a long process, and I needed some help—but *fast*!

In San Francisco there is an organization called Community United Against Violence (CUAV). It's an extremely worthy organization dedicated to eradicating violence toward, and within, the gay community. I'd read about them in the gay press, so I called, and got Greg on the phone. Briefly I outlined the situation.

"This is something big," he said. "You're going to need information about what to expect, and when your friend gets here, he's going to need our services as well. Come by in an hour, and I'll have a packet of information ready. You need to read this tonight. Know what you're getting into. Know that it will eat up a big portion of your life for at least eighteen months."

Greg went on to tell me that gay domestic violence was a dirty little secret in the gay community. There were some who, especially when it concerned two men, didn't want to believe it could happen. These people generally dismissed it as an "S and M" relationship, because they couldn't believe that this sort of thing could happen between *men*—men could fight back, couldn't they? It was thought that this couldn't happen between two women either. In some people's minds, domestic violence, like conception, needed a man and a woman to make it happen.

Since the gay community in the mid-'90s was still reeling from the scourge of AIDS and all of the anti-gay sentiment it aroused in certain right-wing people, the idea of openly discussing domestic violence was too much for the community to contemplate. If anyone acknowledged it, let alone talked about it, well that would give the haters just one more piece of ammunition to use against us. In other words, we weren't supposed to air our dirty laundry, as my grandma would say.

ACT THREE:

To complicate matters, this shame usually keeps the victim silent. This silence means that the victim usually won't report the violence. No reporting, no paper trail—later, the abuser could deny anything ever happened, and there would be no record to contradict him. He could claim to be the one abused and paint the abused as crazy, or just making it all up. Which feeds the shame and silence about the abuse—another cycle.

That was the mind-set that Mark would be up against when he came here, Greg told me. Happily, though, CUAV was there to provide Mark, and me, with whatever help necessary to deal with this. *(And trust me, over time they did!)*

Another complication that comes up with gay domestic violence is the issue of where the abused person goes for shelter. When you have a straight couple, the woman (who is generally the abused partner) can go to a women's shelter. Men aren't allowed there, so it's easier to keep the abuser at bay. For gay men especially, there are no such shelters—this is what Robert discovered when he started trying to get Mark out. And this is precisely why I had to go down to LA and snatch Mark away.

I dropped in to CUAV on my way downtown to buy pajamas and sundries for Mark. Since I was basically kidnapping him, I figured he would have just the clothes on his back.

He needed something to sleep in, brush his teeth with, and shave with. He could wear my clothes during the day until we could get him some.

Later that evening I read the packet of information about domestic violence, and it all sounded really familiar to me. When I was dealing with Mom and Don's chaos as a kid, I didn't know that there was a profile for an abuser and a predictable cycle of violence. The only thing I observed when I was young was that it usually happened late on a Thursday evening, after he drank a bottle of scotch.

In the textbook situation of domestic violence, the abuser isolates the abused, systematically getting rid of the abused person's friends, family, and anyone and anything they hold dear. In Mom's case, we moved to Oklahoma. In Mark's case, they moved all over the country.

After the isolation, a cycle begins—first a honeymoon period, then a building up of tension, then the violence and abuse that releases the tension, followed by a period of remorse and promises to do better, which starts another honeymoon period and another cycle. Since the abused is isolated, it's easy to become lost in this cycle; if you don't have anyone to check reality with, you lose your moorings. Over time, the cycles get shorter and shorter. Just because both partners are of the same sex doesn't mean that it works differently—people are people.

As I said, it all sounded like a replay of Mom and Don. I finished reading and went to bed, feeling a little creeped out. This all felt like I was going back in time, back to the days when we first moved to OKC.

I slept fitfully that night, knowing that I was turning my life upside down for someone who I hadn't talked to in years, and who would, no doubt, be a very changed person from the man I met back in 1980. Eventually I just got up, because I wasn't doing myself any good tossing and turning. I got showered and dressed, walked my sweet, pampered, little buff-colored, rhinestone-collared-princess of a cocker spaniel Daisy, went out for an early breakfast, then took Daisy to the studio, where she would wait for me to come back. While I was getting Daisy settled with a new doggie bone and filling her water dish, I listened to my messages—there were quite a few. They were all from Mark, and all said essentially the same thing.

"Ken, this is Mark," I heard him say urgently." Come get me now! Robert told me what you two are up to. Vic's not here right now. Come get me now before he gets home!"

The clock said 7:10 a.m. I grabbed my keys and the map of LA and ran off to the car. I took off for the airport and fell into a time warp—I was able to get to the airport, park, get through security, and onto the plane by 7:30 a.m. (For those of you who have been to the Bay Area, you will know what a feat *that* was.)

At the Burbank airport, I got the *very spiffy black* Chrysler LeBaron convertible and headed to Mark's place. Driving there, I went over my checklist again in my head. Clean underwear in case a trip in an ambulance was necessary. *Check.* Hair freshly bleached, with only minor scalp burn. *Check.* My new Alain Mikli sunglasses from Paris for the convertible. *Check.* Julie Brown on the stereo singing "Girl Fight Tonight." *Check.* Imagining how cool I looked helped to distract me from thinking about the possibility of getting my brains blown out.

As I turned the corner from Sunset onto Olive, I could see Mark sitting by the curb on a suitcase. I was shocked at his appearance. He looked like a little old man, hunched over, emaciated to the point of being skeletal. I could see the outlines of the bones in his skull through the skin on his face, which itself had gone as gray as his hair. (I relaxed a little, seeing him there. That meant I didn't have to go into their apartment and confront Vic.)

For contrast, imagine me, blasting down the street in a cool convertible with the top down, great sunglasses, the stereo playing really loud, and my white-blond hair sparkling in the LA sun, looking *fabuous*.

I do love an entrance.

Screeching up to a stop, I jumped out of the car, gave Mark a hug, threw his bag in the trunk, him into the front seat, and off we sped to the airport.

During the plane flight back to San Francisco, Mark told me of the harrowing exit he had just made. It seems Victor had come home from another night of carousing to find Mark with a suitcase packed and went ballistic. Mark told Vic that he was just going to visit me for the weekend, that he had to get away for a little while.

The whole time Victor had his gun out of the holster, fondling it and pointing it at Mark.

"Ken, I just had to get him calmed down just so I could get out of there. If he thought I was really leaving for good, he would have killed me. He's said many times that, if I left him, he would kill me, and after he killed me, he would go into my grave to get me!"

He trembled the whole time on the flight back.

Perhaps I should fill in the five-year gap between Act Two and Act Three.

When I last spoke to Mark in 1990, five years before, I was right at the cusp of success. I had a spiffy apartment and sold to the Very Posh Store in Los Angeles, where all of the rich-and-famous bought my work. Eventually there were those who sought me out in my fashionable South-of-Market studio to commission pieces. I had my first pieces go into museum shows and permanent collections. My hats were on music videos and soda commercials played all over the world. My work showed up on the red carpets of the Oscars and Grammys. Life was fun, and I was very pleased with myself. I had become a grown-up, just as I'd imagined when I was a kid.

Because of my choice of career, I had a good life. Once I was able to trade a ball gown for a new convertible. And the checks from the Very Posh Store and private commissions kept me in expensive sunglasses, watches, and shoes. All in all, *good times*.

ACT THREE:

From a fashion standpoint, I had found a "look" for myself—a uniform of sorts—somewhat like Miss Ann had done in the later years of her life. Mine was very short, bleached white-blond hair (to hide the gray), black T-shirts or turtlenecks, black jeans, good tailored jackets, good shoes, good sunglasses, good watches. The watches, in my mind, replaced the jewelry I had to melt down in the lean years to fill orders. It was a look that I could go to work in comfortably, but would look hip and appropriate, if I had to go to lunch with a drop-in customer or to an event after work. It may not have been as whacky or inventive as my clothes from younger years, but it was a look that worked—besides I spent my creative efforts making clothes for other people.

However, things had started crashing to earth of late.

In the fashion biz, people love someone because they're new and different, which was me when I started selling to the Very Posh Store. Then, as it happens in the creative fields, the store wanted to turn me into something *they* thought I should be. Then came the design by committee and then the comment: "*His work has lost its sparkle.*"

That's where I was in early 1995. Creatively I had "said" what I wanted to with this particular body of work, and I was trying out new ideas. The Very Posh Store had its own ideas of my work; they wanted it different, but they wanted it to be the same. (*This is one of the dysfunctions of the fashion industry.*) All of this sucked the joy out of creating, and I increasingly felt like "Why bother trying anything new—they won't like it anyway." The Kiss-o'-Death.

To make matters worse, my agent was siding with them, even though I had to remind her who signed her checks. I realized that if I were going to advance creatively, I'd have to completely leave this entire situation behind. My big mistake in this situation was this: Everybody along the chain needs to make money, but everyone made money *from my creative output.* Everybody forgot this key idea. And by everybody, I include *me.* All the money everybody made was generated by my ideas, and I lost sight of that. HUGE mistake.

So I fired the agent, dropped the store, and cut off 90 percent of my income.

On other fronts, I was chosen to do a sewing show on PBS and made a name for myself in a different arena, so in a sense, I had other options. There was also a sewing book contract in the pipeline. And, traveling to lecture. Offshoots to my main career that didn't involve flipping burgers or scrubbing toilets. So I was lucky.

Creatively, however, my life was dark. I didn't want to create, as all the satisfaction of doing that had been drained away. In later years if one were to put photos from my archive end to end, you would spot this period immediately. Everything I made during that period was black. No color. Eventually some came to believe I had never worked with color.

My last (and final) meeting with the owner of The Very Posh Store was like going twenty rounds with a sumo wrestler. I had dressed in my most intimidating fashion-as-armor outfit: White-blond hair; big-shouldered, navy-blue pinstripe Dolce & Gabbana jacket; black turtleneck; black leather jeans; fast, pointy black boots; Rolex watch.

He was dressed in a nondescript brown schmatte and trousers, surrounded by a cloud of very expensive Scotch fumes.

The beginning went cordially enough, until he started lecturing me about firing Brenda, my agent.

"She was like a sister to me," he boomed. "You have no right to fire someone who has done so much for you. And *after all I've done for you . . .*"

That sent me ballistic. But quietly so.

"That business relationship is between Brenda and me. And besides *you've taken a markup*," I softly said.

"WHAT?!? WHAT DID YOU SAY?!?"

ACT THREE:

"You didn't buy these pieces *just because you're a nice guy*. You made money," I calmly stated. "Quite a lot."

Retail is like a dysfunctional family. In both the dysfunctional family and retail, there are certain issues one shouldn't bring up. In the family it might be that "daddy drinks." In retail any mention of money (as in the making of it, or the paying out of it by the stores) is considered unseemly. The pretense is that we are all just in it for the love of fashion. Indeed.

When I mentioned that he had made money, the tone of the conversation veered 180 degrees. Smiling, he said brightly, "I saw your gown on display at the entrance of the exhibit at the LA County Museum of Art!"

"If I remember correctly, you said that gown was 'stupid'," was my response.

And, as they say, things then went from bad to worse.

When my "audience" was over, I took a deep breath and said a quick prayer that I would get out of there without my knees collapsing, with my dignity intact. Head held high, I walked out of the store, got into the rental car, drove a block or so away, then pulled over and had a good cry. I had just jettisoned 90 percent of my business. I at least had my teaching and private clients. Or so I thought.

The trip to Paris that I had just come back from was also a disaster. I went with one of my top-paying custom clients and learned that one should *never* travel with clients. There was a fundamental miscommunication as to the intent of the trip—she expected that I was just going to follow her around, watching her blow through money.

However, I wasn't made aware of this until I hadn't done it for a few days.

She and I had a spectacular blow-up about all of this, right in the crowded plaza next to the pyramids in front of the Louvre. This resulted in me losing her as a client forever.

Great. Another blow to my cash flow.

All wasn't gloom. I did have the PBS show, the lectures and the book deal. So I could sustain myself while I was finding my way creatively and licking my wounds. Not how I planned my career trajectory, but there you have it.

So there I was, suffering from creative block, facing a complete change in my career, and contemplating possible financial ruin. (Well, perhaps I exaggerate—a bit—but it felt like that.) Life was looking very unstable and unsettled, and I was feeling disoriented and battered by events.

And I now found myself on a plane with this trembling man who I had just impulsively kidnapped. And how did I feel?

In short *I was scared out of my wits*.

We landed in San Francisco to rain and gloom. It seemed somehow fitting for what was happening.

In the car, coming home from the airport, Mark asked, "What can I do to repay you, Ken? You've saved my life."

"Oh, Mark, let's not get so dramatic. I *would* ask that you get into therapy. Therapy can help you recover from this, as well as figure out how you got into it and how not to do it again. I'm not a professional, just a friend, and can help only so much. So get into therapy! That I insist upon."

I knew I didn't have the psychological resources to do the entire job.

ACT THREE:

The first order of business when we got back was to call Robert. I got on first to tell him that Mark was here and OK, and then I handed the phone to Mark. They talked for a while, but soon I heard a change in the tone of Mark's voice. It sounded anxious and a little worried.

"He's not sure the family can give me any help," Mark said after hanging up. "He tells me that David is having none of this drama and won't be sending any money to help out. Ken, what'll I do? I don't have anything!"

"Don't worry about that now. We'll think of something," I responded cheerily. "But now we need to go to CUAV to introduce you to the people there and get you into their system. Then you need to start on the cream cheese and chocolate cake diet. We'll get a good start on that after we visit CUAV."

And away we went, starting the long journey of Mark's escape from Victor.

I realized that I had just ripped Mark out of a really horrible situation. But by doing so, I had removed any trace of normalcy or purpose in his life, such as it was. Mark didn't work the last years in LA, primarily because he was being held a prisoner of sorts by his own doing as well as Victor's. But still, in its horrible way, it was the devil-he-knew, whereas San Francisco was the devil-he-didn't-know. I had to help change that for him.

The next morning, as we were having coffee at the corner café (where I introduced him around), I gave him a task to complete—something to give him focus and purpose. Really I felt responsible for his situation, so I had to give him some structure to work with.

"Here's a map of The City," I said. "Your job this month is to choose a neighborhood, go there, and explore it. You can take more than one day to do a neighborhood if you like, but your first task is to reacquaint yourself with The City."

For the next two weeks, Mark and I had coffee in the morning, then he went off to explore. It was a real challenge for him; of late he wasn't used to even going outside, let alone going to unfamiliar places, by himself. The fear that Victor would appear was a very real one. Since LA wasn't that far away, and with Victor being crazy, it was likely that Vic might appear out of nowhere. But Mark had a task to do, and to his credit, he went out every day and covered The City.

In the meantime I had to deal with his family. The day after Mark arrived, I called Robert.

"What is this I hear about your family not wanting to help out here?" I shouted.

"Well, uh, David, you know, is tired of Mark's dramas, and told everyone else not to help . . ."

"Does David rule over everyone else? What do you think about all this?"

"Well, I'm not rich you know, and can't . . ."

"Can't *WHAT*? When I had you on the phone not two days ago, I told you I'd help, but I'm not rich either. I won't hang Mark out to dry, but I'm not going to do this alone. You blathered on about blood being thicker than water and he's family and all when Mark was still in LA. Was that all talk?

"Uh, no . . ."

"Then put up or shut up. Get them *back* on the phone. Mark is going to need, at least, first and last month's rent for a place to live. He can stay with me for a while, but I live in a *very* small place and will get charged extra rent if he stays too long. Like I said, I'm not going to hang him out to dry. But you have to help."

The very idea! I was really exasperated by this and felt like I'd been given the bait and switch. The jerk—did he think I was just going to let him get off scot-free?

ACT THREE:

It wasn't two hours later that Robert called back, singing a happier tune. It seems he stood up to the hateful David, reminding him that when one goes on and on about "family" as David had a tendency to do, part of that is actually backing words with action. (David sanctimoniously blathered on to me about family a few weeks later, the prick! And then didn't follow through with what he promised to do.) It took a couple of weeks, but Mark had some funds to start looking for a place.

In the meantime Mark slept on a futon on my living room floor. He shared the futon with Daisy,. They took to each other immediately, and Mark became "Uncle Markie" to her. He lavished all sorts of mothering on her, giving her treats, playing ball, and rubbing her tummy when they were both napping on the futon.

Daisy knew something was amiss with him. She hovered protectively, following him around the apartment. The first few nights he was living with us, I would hear him starting into a nightmare; Daisy would jump up, rush onto his futon, and start licking his face to wake him up. I'd watch her, sitting sentry over him, until he went back to sleep.

Mark had had two yorkies, Shayna and Freeway, who were now gone. He kept their photos in his wallet—that was all that was left of them. At first I didn't know what became of them (and knew somehow that it wasn't time to ask), but later Mark told me. Daisy already knew.

One day Victor got it into his head that the dogs had to go, like Mark's dog Danielle when they moved to San Francisco. He took them to the pound and had them put down. When he got home, Vic beat Mark because it cost money to have them killed!

Mark's sleeping in my living room proved fortuitous a few days later. He woke me one morning about six, saying, "Ken, there's something you need to see in the kitchen."

The lights were on. As I walked into the kitchen, I heard water running and looked up to see it cascading out of my upper kitchen cabinets like Niagara Falls. As I dialed the apartment manager, I could see the water starting to drip from the living room ceiling. Daisy started barking and running around, looking really confused.

"Get on the end of that sofa—let's get this outta here!" I shouted. My sofa was the one expensive piece of grown-up furniture I had in the apartment—from the '30s, reupholstered in mohair velvet at great expense. The two of us *just* got it out in time for the storm to break; there started a rainstorm in my apartment that looked like monsoon season in the tropics. But rain in the tropics doesn't look and smell like stale urine.

By that time the apartment manager had come and was furiously emptying out glasses from my kitchen cabinets that were filling with this nasty water. Why, I don't know. He's not too quick, if you know what I mean.

"DON'T YOU THINK YOU SHOULD SHUT OFF THE WATER?!?" I shouted as water poured down around us.

"Uh, I guess so . . . good idea," he stammered.

After the flood abated, I dressed, figuring I was awake and wouldn't be going back to bed soon. Besides, the bed and all the bedding were saturated completely with that nasty, foul-smelling water. As was the closet and all my clothes and shoeboxes. Thankfully I keep my shoes in the boxes. That's what saved them. The rain diminished and eventually stopped, leaving the entire place a wet, skanky-smelling mess, with water-streaked walls, ruined window shades, and nasty sludge on the hardwood floor.

Mark had a panicked look on his face. He looked as if he felt he had done something wrong and started to apologize for waking me.

I started to laugh.

Mark looked confused. Even Daisy looked confused.

"What else can I do?" I asked.

ACT THREE:

"Aren't you upset?"

"Well, Mark, yes, but really now, what else *can* I do? If I didn't laugh right now I could get really upset. So let's go have breakfast and then clean this mess up later."

The trouble with Victor started about a week after Mark arrived.

Victor called the studio (he didn't have my home phone) to ask for Mark.

"He's not here," I said. "He went home to Boston."

"Now, Ken, take a deep breath. You sound nervous," Vic said.

"Anyone would be nervous, talking to a nutcase like you! Victor, go to hell! And don't call back here!" I shouted and hung up.

I felt just like I did in the days when Mom and Don were together and fighting. The same churning of the stomach, the same weak knees. It was *Dances With Land Mines, The Redux*.

Robert and I made an agreement to have Vic send any communication to Robert's fax, and Robert would then forward it to me.

That way I wouldn't have to give out a fax number, as I was sharing one with my studio partner, Marshall.

The faxes started in earnest on day six and were a regular occurrence for the next six weeks, drastically increasing my expense for fax paper. They centered on several themes:

"I love you so much and want you back, and I'll be good, I promise!"

And:

"You had this whole thing planned for a long time because you've been playing around on me, you devious SOB!"

And:

"I've been so good to you for all these years, to be so cruelly treated now .

And finally:

"I'll get you back one way or another. You'll never get away!"

It was astonishing to read some of these missives, as they would whipsaw back and forth from one theme to another, sometimes in mid-sentence. Usually they were written in Vic's psychotic scrawl on unlined paper but occasionally were typed. When they were typed, there was usually an attachment of some computer chat-line conversation, "proof" that Mark was out there in cyberspace hustling guys and making fun of Vic.

(I was not online then, as this *was* 1995. My computer was one step up from the stone tablet and chisel. Mark had no access to any other computer but mine.)

Then there were the accusations that I had stolen Mark away to have him for myself.

Victor wasn't the only one who thought Mark and I were an item. Casual acquaintances, and some of the people we needed to interact with to get Mark help, assumed that I was his new significant other. The assumption was that the only reason I was helping out was that we were sleeping together. Several times I was asked about this.

My response was always an exasperated variation of "I'm good-looking enough, with enough on the ball, that I don't have to go to such extraordinary lengths to get a boyfriend!" Jeez!

ACT THREE:

I never had any interest in him "that way," absolutely not! But now, *especially* now, Mark was too damaged. I knew what he would put up with (and over time found out more about this than I ever wanted to know, oh my god!) and knew that any relatively sane man would seem to him like heaven, compared to Victor.

Sadly, though, Mark got it into his head that we might one day become an item. He broached the subject one day, by telling me of a dream he had the previous night. (*I could see what was coming a mile away.*) In this dream we ended up "doing it" after circumstances I don't remember. Then there was a tentative inquiry as to if it might be possible one day, as he felt safe with me . . .

"Mark, you're a nice guy, but ONLY IN YOUR DREAMS!" I said firmly. "It wouldn't work for me, and it wouldn't be good for you. Besides, some of the things I like to do would scare you so bad you'd flee the continent."

(Little did I know, until he told me later, that some of what Victor put him through made *me* want to flee the continent!)

Victor had a burglar alarm business with a guy I'll refer to as Big-and-Dumb. Big-and-Dumb was a former child actor who didn't make the transition to grown-up roles, probably because he was, well, *dumb*.

Mark called Big-and-Dumb one day after he arrived in San Francisco to tell him that he (Mark) wasn't with Victor any more and, therefore, wasn't watching the business. That's what Mark did during his last years in LA. While Victor would go out and carouse, Mark was the man on call if there was a problem with the burglar alarms. He also dealt with all of the books and accounts, so he had intimate knowledge of how it all worked.

What Mark also let Big-and-Dumb know was that Big-and-Dumb should do some research into how the business was set up. Victor set things up so that only HE had access to the accounts and didn't do any kind of regular reporting to Big-and-Dumb or any outside auditor. Big-and-Dumb was OK with this because he trusted Victor. (*See why I call him Big-and-Dumb?*) Also Big-and-Dumb worked for a competing burglar alarm company and had a no-compete clause in his contract. If they knew he was a partner in a competing concern, he'd get fired. So Victor agreed to keep quiet about that. Indeed.

This is what is called "plot material."

Big-and-Dumb thought that Victor was piling up all of B-&-D's share of the profits in the bank account, so he could claim them in the future. Until then they were safe, weren't they? Victor wouldn't steal from him!

Mark tried to let B-&-D know that no, they weren't safe. Vic was spending the money and not setting anything aside.

"Well, I don't wanna get involved in your disagreement," Big-and-Dumb drawled.

""I'm not asking you that; I just want to tell you to watch out for yourself, or you'll have nothing!" Mark shouted.

A month after Mark got to San Francisco, he found an apartment right across the street. He felt he wanted to be close to me for safety's sake. It was convenient, and I too felt I could keep an eye on him. And my doggie, Daisy, could go visit Uncle Markie easily. She loved her Uncle Markie already.

When he moved in, the place was painted the most abhorrent color—a cross between Pepto-Bismol-pink and lobster orange. Walls, trim, and ceilings all were painted this vile color. (*The previous tenant, who we met, was a bit peculiar.*) I thought we'd have to rip the plaster out to get rid of this hateful color, as it bled through two coats of good paint; but finally after coat three, we were able to subdue it. Then there was the issue of furniture or lack thereof.

ACT THREE:

"Great! Here I am with a place to live and not even a chair to sit on," Mark said sadly, after looking around at all the new paint. All he had then was the futon he had been sleeping on, which my friend Meryle had given him.

"Not to worry! This neighborhood is great for abandoned furniture!" I exclaimed enthusiastically.

Until it got all fancy and they started calling it "Hayes Valley," this neighborhood was known as part of the Western Addition and, therefore, a slum. When it became Hayes Valley, the quality of the abandoned furniture declined drastically. I could see Mark's nose turn up a millimeter at the idea of actually owning abandoned furniture. He raised The Eyebrow (as I took to calling it) and looked somewhat horrified.

"Now, don't worry, you'll see," I protested. "And don't get all snobby! You'll have furniture in no time."

Which we did, to Mark's astonishment. Within two weeks he had a sofa (from the freeway on-ramp across the street), an easy chair and kitchen table (from my friends Meryle and Jennifer), kitchen chairs (a neighbor sent them over), a nice occasional chair (the sidewalk), and a bed (an early birthday gift from me). Another friend of Jennifer's contributed several bolts of unbleached cotton canvas scavenged from a store going out of business, which did well for making window treatments and slipcovers. When it was all done, Mark was astonished. His place looked like a chic-on-a-budget spread in *Apartment Living* magazine. All that was missing was art on the walls and all his personal things.

Which was a problem. Victor wasn't going to let Mark come get his things. He claimed that Mark gave him everything and, therefore, Mark had nothing to come get. This we first learned from one of the many faxes, and Mark confirmed it during a phone call to Vic from my studio, with me listening on the extension. All of Mark's portfolios of work, art supplies, the remainder of his art collection (sadly diminished by years of selling things off), his clothes, his Lalique, everything—it was all in Victor's possession. Vic was using it all as a bargaining chip to get Mark back.

"Mark, this is terrible, but just pretend there was a horrible fire. You have a choice between *things* and your freedom. You can make more art. You can get more things. The family heirlooms are painful to lose, but if you pretend there was a fire, it may make it a little easier. After all, living with Victor WAS hell! And Hell has fire . . . "

Time went on, and Mark got settled into his new place.

Mark had to have a job. I helped him with a resume, but it was very difficult to make it sound coherent. There were too many long, unexplained gaps and too many jobs in too many locations that were left after a few months. Mark was trying for a position teaching art (he had taught art in a community college in Boston many years before), but the resume, however creative I was, just didn't support it. Eventually he answered an ad for catalog sales for Williams-Sonoma and got hired. He worked the telephones, selling upscale goods to bored people at all hours of the night. It was soon after getting this job that Victor started turning up in The City.

Mark called late one night really freaked out. Victor had met him at the door to his apartment building when he came home from work. It was about three in the morning, and no doubt Victor had been up here carousing—we lived near a sex club, which closed at two. (*I prefer not to say how I knew that.*) This visit started a higher level of craziness, because Vic had now come onto Mark's turf.

The phone calls continued in earnest, filling my answering machine up with crazy messages to Mark about how he had better come back or else. I had quite a file of answering machine tapes (I ended up buying them in bulk), which the people at CUAV advised us to save "just in case." It finally came to the point where Mark was advised to get a restraining order.

ACT THREE:

Since I had taken basic business law in college, it fell to me to write the statement requesting the restraining order. Mark could be his own counsel at the hearing, but he needed a statement. So one Sunday afternoon we hammered it out. As an afterthought I put in the statement a request for police protection for Mark to go get his belongings. The next day he went down to the courthouse to file it.

A restraining order, I discovered, is not worth the paper it is printed on. It works with civilized people who respect the law, but these people rarely need restraining. The crazy people, who it is supposed to protect against, are too crazy to care about any negative consequences of violating the law, and by the time they are busted, they have managed to do some damage. Restraining orders are not bulletproof, nor do they come with bodyguards. But it's the best the law can do, we were told. Cold comfort for someone fearing for his life.

The day finally came in the early summer, when Mark and I went to the courthouse to deal with the hearing. Jennifer, Mark's counselor from CUAV, was there for moral support and advice as well.

Mark was scared that Victor would show up, but thankfully Vic sent a lawyer and stayed home.

I was really nervous as well, but felt a little better when the judge came in. She was wearing a "Star Trek" badge on her robe. This was a good sign, I thought.

The hearing got underway, with Mark pleading his case and Victor's lawyer scoffing and denying everything. One point of contention was Mark's request that Victor's guns be taken away, as they posed a danger to him. Victor's lawyer claimed that Vic needed the guns for his "security" business (which was burglar alarms, not guarding property). The judge went out of the courtroom to deliberate, then came back with her decision.

"Restraining order granted but without the restriction on the guns, as Mr. Smith needs them for his business." I could see Mark blanch at that.

"Grant permission to let plaintiff go into the apartment, with police protection, to get his belongings." A murmur ran through the crowd. One lady next to me remarked at how unusual that was. Later I realized that, in the statement I wrote, it wasn't clear that the apartment was in West Hollywood, which would have been out of her jurisdiction. Victor's lawyer was indignant but signed off on the documents presented to him.

As Mark, Jennifer, and I were leaving, I stopped Victor's lawyer. I said, "We will be calling you tomorrow morning at nine, to set up a time to go get Mark's things."

With that, the three of us left the courthouse, feeling like winners.

After a light breakfast at the café the next morning (biscotti and coffee, actually), Mark and I went to my studio to call the lawyer. As Mark talked I listened on the extension. The guy wasn't very nice, nor did he want to make things easy.

Mark asked when we could go down to get his things.

"Well, I'm going to file an injunction in court tomorrow to separate this part of the decision from the restraining order, so *you're just going to have to wait!*" He had a snotty tone that implied "you stupid faggot!"

Which *PISSED! ME! OFF!* I'm one of those people who makes friends slowly, but once someone is my friend, if you mess with them, you've messed with me. That this shithead took that tone with Mark, well, that was enough to get me mad. Fighting words, for sure. Even before Mark hung up the phone, I had a plan.

Mark hung up and looked like he was going to cry.

ACT THREE:

"Hey!" I said. "He's going to court tomorrow."

"Yeah," Mark sighed.

"So *we're* going to court TODAY! Get your coat—let's go!"

Down to the courthouse we ran and to the courtroom where we were the day before. Thankfully the clerk (who plays on our team, so to speak) was there, and he remembered us.

"He's going to get some sort of injunction," Mark said.

"I cannot give you any legal advice, but you do have a valid court order," the clerk said evenly.

"But he's going to file . . ."

"I cannot give you any legal advice, but you *do* have a valid court order," he said again, more pointedly.

Doing my best Eve Arden, I perched on the corner of his desk, leaned over real close, smiled, and said, "So, Doll, if we just flew down today and *showed up* with a U-haul, this thing would work?"

"I CANNOT GIVE YOU ANY LEGAL ADVICE, BUT YOU DO HAVE A VALID COURT ORDER! " he said brightly, slightly nodding and smiling at me all the while.

"Thanks, Doll! You've been *most* helpful!" I said as I pinched his cheek. "Come on, Mark, let's go!"

As we walked briskly out of the courthouse, Mark looked bewildered. "What are you up to?" he asked.

"Correction. What are *we* up to? We have a court order, a credit card, and twenty-four hours. We'd best get busy!"

ALL GROWN UP NOW

We got to the airport at noon, after arranging for a U-Haul truck and a rental car to be waiting when we arrived in LA. While we sat at the gate waiting for the plane, I noticed that Mark had gone completely white.

It didn't take too many smarts to realize what was going through his head. He was going back into the Chamber of Horrors. I was concerned because I needed him to be present; I couldn't pull this off alone. Because, I must confess, I was feeling like I'd gotten in over my head.

I had to do something and fast.

"OK, Mark. We're in a movie," I said. "In this scene in the movie, we're going to get this guy's stuff. In the movie, you're Antonio Banderas, and I'm Brad Pitt."

He looked at me and arched The Eyebrow. Right then I knew then he was going to be OK.

"OK, OK, so I'm Tom Hanks!" I shouted. "But we're in a movie . . ."

As we were landing at the Burbank airport, the flight attendant announced, "The temperature in Burbank today is 108 degrees. Welcome to the Los Angeles area!"

Welcome indeed.

"Well, we're going into hell, so it figures it'll be hot!" Mark said.

We got the rental car from the airport and went to the U-Haul place. Once we got to the U-Haul place, Mark and I split up. While I was signing the papers and such, Mark

ACT THREE:

was talking up the Latino day laborers to get some help. Since the police were going to be involved, he made sure not to get any guys who might be wanted by "immigration."

Thankfully I had gone to the ATM to get a big wad of cash—I was sure these guys wouldn't take checks.

With all that done, Mark called the West Hollywood Sheriff's office to tell them what we were up to. We all went to the apartment, Mark in the rental car with The Laborers and me following, driving the big truck. We waited in front of the apartment building until the cops arrived.

While we were waiting, the "leader" of The Laborers asked me, "Hey, man, what's going on?"

"You know, there are times when it's better not to know?" I said.

"Yeah . . ."

"This is one of them. When this is over, you guys never saw us, and you'll get lost fast. Get it? You'll be paid well."

"OK, man . . ."

The sheriff finally arrived about 3:10 p.m. Mark went over to talk to him and show him the court order.

"I can only give you fifteen minutes," the cop said, bored. "Then you're on your own."

"You can't do that!" I insisted. "The guy is CRAZY! And he has *GUNS! LOTS* of them!" The cop perked up at that.

The local cop in my neighborhood told me once that, if you say to a cop that someone has guns, he'll get a hard-on and call all his friends to come see. That's *exactly* what happened. Within three minutes there was another cop car parked in front of the building and four officers at our service.

We all went into the building, Mark taking two of them to the back entrance, and the other two going with me to the front door. They knocked with the usual "Police, open up!"

Nothing.

They knocked again.

Nothing. We could hear Victor moving around inside.

"Break the door down," I demanded.

"We can't do that."

"Why not?"

"You have a court order to be escorted IN. If he doesn't open the door, you're out of luck."

"No way!"

"That's the way it works."

"What if I broke the door down?"

"Then we'd have to arrest you for breaking and entering."

"So if he doesn't open the door, we're screwed."

"Yeah."

Oh, *goddamn* that made me mad! I had just ripped through God-only-knows how much money on my credit card (*Visa called me the next day to see if the card had been stolen*), and there was NO. FUCKING. WAY! I was going to leave empty-handed. I had gotten this far, and I *wasn't* giving up now!

ACT THREE:

"VICTOR, YOU SPOUSE-BEATING SON-OF-A-BITCH, YOU OPEN THIS DOOR!" I shouted repeatedly while pounding loudly on the door, making as much noise as possible. If nothing else I wanted to make a stir that would attract as much as attention as possible from the neighbors. Bullies don't like people to pay attention—they might be witnesses later. So I continued pounding and yelling until we all heard a lock clicking. One officer got on his radio:

"He's opening up!" And after three more locks clicking, the door swung open . . .

At which point both cops drew their guns, pushed me aside (*very* "reality TV") and stuck the guns in Victor's face. They grabbed him and pushed him up against the wall to frisk him. Mark came around with the two other officers, and we all got inside.

What a fright the place was! It looked like an insane wild animal lived there—there was debris at least a foot deep on the floor. A scrawny black cat scampered about. From the smell of things, the cat had used the entire apartment as a litter box. (Mark told me once that the former tenant performed animal sacrifices in that apartment, why am I not surprised? The black cat and the mess reminded me of that choice bit of information.)

Two of the dining room chairs were in splinters, and there were stacks of moldy, unwashed dishes—including Mark's expensive Block china, which he left behind because it looked so thoroughly revolting. The "office" looked as if someone had pulled everything out of the filing cabinets in a rage and threw it around like confetti.

Mark started apologizing to everyone about how the place looked (it seems he cleaned one last time before he left), until I reminded him to keep on task—we weren't there to do a spread for *Architectural Digest*!

Even more frightening was how Victor looked! He was my height and usually outweighed me by at least thirty pounds, but today his skin hung on him like saggy underwear. He looked obviously ill, and for a brief moment,

I thought that he might have AIDS. I was alarmed for Mark, as with all his other troubles, to have to worry about that one as well—oh, man!

Vic demanded to call his lawyer. I wasn't too worried at this point. It was 3:30 p.m., and by the time he got the lawyer on the phone and rallied the guy to actually get to the courthouse to *do* something, it would be too late, and we would be gone. Happily, though, my mental calculations were unnecessary—Vic got the guy's answering machine! Touchdown!

I started with telling The Laborers what to take out and filling boxes as fast as I could. The "leader" was a real godsend—he had obviously done some of this before and kept the other two hopping, packing the truck like a pro.

At one point I looked up to see eight officers in that apartment. It took me by surprise, but one of them told me that they had discovered armor-piercing bullets (*very illegal*) in one of the guns. And here they were, sweltering in 108 degrees with bulletproof vests on, no doubt wanting to do some serious harm to Victor. I gave them all something cool to drink, turned up the air conditioning, and even turned on the big-screen TV for their viewing pleasure.

The "main cop" came out and said to one of the others, "We can't find all the guns registered to this creep. That means they're hidden somewhere around here. We can't leave until they're finished packing because he could still be dangerous." Such a comfort.

The Laborers and I packed up Mark's things, and Mark dealt with Victor and the police. Mark showed the police where the video cameras were hidden (one was in the thermostat that was directly in front of the front door, and the recorders were in the hall closet), and he also showed them the fake clock where Vic hid the Beretta (with no safety, Mark discovered). It was a wild afternoon. I'd love to see the videos of it—I know they exist somewhere.

At one point one of the officers asked me, "How do you know what's your friend's and what's the other guy's?"

ACT THREE:

"See this lovely piece of Lalique crystal? That's my friend's. See that photo of the naked man with the erection? That's the other guy's. I know Mark's taste. He would never display a picture like that."

"Oh."

"Now I have to get back to work!" I said as I raked off a table-full of Mark's elephant collection into a box. Not a time for idle conversation.

I made sure not to take anything that looked remotely like something Victor owned. (As you can see, it was easy to tell what was his.) If I had questions, I asked Mark, so there was a lot of stuff left when we finished up. We didn't take the big furniture like the living room, dining room, and bedroom furniture, or the big screen TV. What Mark wanted was his art collection, his portfolios, his family heirlooms, his books, his things. Victor was left with more than enough to keep on living there.

The Laborers and I were finishing up when I heard Mark get loud with Victor. "Where's the silver?" he demanded. "Victor, *WHERE'S THE SILVER?!?*"

Mumble . . .

"Ken, let's look out in the garage. His car is a beat-up VW bug."

Sure enough the silver was out in the car. Victor had some story about bringing it back from a "friend's" house, but it was obvious that he was in the process of taking things out of the house so as not to let Mark have them.

Eventually we got everything loaded, and as Mark was finishing up with the police, I was paying off The Laborers and telling them to get lost. It cost plenty, but it was worth it. They had really earned their money, make no mistake about it.

"Here you are, gentlemen," I said. "Good job, thank you very much. Now goodbye—you never saw us."

The cops waited and held Victor to give us a good fifteen minutes head start.

Mark and I had to take the rental car back to the airport before we headed back north. About a block from the airport, it finally dawned on me just what we had done. Up until that point, I was sort of on autopilot and taking care of things moment by moment. I hadn't had time to reflect on the big picture.

This was a caper that could have gone horribly wrong, getting Mark's and my brains blown out, to say nothing of the police officers'.

This was a possibility, what with the small arsenal of guns in that apartment. And the unbalanced man who possessed them. I was so overcome with what we had just accomplished (and the metaphorical bullet we had dodged) that I got dizzy, had to stop the truck, and get out. I walked back to Mark in the car. He gave me one of those "What, already?" looks.

"We did it!" I shouted. "OH. MY. GOD. WE DID IT!"

With that I got back into the truck, so we could drop off the rental car and begin the drive back to San Francisco. After we got rid of the rental car and started to get on the freeway, I suddenly felt faint.

"Mark, do you realize that we've only had biscotti and the pretzels on the plane? I can't go any further until I get something to eat!"

So after a quick stop at the In-And-Out Burger, we headed up I-5 to San Francisco.

It was midnight before we pulled up to Mark's place. Once we got home, we realized the one tiny flaw in our plan; it dawned on us that we didn't have The Laborers to help unload that damn truck. Mark had to be at work at 9:00 the next morning, so for the next five hours, we schlepped things into Mark's apartment. But when it was all said and done, we both felt pretty satisfied with the full day's work we had just finished.

A few days later, on a sunny Sunday afternoon, I was over at Mark's place, helping him unpack boxes. Looking out the window, I saw a big, ugly man,

ACT THREE:

built like a fireplug, bald, wearing a Fu Manchu moustache and mirrored aviator sunglasses. He was headed towards the building, and my hunch was that he was up to no good. I pointed him out to Mark.

"Oh, that's Ace! You remember him? He was with Julio, and they lived in the building on Burnett Street," Mark said calmly.

"You mean the private eye who used to work in a mortuary? The one with the gold-nugget pendant he wore around his neck?"

"Yeah, that's him!"

"YIKES! SHIT! Pull down the shades! Don't answer the door!" I shouted, as I ran to pull the window shades down.

I had spoken with Ace-the-Gumshoe a few days after Mark arrived. He called me at the studio and seemed to know where I lived and what was what. Ace-the-Gumshoe was also talking to Victor. Mark had told me some about him, and I remember thinking that he was someone I wouldn't want mad at *me*. Knowing his history and knowing he was a private eye, when he started calling Mark, I suggested that, however cozy the conversations got, to remember that Ace spoke with Vic as well.

"We can't *not* answer the door!" Mark said. "Besides, he's not someone to have mad at me, even though I suspect he's playing both sides."

About that time the buzzer went off. I about jumped out of my skin! Mark calmly buzzed Ace in, and I could hear him clumping up the stairs as I sat down at the kitchen table. I was feeling a little weak in the knees. Somehow facing down Victor and the possibility of getting my head blasted off wasn't as scary as this. Don't know why.

Mark let him in, and after the usual pleasantries, he introduced Ace to me, and we shook hands.

"So *you're* the guardian angel!" Ace said, grinning, his gold tooth glinting in the late afternoon sun.

"No, I'm just the one who drove the get-away car!" I shot back.

Ace stood there a few moments, hands in his pockets, coolly surveying me through the mirrored sunglasses. He finally chuckled and said,

"I have to say, as a professional . . . That. Was. GOOD!"

"Why, thanks, Ace! It's so nice to hear, coming from one who does this for a living!"

"I'm here to tell ya, Ken, Vic didn't know whether to shit or go blind! He had *no idea* that you were going to just show up like that."

"Neither did *we* until about three hours before we got there."

So Ace regaled us with tales of Victor's version of the events: about how we descended on the place like locusts (all ten—*TEN* laborers! And Mark's new boyfriend?—as well as me) and stripped the apartment of every stick of furniture, every scrap of clothing, EVERYTHING. I had to correct this version; we left quite a lot of stuff, and he could go on living there. Mark didn't *want* the soiled furniture or have *room* for a big-screen TV.

Vic was convinced that Mark and I went down to LA directly from the courthouse and had plotted and prepared for weeks to pull off this caper.

Though I was flattered that it looked like it was a more well-thought-out and planned commando raid than it was; I had to confess to Ace that it was just a last-minute thing, with no thought put into it, really. Just two pissed-off queens with a court order, a credit card, and twenty-four hours.

Our victory was short-lived. Mark got notice of a lawsuit in the mail about a week later. It was a new lawyer, and the long-and-short of it was that Victor

ACT THREE:

wanted everything back as well as damages. The text in the action said that Mark and I had taken everything when we were there—every single stick of furniture, dishes, clothing, even the last roll of toilet paper—totally cleaned out the place. Victor claimed that we left him with nothing at all. It seems he was mad as hell and wanting it all back.

Victor had lots to spend on a protracted legal hassle, what with Big-and-Dumb's profits that he was embezzling, and he was determined to either drag Mark back to LA or make his life miserable.

We went to Susan's brother-in-law, Milt-the-lawyer, who took on the case. Sadly, though, over time, Milt proved to be a huge disappointment.

It was during this period when I became an advocate for gay marriage. If Mark had been in a straight marriage, there was a body of family law to go by for the distribution of property and so forth. Their relationship would have been recognized in the eyes of the law. As it was even Mark's lawyer felt that this was just a dispute between roommates and suggested that if Mark gave back a few things, Vic would be mollified and go away.

"You don't understand," I said. "We're dealing with a nutcase here. The rules don't apply. Give him an inch, and he'll take the whole continent!"

"Aaahhh, yeah, yeah" was his very learned answer.

We were back in court and got to see Vic's new lawyer. I immediately dubbed him "Pizzaface" because he had horrible acne on his evil face. Pizzaface was a real asshole. Sadly Milt was no match for this guy, and if I didn't know he was straight, I would think he had the hots for ol' Pizzaface. He sure spent enough time with his lips puckered up against Pizzaface's ass.

The first round of court ended up with Milt agreeing to ask Mark to give up some things (above my protests). Victor had said that if Mark gave him the opals that Mrs. Thames had given them, then he would call the whole thing off.

"So why don't you just give up the opals?" Milt asked Mark.

"BECAUSE THERE ARE NO OPALS, MILT! He's crazy and knows there are no opals. This is his way of manipulating! You're dealing with a crazy man!"

"Could you get a statement from Mrs. Thames, telling the court that she didn't give any opals?"

"I'll try. But Milt—THERE. ARE. NO. OPALS. NONE."

Mrs. Thames, if you may remember, was my first customer. To refresh your memory about Mrs. Thames and her family:

As I hinted at before, Gordon was a bit of a problem for them, as he was, well, a monster. *Really Faggy*. (*REALLY, REALLY FAGGY*. You know, the kind that walks with an audible swish.) Full-on makeup before five in the evening, tons of gold chains, frosted hair, and lots of silk shirts—as Armistead Maupin would say, Gordon even had limp ankles. He was the only fag I knew who could turn an ankle while wearing flats.

Remember he had his first face-lift at age twenty-six.

Gordon claimed to be an artist, but between you and me, let's just say that an artist usually has something to say in his or her work; Gordon was still working on crudely forming the alphabet with a blunt crayon, metaphorically speaking. But that's just my opinion—his real oeuvre was cosmetic surgery.

To further refresh your memory, Mark and Vic met Gordon at a sex club in Austin, and they all had a sort of "design for living." Gordon followed them out to San Francisco, where Mark became Gordon's unofficial babysitter. (Gordon needed watching for his own good. He came up with the idea for the face-lift when left to his own devices.)

Gordon followed Mark and Vic from Austin to San Francisco and then to Long Beach, before moving to some godforsaken hamlet (spelled with twenty consonants and not a vowel in sight) outside The Hague (the one in The Netherlands) to live with a guy named Ruloph. (*No information on the color of Ruloph's nose.*)

ACT THREE:

Mark had gotten Gordon out of some serious scrapes with the law and otherwise, while he was Gordon's keeper. It was Mark who Mrs. Thames called whenever Gordon was in trouble.

So now that Mark needed help, what was her response?

"I don't really want to get involved with your quarrel. Besides, I don't make statements in writing. If you want the judge to call me, I'll talk to him, but that's the best I can do."

THAT. BITCH.

Victor had banked on that. Rats recognize weasels. It's because they're both vermin.

Even though I had given up ushering at the Opera House just a couple of years before, that didn't diminish my privileges there. As long as Susan and George worked at the Opera House, I could go any time I wanted for free. They *saw* to it that I could. And I made frequent use of this privilege. I was spoiled. I can say it now–I took it for granted.

Since Susan was keeping track of the situation with Mark, she decided that we needed an antidote to some of the drama going on.

"Darling Angel! *Do* come this Tuesday, and bring your friend Mark!" she insisted on my answering machine one day. "The Opera de Lyon is performing For the Love of Three Oranges, and it's a *must-see!* Absolutely *divine!* Come to the front door, and George will get you seats in the orchestra. We'll have drinks at intermission."

So off Mark and I went in our good clothes to see an opera I had no clue about, except to know that Susan had pronounced it "absolutely *divine.*" That's all the recommendation it needed. That and knowing that we would get to hang out for drinks with Susan and George in the bar on the box level. This in itself was worth the trip, as there was always good and lively conversation when Susan and George were around.

What an evening! Indescribable! Magical! If I could go back in time to see a performance again, this would be right up there in the top ten. Speaking of performances, Susan was in fine form during the intermission, entertaining George, Mark, and me with a funny, juicy, gossipy behind-the-scenes story about the latest opera she was performing in.

As we were walking home after the performance, Mark suddenly stopped in his tracks. I looked over to him to see what was up; he was looking back at the Opera House, which was bathed in light diffused by a veil of fog as was all of the Civic Center. This big bunch of Beaux Arts splendor was, indeed, a beautiful sight, though one that I took for granted.

There were tears in his eyes.

"It was all so beautiful," he said tearfully. "I'd forgotten how wonderful it all is."

"What do you mean?" I asked.

"This evening—you don't see it like I do. This is a regular part of your life, and for you, this is nothing special. I haven't been to an opera for eighteen years. *Eighteen years!* I haven't been out with people like Susan and George, having drinks and talking, and enjoying a wonderful opera. Like normal people. *Eighteen years!*"

"I see . . ."

"Ken, it makes me realize just how bleak my life has been. What I've missed."

Right then, I was mightily ashamed that I had taken it all for granted—now that I saw it from his point of view.

ACT THREE:

But when I thought about it later, I was thankful that I had lived the life I had lived and made the choices that brought me to this place—where the life I took for granted wasn't grim or poor, but quite the opposite. Mark helped me to see and appreciate that.

A few days later, Milt-the-idiot-lawyer called Mark to discuss the hated settlement that Mark had agreed to. He tried assuring Mark that if Mark agreed to give Vic a few things (a list was in the mail), this would settle things. Victor would be able to save face and quit his claim and be off Mark's back. Mark tried to explain to Milt that if one gave Victor an inch, he would want the whole continent. This wouldn't end things—it would just get another demand for even more stuff.

The list arrived in the mail the next day, and some of the things Vic was asking for were things he knew it would pain Mark to give up—like his mother's silver, the good Russian lacquer boxes, and some paintings Mark had done that Victor claimed Mark had given him. Other things Vic wanted were just foolishness—like the set of little gold leaf-framed mirrors.

The paintings Mark couldn't fake, but he *could* modify them in unflattering ways, which he did. For the rest I suggested that we go shopping to buy old silver plate at the thrift stores, cheap mirrors at the Goodwill that we could spray-paint gold, and fake Russian lacquer boxes from Cost Plus. Since Victor didn't have photographs of any of these items (and he certainly didn't have a discerning eye), how could he prove they *weren't* the ones he was claiming?

And since Vic was adamantly denying to his lawyer that he had video cameras around his place, I felt that these were not a threat. To present them as evidence would have been really inconvenient—it would have also shown that we hadn't completely cleaned out the house. Which is what he was alleging that we did.

I had learned my lesson with the opals. If I had been thinking better or faster, we might have ended this bullshit by just asking for an accurate description of the opals (so we knew what to get), and then going down to the wholesale jewelry suppliers and buying them cheap. It would have certainly been less expensive than burning through money in legal fees.

When the day came for the "handoff," I was out of town, so one of the guys from Mark's counseling group (*Butch, a big, solidly built, burly Texan with blond hair, blue eyes, a big smile, arms like tree trunks, and an ass you could crack walnuts on—woof!*) was there with Mark to head off trouble. Vic had come up from LA with some kid, who was about twenty-two years old and looked a lot like Mark (as they told me later). Apparently, from what the kid said, he and Vic were an item. The kid was the one appointed to collect all of the goods as the restraining order prevented Victor from doing it himself.

When it was all said and done, Vic never caught on that we had substituted quite a number of items with counterfeits. And true to form, after the handoff, Victor's lawyer, Pizzaface, called Milt and demanded yet more things, completely ignoring the agreement Mark and Vic had entered into.

After telling Milt that this was exactly what he had told him would happen, Mark fired him. (*And, I hope, stiffed him as well.*) From then on Mark would be representing himself.

The person who said that one who represents himself before the law is being represented by a fool *never had Milt for a lawyer.*

Later that first year Mark was in San Francisco, his brother Robert came out to visit. I knew Robert and his wife, Betty, on the phone but had

ACT THREE:

never met either one in person. Mark and I both were looking forward to it.

Seeing Mark and Robert together for the first time at the airport was fun and an interesting study in contrasts. Where Mark was thin and refined, Robert was robust and sporty. Mark was more quiet-spoken, while Robert was larger than life. And funny. I liked Robert immediately. On the way back from the airport, he jokingly commented in the car that I drove really fast, just like his wife, Betty, and what was all the hurry anyway?

Robert was staying only a couple of days, and Mark put him up at his place. But during this visit, a strange change came over Mark.

Mark turned into a neurotic mess, not sleeping and getting somewhat argumentative. This didn't seem to be the behavior of one who was glad to see his brother. It was most unattractive, and I was really irritated at Mark.

I found this very troubling and somewhat astonishing, as Robert was the good brother, the one who was helping out. Regular care packages would arrive from Florida, and they would contain useful things like towels and socks and soaps, as well as a good supply of really beautiful chocolates. (Robert owned a fancy candy store.) I'm sure the packages contained money as well— that would be like Robert. So to have Mark acting this way toward him was extremely puzzling.

It puzzled Robert as well.

The last day he was here, Robert wanted to take Mark to the Safeway to stock his pantry with lots of staples like flour, sugar, and what not. He asked me if I wanted to go as well, but I begged off.

"Just call me when you're done, and I'll bring the car around to drive you home," I said brightly as I waved them off.

Two hours later I got the call. When I pulled up in front of the store, what I sight I saw: Mark looking somewhat comatose and Robert looking steamed, with his eyebrows meeting in the middle he was scowling so hard.

I hopped out of the car and said, "Hello, boys! Have fun?"

Robert, looking now like something out of the Old Testament, pointed one of his thick, hairy fingers at me and boomed, "NOT A MORSEL! NOT A MORSEL SHOULD YOU HAVE FOR PUTTING ME THROUGH THIS ALONE!"

Laughing, I helped load the car. We drove home and hauled the groceries up to Mark's place in silence.

Once we got everything upstairs, I said to Mark, "You know where you want to put all of this, so I think I'm going to take Robert down to the café for some coffee. How's that? Come on, Robert, let's go!" And we got out of there and down to the café in a hurry.

Robert and I got along like a house-afire. We were gone for a couple of hours, talking about his family history and getting his side of events. I filled him in on what was going on here as well. We probably would still be there at the café talking, if it were not for my friend Meryle coming in to get us—we had forgotten that Meryle and her girlfriend Jennifer were coming over for dinner.

Next day we drove Robert to the airport. On the way back, Mark, who by this time hadn't slept in four days, was passing in and out of consciousness. At one point he mumbled, "Ken, was I a bad boy?"

"Bad boy? Mark, I think you need to get some sleep. Later, though, we need to talk."

Late in the afternoon he called me over.

"Mark," I started. "What I think you really need to explore in therapy is what is the payoff you get from suffering? I don't mean payoff in the posi-

ACT THREE:

tive sense, but there's something deep in you that needs to suffer. All you put yourself through this weekend was really unnecessary."

"I don't know what I get . . . " he said exhaustedly.

"You don't have to answer me. It's not an easy answer, I'm sure. But in therapy it might be really useful to look at this question. It might answer a lot of questions."

This period of my life wasn't all drama; there were some funny times as well.

I would occasionally drive Mark to his job working the phones at Williams-Sonoma. It was down by Fisherman's Wharf, and usually he got off late at night. The buses were somewhat erratic, so occasionally I would drive round to pick him up, even though I detested driving down there with all the tourists. There should be a bumper sticker for tourists, saying, *"I'm on vacation and so is my brain."* It would warn the locals who to watch out for.

One Friday night, though, I told Mark to take the bus home as I had a date. There was a guy in the neighborhood who I had been eyeing for some time. He worked downstairs at Stormy Leather.

Stormy Leather sold the kind of goods you might expect from a place with that name. The clothes were the usual kinky goods, but it was really fun to see how the help put their spin on the basic look. They each had their own look—there was one Betty Page wannabe complete with the black hair cut in bangs and leopard print, Jantzen-style bathing suits worn with fishnet stockings and high-heeled platform pumps; one gal had fluorescent magenta hair and wore black bustiers with black PVC circle skirts and towering fetish boots; there was another gal who had the "Heidi-Gone-Bad" thing going with the blonde braids, dirndl, and black combat boots. It was a fun, kinky fashion show down there. Good neighbors, too.

In our building my floorboards were *literally* their ceiling—no insulation or anything, so sound traveled. I got to hear lots of "product testing" after hours. (Most distracting.) They also had seminars on aspects of the S&M culture. (Most informative—I learned that cotton clothesline, when run through the washer and dryer, gets really soft and pliable, making *excellent* bindings.)

More entertaining, though, were those times when suburbanite couples from Walnut Creek went there to "walk on the wild side," only to get stuck inside a latex outfit one or the other had been trying on. (No talcum powder.) I'd hear the cries for help and laugh about the commotion made to get the poor unfortunate out of the outfit without cutting it apart. (*How humiliating for them.*)

Anyway this guy worked at Stormy Leather, so I would see him on a regular basis. Going to work or leaving. Big, burly, hairy, rode a Harley—well, I worked up the nerve to say to him one day that he looked like he would be a fun ride, on or off the motorcycle, and where could I get my ticket? He blushed when I said that (*quite refreshing, I thought*), so we set a date for that Friday.

Mark was a bit surprised to see me waiting for him when he got off work and started quizzing me about the date in the car on the way home. It was one of those rare balmy nights in the summer in The City, and I had the top down with the windows down as well. Every other car seemed to have the windows down as well—it was really balmy.

"Well, how did the date go?" he asked with that "Tell!" tone of voice.

"I don't want to talk about it."

"Oh."

We rode on in silence, but Mark practically bored a hole in the side of my head with that stare of his. He asked again, this time at a stoplight on a crowded intersection on Van Ness. He wasn't giving up.

ACT THREE:

"He was, well, *lacking*," I responded.

"Lacking? Lacking what? Was he nice?"

"Yes."

"Then, what?"

"HE DIDN'T HAVE A PENIS!" I shouted.

Not one but both of Mark's eyebrows shot up at this. Heads turned in all the surrounding cars (*remember, windows down*), and no one moved when the light turned green. They were all listening.

I had to shout and pound the steering wheel, I was so exasperated at the turn of events.

"IT'S NOT ENOUGH THAT I HAVE TO MAKE A LIST OF WHAT I'M LOOKING FOR IN THE IDEAL MATE, BUT NOW I HAVE TO PUT ON THAT LIST THAT *HE MUST HAVE BEEN BORN WITH HIS OWN PENIS!*"

What I found out (thankfully before things got too far) was that my dream date turned out to be a female-to-male transsexual. (My thought was *"Do the math—is this addition or subtraction?"*) Now I don't have anything against gender reassignment, but conceptually most of the plans I had for the "shared activity" portion of the date involved a working penis and not the latex, detachable model.

With that we had to change subjects as we were creating a traffic jam.

Another night the director's cut of David Bowie in *The Man Who Fell to Earth* was playing at the Castro Theater. Since I had never seen it, and knowing that a director's cut of a movie gives one more points when renewing one's Gay Card, I suggested to Mark that we go. He was game for seeing it, since, with his recent background, he had little opportunity to get the required number of points to keep his Gay Card current. He was seriously in arrears.

We ran into Jennifer, his counselor at CUAV, and her partner, Diane, in the street before the movie. When I told them what we were seeing, they gave me a funny look, which I just interpreted as puzzlement about the Gay Card thing. Lesbians don't have to get a Gay Card—there's a special exemption.

So here we were in this movie, which I can only describe nicely as interminable. At one point I thought I had died and gone to Hell, only to watch this cipher of a film into eternity.

We were into the film at two hours forty minutes when it happened:

For those not familiar with the "story," Bowie is an alien (what a stretch!) who somewhere in the first hour or so gets involved with this neurotic brunette. At one point she sees him without his "human suit," looking all slimy and repulsive.

After screaming in terror, she decides he looks really hot after all and "does it" with him.

(I'm sure this is the inspiration for the line in Julie Brown's song "Earth Girls Are Easy," where she says, "He still was disgusting, but I didn't CARE!")

Later in the "story," Bowie is captured by the government and is going quickly off his head. The girl comes to rescue him, and when she gets there, she finds him in a bedroom watching a television, holding a highball glass filled with scotch. He's stirring it with a gun.

OH. MY. *GOD!*

I was horrified!

ACT THREE:

I looked over at Mark, who had gone completely WHITE!

Bowie put the gun to the girl's head and said, "You know, I could kill you right now, and nobody could do anything about it."

Appalled, I looked over again to see sweat pouring off Mark's face.

"Come on, let's go!" I said, pulling on Mark's sleeve. "Let's GO!"

So the two of us fled the theater and stopped on the sidewalk. I started apologizing. I felt like I had just taken a Holocaust survivor to a castration film.

Mark started laughing, even though he was still shaking. Nervously so did I. It was both funny and horrible at the same time, and I was glad that Mark had a sense of humor even as he shook off the trauma the movie had reminded him of.

And he had gone through some trauma, oh-my-god.

As I said earlier, I had asked him to get some therapy to recover from his ordeal, and Jennifer at CUAV got him into a group of gay men survivors of domestic violence. This was good for him, but at the same time it caused him to face what had happened to him. There were times that he would recover a memory during the meeting; these were times he would ask me over to his place afterwards, just because he didn't want to be alone. He would just want to talk, so I let him talk.

Remember the cycle of violence I told you about earlier? It seems that the first cycles are of long duration (over months) and get progressively shorter over time. In Mark's case, the cycles started out happening over a very long period, so he couldn't see the pattern. Later, though, near the end before I went to get him, the cycles became so short that life looked like the spin cycle in the washing machine. The things Mark told me about what he went through during these cycles at Victor's hands—*they* made my head spin!

CUAV told me that when dealing with someone who was going through this ordeal, one shouldn't react to what is said. If one were to get upset at hearing what the person had gone through, they may be reticent to tell any more in fear of upsetting. The proper reaction was one of concern but not upset.

This tested me on a regular basis! It was beyond my comprehension that someone who claimed to love someone could do some of the things Vic did to Mark, and also beyond my comprehension that someone could sit still for them. It was difficult enough to sit still while *hearing* about them. It was a thorough look into the deep recesses of the human mind, those cesspools where invention turns ugly and evil with ways to harm and torture.

This I contrasted with some of the supposed "tortures" that I heard about from some of my idle women customers.

One woman, who I'll call Meg, used to complain that her husband made her drive a car (a Jag convertible at that) that was three years old! And she was only limited to two trips to San Francisco from Southern California a month! She was obviously hard done by. So Meg would complain bitterly to me about how abused she was. Until one day.

I had not gotten to sleep the night before because Mark had been up talking half the night, telling me of one particularly gruesome torture he had remembered.

"I was raped WITH A LOADED GUN by my spouse, and he had his finger on the trigger the whole time, and said to me, 'keep your legs in the air so I can keep my finger in the trigger' ", he said.

I spent the other half of the might walking the streets, trying not to go buy a gun to go kill Victor after what Mark had just told me. So I wasn't feeling up to any nonsense when the phone rang.

ACT THREE:

It was Meg, and she started in. When she got good and wound up, I stopped her and asked, "Meg, have you considered volunteering in a women's shelter?"

"Why, no. But funny you should say that—my therapist suggested it just the other day," she said *totally without irony*.

"Perhaps you might consider it. When you hear something like 'I was raped at gunpoint by my spouse,' or better yet, 'I was raped WITH A LOADED GUN by my spouse, it might just give you a little perspective on your own situation. I know that when I hear something like THAT, my life looks PERFECT!"

And then I slammed the phone down.

There were the triumphs . . .

When Mark got to San Francisco, we would go to the corner café; he hung out there a lot more than I did, as his schedule made it possible. In this café all the neighborhood artists hung their work on a rotating basis.

One day I suggested that he might want to exhibit. At first he was reluctant; it had been quite a few years since he had done any art and was afraid that he might not be able to do anything.

"There's no reason not to start!" I said. "You won't know if you don't try. Besides, since you have trouble sleeping anyway, why not do something you might enjoy to keep you company? It's better than pacing the floor and stewing!"

So he rounded up some art supplies and started making art. At first I could tell he was self-conscious about it, but as time went on and he built up some new work, I could tell he was feeling more confident.

Then one day he called with the announcement:

"I'm showing at the café in April!" he crowed. "We're opening on April 7th."

It would be one year to the day from when he left Victor.

One of the baristas at the café was a guy named Bill. Bill was a nice-enough guy, but he happened to be a heroin addict. Now I think it's OK to be friendly to a heroin addict, but one is not *friends* with a heroin addict. Since Mark was hanging around the café a lot, he got to know Bill-the-Junkie and eventually invited him over for dinner.

Mark was taking Clonapin, a very expensive anti-anxiety drug. I'm sure this fact came out in conversations with Bill-the-Junkie. It seems that heroin addicts really like this stuff if they can't get the heroin.

Mark cooked him dinner that evening and the next day discovered a whole bottle of the Clonapin—which Mark was paying for out of his own pocket as he had no health insurance—missing from his medicine cabinet. This caused Mark some more anxiety.

Mark asked Bill-the-Junkie if he took the bottle, and to his credit, Bill-the-Junkie owned up to it, saying something like he did it to sell for some more junk. Sadly he didn't bring it back or offer to replace it. What amazed me was that Mark still spoke to him after that, let alone still regarded him as a friend!

ACT THREE:

About the time this happened, one of the guys from Mark's support group, who I'll call Charlie, needed a place to stay. He was changing apartments (to flee the abuser he was saddled with), and Mark took him in.

One night I was over visiting (I did that a lot because Mark was a good cook and let me do my "Kitchen Blonde" routine without rolling his eyes), and the three of us were sitting around after dinner talking. I casually asked Mark about a date he had recently set up (with a doctor! Definitely a good candidate!).

Mark hesitated. I looked at Charlie, who was giving him a look.

"Well, how did it go?" I insisted, smelling a rat.

"Oh, you know . . ." He avoided my gaze, waving the question away.

"Oh, c'mon, Mark. Tell 'im!" Charlie said.

"Tell me what?"

"I didn't go."

"And *why*, may I ask? Were you ill?"

"No . . ."

"What, then?"

Charlie piped up.

"He was haulin' Bill outta jail."

"What? And why, may I ask yet again?"

The story tumbled out that Bill-the-Junkie had gotten strung out and was found unconscious, facedown in a gutter somewhere, and hauled in as a nuisance. Mark got the call to help out, as Bill-the-Junkie had nobody else he could call, what a surprise.

Boy, that got me mad. "So you're telling me that, given the choice between going on a date with a doctor who was probably very nice and bailing out this junkie who, if you don't recall, STOLE FROM YOU, you chose the junkie!"

Silence. Charlie was watching all of this intently.

"Well, he needed help," Mark ventured weakly.

"And didn't *you* need help in the form of that very expensive prescription he stole? And did he offer to either give it back or replace it? I think not."

"Well . . ."

Charlie was still very quiet. He was no weatherman but no doubt sensed a storm was brewing.

"Well, I'm mad now, and I have to say something, and you're going to listen. Mark, what IS it you like about fixer-uppers?"

"Fixer-uppers? What do you mean?"

"Victor was a fixer-upper. I remember you telling me that he didn't even have a decent pair of shoes that wasn't duct-taped together until you bought him some. You came from a good family; he was white trash. You enjoyed art and opera; he favored video games and sex clubs. Your entire relationship, from where I was standing, looked like an exercise in ignoring facts and trying like hell to fix him. Something that you never could do. Never *can* do."

"Uh . . ."

"I'm not finished! So here you are now, and you chose a junkie WHO STOLE FROM YOU as a friend, and chose to haul him out of jail over a doctor who was probably very nice and would have treated you well, and if he had

ACT THREE:

turned out to be a junkie no doubt *HAD HIS OWN SOURCE OF DRUGS*, thank you very much! What were you thinking!"

Charlie spoke. "What do ya mean by 'fixer-upper'? I haven't heard that before."

"It's a real estate term, meaning you buy something cheap that has potential and fix it up. It works with real estate and sometimes with furniture you find on the street, but not with men like Victor or Bill-the-Junkie—no potential."

"Mark," Charlie said. "Ken has a point! I hadn't thought about it myself, but that's what I was doin'. I kept hopin' that I could make 'im better until he pushed me down the stairs and broke my arm."

Mark sat silent throughout all of this, chain-smoking, with his arms and legs crossed. He didn't look at either of us.

"Forgive me if I sound like your parents or like I'm lecturing, but I just don't understand. Help me understand why you made that choice, Mark," I said.

"Because he needed help. You've helped me, and I want to help someone else. Bill needed help, and that's why I helped him. You yourself said that as payback you wanted me to help someone else."

"Yes, I did. And I wasn't specific about who and why. My mistake. So now I'll clarify. I chose to help you because I knew that you were someone who would actually DO something with the help. Your show at the café is evidence of that. But when you decide to help someone, it needs to be someone who the help will benefit. In Bill's case you didn't really help him, you just got him out of a jam. There's a difference. He'll do this again. He's a junkie. A lost cause."

Silence from Mark.

"Besides I helped you because I had gotten to a point in my life where I had built up enough—for lack of a better way of putting it—capital, emotional capital.

I could spend a little of the interest helping you and not dip into principal. You need to spend the time to develop the principal. Once you're on a firmer footing, then help someone; but don't dip into principal, and don't squander it on lost causes."

Mark's taste for drama made me crazy sometimes.

There appeared a guy who Victor hired to come beat Mark up. I found out about the first time when I returned from a business trip. Mark mentioned it in a casual offhand manner during coffee, after picking me up from the airport, causing me to choke on my scone.

It seems the guy approached him at the bus stop and asked Mark if he was, indeed, the Mark who was showing at the café. Since Mark's show was still hanging at the café, this didn't seem strange, and Mark let down his guard. When Mark told him "yes," the guy told Mark that Victor had sent him, that he would come back again and again until Mark returned to Victor. Then, in broad daylight at a bus stop, he proceeded to attack Mark. What astonished me was that nobody helped out or called the police.

Since it was only hours since this happened, I insisted that Mark file a police report. One thing I learned from all of this was that if there is no paper trail, an abuser will hide behind the "there's no proof!" defense. Victor's lawyer, Pizzaface, was playing this one to the hilt, saying that Mark was making up all of this and poor Victor was the real victim. So off to the police station we went.

About a week later Mark came home from work and related the most recent ordeal. That morning when he was getting ready for work, Mark looked out the window to see the very same thug leaning against *my* building, swinging an aluminum baseball bat and waiting. And what did Mark do?

He went out.

ACT THREE:

I was so mad that I could hardly restrain myself.

"Why didn't you call me? We could have both ganged up on him, caught him, and called the police. Then this business with Victor could have ended. Guys like that thug wouldn't hesitate to rat Victor out if it meant they would get a better deal, and it would prove to the court that you're telling the truth."

"I didn't want to upset you."

"Well, I'm *more* upset NOW! We lost a good opportunity to end this stupid legal battle. Between the two of us we could've captured him! Dammit!"

There were a couple more incidents, which were duly reported to the authorities, but the police never got the guy. I'm sure they get these types of things all the time. It *is* galling though. But at least there was a paper trail, which I was grateful for later.

These attacks were mentioned in court but by Mark instead of Milt. Milt had been fired because he still insisted on defending Pizzaface to Mark instead of the other way around. The legal battles that started with the restraining order were incessant, with no end in sight. Mark said Vic probably thought that Mark would get tired of the harassment and go back to LA, just to get Victor off his back.

This whole drama with Mark and Vic played out during the time of the O. J. murder trial and all of the publicity it generated. One couldn't escape it, which I wanted to do—I had my own drama to deal with. Daily on the radio and TV (I didn't have a TV and was glad of that) we heard all the grisly details of how Ms. Simpson and her friend were brutally murdered. Mark and I didn't discuss it—the topic was too close to the bone for him. But, of course, there would arrive the day of the verdict.

I remember where I was when I heard the O. J. verdict—I was standing in my studio, working on a project, when I heard it over the radio. I was dumbstruck, to say the least. To me it was obvious that someone with tons of money just got away with murder.

Later I went over to visit Mark and found him in a real state. Obviously he had a better understanding than I did about these things. He was sure thinking about the issue, to be sure.

"Ken, Victor is going to get away with all of this," he said in a small, scared voice. "He has lots more money than I do, and that's really what this is all about."

"No, I can't believe that," I said, not too convincingly. I didn't want to believe that money trumps justice, despite the evidence of the O. J. verdict.

Victor wasn't wealthy, but he did, indeed, have more resources at his disposal than Mark did. Vic also had a lack of mental stability, which made him unpredictable at best and dangerous at worst. This lack of stability seems to give these people the persistence and stamina to keep going when sane people would have given up or resolved a dispute.

A friend of mine tells me there are four kinds of outcomes: I win, you win; *or* I lose, you win; *or* I win, you lose; *or* I lose, you lose. The first three outcomes are for rational people. But the "I lose, you lose" combination is the irrational outcome. When confronted by someone who has that "I lose, you lose" mentality (like Victor), know that he or she is crazy. The only defense is to get away as far and as fast as possible. There's no defending against these types of people—there's no reasoning with them—and there's no way of coming to any sort of agreement.

This is what I was slowly learning during this whole hateful legal tangle—when dealing with crazy people, you just need to get far away. There's no predicting what they will do and no fighting them, unless you are part of the Mafia and have no qualms about fitting someone with cement shoes. Now *there's* a solution.

ACT THREE:

In the fall of '96, Big-and-Dumb started calling Mark. Remember Big-and-Dumb? The one Mark tried to warn about Victor? Well the predictions Mark made came true, and Victor had siphoned off all the profit that was due Big-and-Dumb. No doubt part of it went to pay the hourly rates of Pizzaface, which was what Mark feared would happen.

Big-and-Dumb wanted Mark's help in getting the goods on Victor. Mark had literally run the business while he was still in West Hollywood, since Victor spent most of his time in sex clubs or otherwise cruising for men. So Mark knew how the accounts were set up, where they were, all of that. Big-and-Dumb's lawyers wanted Mark to tell all. Mark told them, under one condition: they had to put Victor in jail. If they didn't, he told them, Victor would surely do harm, and no doubt, it would be fatal. Big-and-Dumb promised to do just that, so Mark began a series of conversations with them to help crack the case. It was determined that Vic had gotten about $200,000. So far.

A few weeks later Mark called me at work—he was in a panic.

"Ken, they're not going to put Vic in jail!"

"WHAT?!?"

"Pizzaface recommended some sleazy, killer lawyers down there, and they are saying that, yes, Vic did take all that. Now if Big-and-Dumb doesn't sell the business and give Vic half, he is going to tell Big-and-Dumb's boss, and with the no-compete clause, Big-and-Dumb will be out of a job."

"Good God! This is terrible! What's his phone number?"

After I got off the phone, I called the idiot. After a few pleasantries, I got down to business.

"What's this I hear that you're giving in to Victor's blackmail demands?"

"There's nothing I can do," he whined. "I need the job."

"You should have thought about that when you started doing business, knowing that you had a no-compete clause. Besides Mark tried to warn you over a year ago that Victor was robbing you blind, but you wouldn't hear any of it. Now you've not only lost a business, but you've put my friend in danger."

"I think you're exaggerating," he said petulantly.

"I'm surprised that you know HOW to think. Know, sir, that paying blackmail will never make them go away; it just puts them on the payroll. And as for Mark, know this: IF ANYTHING HAPPENS TO HIM, HIS DEATH WILL BE ON YOUR SOUL."

And I slammed down the phone.

Remember Mrs. Thames? She popped up as well during that time. It started with a call about Gordon.

"She thinks Gordon has AIDS," Mark told me. "Ruloph isn't allowing him to go to the doctor for any kind of treatment; he says he can handle things because he's a nurse."

"Sounds like he wants to snatch the house and the bank accounts. Don't they have marriage for gays there?"

"Yeah. And he stands to get the house, all the art, the jewelry, and the bank accounts. So he has a reason not to get Gordon to a doctor."

ACT THREE:

"So what did you say to her?" I asked.

"What could I say? I told her about the new drugs to combat AIDS, but Gordon has to be here to get them. She, of course, wants to talk to her daughter who's a nurse in Texas about all of this. Texas, the center of the universe when it comes to AIDS research."

A few days later Mrs. Thames called back. She was more insistent this time that Mark help her out. Mark told me of the phone conversation over dinner at his place one evening.

"Fuck her! She has one helluva nerve!" I yelled. "When *you* needed HER help, all she could do was make excuses. She 'didn't want to get involved'."

"But she needs help . . . "

"And this time, Mark, if you help her it will cost her. She's gotten the free ride long enough."

"Ken, she wants me to go to The Netherlands to try to talk Gordon into coming back to the States. But I don't think he could be convinced as long as Ruloph is there."

"Well, Doll, we could kidnap him. Like I did with you. It would be a little more complicated, crossing the International Date Line and all that, but we could do it. BUT *not until you see a briefcase with $50,000. In cash.* And expenses. That cash could be your nest egg."

"Are you serious?" Mark gave me The Eyebrow.

"Sure I am! We could do it. Let's see, in the movies, for something like this, they would call Interpol. Call Ace and ask him about Interpol, if it's a real thing, and how he would pull this one off. I'm sure we would need someone who spoke the language to meet us there, and a car and all that, but we could do it. Ace will know how to arrange it—besides it's one of the expenses. *BUT* I want to see that briefcase full of cash. I think that would be a cool sight."

Mark made calls to Ace-the-Gumshoe and Mrs. Thames. Mark felt this was a good time to do it for a lot of reasons. First, Victor had been calling him, threatening again, after Big-and-Dumb paid off. Mark would be out of town for a while, far, far away. Out of Victor's reach.

Second, it was nearing the Christmas season, and that was a good cover for the visit. We would buy a lot of presents to bring Gordon and Ruloph, and nobody would refuse friends who showed up at the house unexpectedly with armloads of gifts. That would get us in. We would have some expendable luggage, as we would eventually be leaving all our clothes there when we snatched Gordon, so as not to arouse suspicion.

Once we were in, we would take Gordon out alone for drinks or shopping and get him to go with us. Mrs. Thames could arrange for a new passport for Gordon, as he would no doubt not have his on him when we snatched him. She had the connections to do that. It could work.

Mark made the final phone call to the Thames household one evening, and I sat in his living room while he was talking. From the one side of the conversation I was hearing, it sounded like they were having second thoughts. It took awhile, but eventually Mark got off the phone with a bewildered and somewhat horrified look on his face.

"They're going to let him die," he said quietly.

"Oh, no!"

"Yes. They didn't come out and say it in so many words, but between the lines, they said that if they brought him back home, they then would have to deal with the monster they had created, throwing money at him all those years. Mrs. Thames claimed that they didn't have the money, but I know she does, in an account she keeps in Saskatchewan—an account I reminded her of while I was still on the phone."

I wondered while listening to Mark's side of the conversation just what that comment meant, but Mark explained later. What Mrs. Thames didn't know was that by this time Mark had a better job, working in the online banking department at Wells Fargo. He worked the phones on the late shift so had time to do some snooping in his spare time. That's how he found out that little tidbit. Mrs. Thames had a million five in that account.

That Thursday during the second week in December was unexceptional. Mark was cooking dinner for me and two of his friends. Nothing special, just roast chicken and vegetables. Four guys hanging around a kitchen table, eating and gossiping, the most normal thing in the world. The main entertainment was my purple hair, which I had dyed just the day before. It was, as my friend Susan would say, an *unfortunate* choice.

Mark was excited as he had just talked to the head of the fashion department at Cañada College, and they had set up an interview—he would be teaching draping in the spring. Things were finally going in the right direction for him!

I noticed something different about Mark that evening. Usually he was the consummate host, always hopping up to get something, worrying over his guests, but at the same time, a bit anxious. This evening, though, he was relaxed, laughing, just hanging out with his friends, and didn't seem to have a care in the world.

Looking at him across the table, I thought to myself, "He's going to be OK now. This is the Mark I remember from all those years ago."

This is what Mark wanted in life: to do his art and enjoy his friends, the most normal, ordinary things in the world. That evening it looked like he was going to be OK no matter what.

We all left about ten thirty.

ALL GROWN UP NOW

I had just gotten into bed when he called.

"Ken, I'm having the mother of all anxiety attacks! Victor just called, and the pain in my arm is unbearable. Could you come over?"

It took me a few minutes to dress and go over, and I must admit I was feeling a bit exasperated. Mark had had many of these anxiety attacks during the past few months—they manifested themselves as a severe pain in the right arm. Many times he couldn't hold so much as a pencil or paintbrush, but eventually the attack would go away, leaving him weak for a few days. Since he didn't have health insurance and couldn't afford a visit to the doctor, he didn't go have this checked out—just thought that they were anxiety attacks and left it at that.

So, as I said, I was a little exasperated as I went across the street. This lasted until I went in.

Mark didn't look good. He'd gone all gray and sweaty, and was throwing up in the bathroom, and his arm was really hurting him. I asked him what he wanted me to do, and he said he didn't know, so I called 911.

"I think he's having a heart attack," I said to the dispatcher.

"Well do you know for sure whether he is or not?"

"That's a stupid question. I'm not a doctor, but his right arm is hurting and he's throwing up; could you get someone here NOW?"

While we waited for the paramedics to arrive, Mark looked at me and said, "Ken, you don't know what it's like, knowing that one day I'm going to walk round a corner and have my brains blown out. You can't understand what that's like."

It took about five minutes for the paramedics to arrive; the buzzer rang and I went to greet them. One of the guys was obviously straight. He took one look at my purple hair and copped an attitude. When he saw Mark, who,

ACT THREE:

you remember, weighed all of 105 dripping wet, you could see it on this guy's face: "AIDS." His expression was one of someone who was being subjected to an unpleasant smell.

They made a show of examining Mark and had him sign some sort of disclaimer. Straight-guy said to me, "We can take 'im in, but it's a real expensive cab ride..."

"Then goddamn get outta here! I'll take him in myself!"

I bundled Mark up and took him to the emergency room, where the (really good-looking and very hunky) doctor and two nurses started moving real fast.

I sat with Mark in the emergency room while they were working on him. He was feeling really cold, so one of the nurses got every blanket she could lay her hands on to cover him, all the while joking that when he got out of there he should EAT SOMETHING, as she could play xylophone on his ribs. The nurse and I joked about whether or not the doctor might be persuaded to ask Mark out once all of this was over—it would give him a reason to get better quickly, I thought. The nurse joked that more than one cardiac patient's heart beat much stronger when that particular doctor was in the room. Woof!

Really, though, I was joking because it never occurred to me that anything could happen to Mark—he was in good hands now. In a bad way for the time being, of course, but once they got him the proper care, he'd be OK. Distracting him by joking about the doctor also kept him from mentally starting down the road of how he didn't have any insurance, and how could he pay for this?

Later they put Mark in intensive care and got him settled in for the night. Night really was turning into early morning—it was about 4:30 when I left to go home. I stopped for breakfast on the way home, as I figured that the morning would be busy, what with calling Robert and getting Mark's personal things up to the hospital. After breakfast I went home and to bed.

About seven o'clock I awoke from a dream I was having. In the dream Mark was telling me that he had to go. I was arguing that, no, this wasn't AIDS; it was a heart attack. The doctors could fix it! Don't go! They can do something about heart attacks!

But in the dream Mark looked at me and said, "No, Ken, it's time for me to go."

And I woke up.

Bummed by that bad dream, I got out of bed, got dressed, and took Daisy out for a walk. We went over to Mark's place to call Robert and pick up some things to take over to Mark. I picked up the phone, and there was a message.

It was the hospital.

I called and asked for the nurse in charge, and they rang me through to him.

"Mr. King, your friend died at 6:57 this morning. I'm so sorry."

I couldn't speak. That knocked the wind out of me.

"Are you all right?" he asked.

I took a breath.

"As well as can be expected," I gasped.

"We need for you to come over and take care of a few matters sometime this morning, when you feel up to it."

ACT THREE:

So this is was how it was going to end.

Surprised!

Angry!

Abandoned.

Widowed. (*There—I said it.*)

Even though we weren't "an item," we were a couple in a way. That I went through all of the chaos and the disruption, only to have him die on me—that was hard to take. (Hard to take? *Hard to take!?* Actually it hit me like a linebacker in the stomach.) This wasn't the way it was supposed to end.

Looking back, though, I can understand why he didn't want to go on. It took tremendous courage to leave Victor and even more courage to try to make up for lost time, to rebuild a life that was scattered and squandered on a relationship that, at best, didn't make sense, and at worst, was a living nightmare. The abuse started soon after Mark and Vic moved to San Francisco, so violence and abuse were all Mark knew for almost two decades. Everything else that he valued or enjoyed was drowned in that vortex of psychosis.

Mark felt that he would never escape Victor as long as he was alive, and perhaps dying free was the best he could do. He was certainly free of Victor now.

The one thing I wanted to do for him was to make him feel safe, so he could work to rekindle any sparks of his spirit and his art that may have survived the cold decades of his life with Victor.

But I took on a job that I couldn't do, and in the end, I felt impotent. I couldn't fix Mark's situation, just as I couldn't fix my mother all those years ago. I thought back all those years to my therapist, Dennis, who made that particular connection for me.

Mark did fix the situation in the best way he knew how—he left. He's safe now.

As it was, I couldn't break down, as there were practical matters to attend to. (I get criticized for this sometimes. People think I'm cold and heartless—I'm not. It's just that when things need to be taken care of, I learned long ago, to set the immediate feelings aside, to deal with later, offstage, out of public view.)

First I had to call Robert to break the news. This was really hard; at first Robert assumed that Vic had killed Mark. (I truly believe Victor killed Mark but not in the usual way.) Then there was going over to deal with the business at the hospital, which I had to do myself. Back from there I had to clean Mark's place, because he hadn't had time to clean up after the dinner. I didn't want Robert to see the place a mess—Mark would have died all over again of embarrassment! I had to clean my place as well, just in case Robert wasn't comfortable sleeping at Mark's.

Then there was the issue of my hair.

It wouldn't have been fitting to meet Robert, who had just lost his brother, wearing my fluorescent purple hair. There was no time to bleach it out or dye it, so I just shaved my head. To my horror I discovered that I had *a hairstyle-shaped purple stain on my scalp*. I spent the next thirty minutes scrubbing my scalp with a Scotchbrite pad and Comet. Most of it came off—the stain, not the scalp.

ACT THREE:

It's astonishing how estranged families come out of the woodwork to stake their claim to the dead. In Mark's case, David-the-hated-brother decided, while Robert was in the airplane and, therefore, not able to communicate, that he would make all the burial arrangements. He called me to tell me what he had decided.

"Does Robert know about any of this?" I asked.

"Well, no, because we can't reach him."

"I find this interesting that you made decisions without asking Robert, knowing he couldn't be reached."

"Well, you've been a good friend to Mark, but now we'll take over from here."

Boy, *that* felt like a pat on the head and a thank-you-very-much-now-go-away. With that I think David felt he had dismissed me, and I would go away quietly— he was used to the people in his life doing just that. Instead, very pissed-off, I rang up the hospital and informed the man in charge that Robert had the power of attorney, and if the body was relinquished to David, there would be hell to pay. It was Robert who would decide, as it was Robert who was there for Mark.

"We get this all the time," the man at the hospital said wearily. "It happens every day. I'll make sure your wishes are respected—we know how to deal with people like him."

Not twenty minutes later, I got another call from David, telling me in his voice-of-god-lawyer-voice not to interfere with their wishes, how dare I! Happily my machine picked it up, so I didn't have to deal with that odious man.

Robert came into the same terminal as he did the last visit. We hugged and went down to get his luggage. Watching for his bags at the carousel, I at first didn't notice him—he was closely inspecting the side of my head with a quizzical expression.

"What?" I asked.

"Purple?"

"So I missed a few spots with the Comet." We both laughed. Robert still had a sense of humor, even in such a situation.

In the car on the way home, I filled Robert in on what had transpired while he was on the plane, and he anxiously joked about how fast I was driving—what was the hurry? When we got in, he called Betty, his wife, to check in as well. She gave him the rest of the dish about what David was up to. It seems David had decided that Mark would be buried next to his mother after a big, orthodox funeral in Boston.

I'm sure *that* would be a strange affair. Mark hadn't been back to Boston since the early 1980s, right before he moved to Long Beach. When he visited then, it was suspected that he had "GRID," which is what they called AIDS before AIDS. Mark was treated as a pariah and a leper, and I'm sure any linens he touched were burned, any dishes he used broken or thrown away. So now all these people from his distant past would be invited to this memorial, and no doubt would be puzzled as to: Why? What? Who was he? Did he die of AIDS?

Not much information would be forthcoming from the family (Robert wasn't going to be there, and David had no clue). All sorts of speculation would hover unspoken over that particular funeral. I felt bad for Mark, even though he wasn't going to be there. The idea of strangers gawping at his "funeral" was too unseemly to contemplate.

"The rabbi wasn't even born when we went to Temple there," Robert fumed. "How could he know Mark? What could he say about him? This is just a show for David! Nothing more!"

Robert and I decided to have a memorial in my studio for Mark, which I hastily assembled. It was to be the following Sunday, two days hence.

ACT THREE:

There was the apartment to empty out and Mark's affairs to settle. He died with no will but also no assets, so it was pretty easy to do. Robert and I went to the Social Security office to declare Mark dead, so Victor couldn't use Mark's Social Security number. There also was the funeral home to deal with, to get the body shipped back to Boston (Robert agreed to David's plan), and to get the death certificates. On them Robert saw that David had listed Mark as "single."

"Shows how well David knew Mark! Mark was married, and David handled the divorce!" Robert snorted. "I can imagine what that memorial service is going to be like! Glad I'm not going! The *real* memorial service will be here with his friends."

Norma, from Amron Metaphysical Center, where Mark had gone to church with me, officiated at the small memorial I set up in my studio. I made an altar of sorts, with Mark's picture on it, and stood one of his paintings behind it.

Stood being the operative word here. That particular painting was 8 feet high by 6 feet wide. When I encouraged Mark to paint—BIG! BIG!— it never occurred to me that I would have to figure out what to do with all of those oversized canvases. Had I known I would have suggested miniatures.

It was a small affair, with the guys from Mark's support group and a few people he made friends with from Amron and from the neighborhood. One woman sang "Ave Maria" (for the nice Jewish boy), and I made the closing remarks.

I started by telling how Mark and I had met, and how in those early years, he had taught me so much. He taught me display, he taught me about opera, and about how the upper class lives. There were the fun times, the humor, and the conflicts as well. Mark wasn't always easy—he could be maddening, overly dramatic, and a bit predatory at times. It was a complicated friendship, and for me, it was one of the more profound learning experiences I've lived through.

Most importantly, though, Mark taught me not to just look at something but to see it as well. See things as they are—curves, shapes, colors, people—observe and see. Don't just cast your eyes on something (or someone), but take it in. *See it.*

The irony here is not lost on me. Painful but not lost.

For someone who taught the value of seeing, Mark lived a life full of what could happen when one doesn't, or won't see.

I miss him terribly to this day.

Mark was my opposite—educated, well-to-do, well-traveled, refined, from a prominent family—while I was the wet-behind-the-ears country boy just out of college, having never really been out of the Midwest, living in a very narrow world. Mark was the person I aspired to be—*hungered* to be, actually. A *grown-up.*

Mark opened a window for me—a window into a life and a wide world that I suspected was out there but didn't know how to get to. I got a good look and desperately wanted to get through that window, to go live that life.

It's like we traded places. He opened that window for me, and I flew through. My life and world opened up because of Mark's help. But what I wasn't aware of was that Mark flew the opposite way through the window, and his world slowly narrowed. It almost choked the life out of him before I got there to bring him back to San Francisco, but in the end, Victor did the rest from long-distance. But at least he died free.

THE EPILOGUE:

After the memorial service, Norma pulled me aside and reminded me of that first reading she had given me, all those years ago.

"Remember I said there would be one day when he would come to you in a more humble position, and you would have the power? Then the friendship would be on a more equal footing?" she asked.

"Yes, now you mention it, I do. There were some years when I thought that might not come true. I thought I'd never see Mark alive again, after I told him not to call unless he was ready to leave Victor."

"Well, Schweetie the karma is balanced here." She smiled and hugged me. And that felt good.

Robert had a friend in The City who wrote for the *Examiner*, a Hearst paper at the time. This woman did a story on Mark after he died, telling a bit of what he went through, trying to get away from Victor. Since I had inherited all of the piles of documentation, answering machine tapes, and paper from the various court dates and actions, I went through and annotated everything for her. When I gave it all over, I told her that before this went to press, she needed the lawyers to go over everything—Victor would indeed sue. She used this stack of documents as source material for the article. After vetting by the *Examiner's* legal department, the article went to press.

Victor sued. (*No surprise. I told her he would.*) He sued the *Examiner*, the columnist, and ME, each for $1.5 million. Since this was the first time (and I hope the last) I had ever been sued, it turned my legs to rubber.

This caused me to wake up with a start every two hours at night, thinking, "I'm so screwed." After all the money I'd burned through during this chapter with Mark, I was tapped out. Happily a lawyer from a Very Very Good High-Powered Expensive Law Firm stepped up to defend me, pro bono, and we had the legal talent from the *Examiner* on our side as well. All that said I still didn't relax totally until it was all over.

The long and short of it was that Pizzaface was humiliated in court. He was humiliated because he didn't call the day before to argue that the case shouldn't have been thrown out of court, which it was. (The excuse was that he couldn't call because he was on an airplane—one with no phone. Perhaps it was Air Estonia.) Since Pizzaface failed to do this, and the case was thrown out of court, under the California Anti-SLAPP statutes, Victor had to pay *all* costs, which were considerable.

As for Mrs. Thames and Gordon:

About a month after Mark died, Gordon phoned me from that godforsaken hamlet outside of The Hague, you know, the one spelled with all consonants. Mrs. Thames had told him to phone me.

After a very brief and passing mention of Mark's death, he plunged into a long, torturous cataloguing of the cosmetic surgeries and procedures he had undergone since we had last spoken—*IN 1983!* He kept saying things like "you know," as if everyone engaged in recreational cosmetic surgery. At one point I was so exasperated, I said, "Gordon, I *don't* know. I haven't had any work done. I don't need it—I look really good!"

The statement that got me off the phone in a hurry was "I just wanted to be fabulous, and—*I've suffered.*"

He's suffered!? Dear God in Heaven!

Once I got off the phone, I got down on my knees and prayed to God, "Thank you, God, that I'm not HIM! Thank you that my parents were who they were and not those monsters who watered Gordon and watched him grow, instead of *raising* him!"

The AIDS got Gordon about a month after that. After he died I started getting phone calls and letters from Mrs. Thames, pleading for help. It seemed like she was now feeling guilty for letting Gordon stay with bad nurse Ruloph, who now had, no doubt, inherited the house, the bank accounts, and everything else.

Hearing her plead for help (usually on the answering machine—I was screening) or reading it in the letters (which I didn't answer), it sounded like Mrs. Thames needed absolution and wanted it from me. I wasn't feeling like giving it to her. She had her chances, first to help Mark get that nutcase Victor off his back and then to help Mark bring Gordon back to get him on the AIDS drugs. She made her choices, and I hoped she somehow gained some insight from the results. Sadly, though, she didn't.

I didn't ever return her calls and had heard nothing more from her. Until this morning.

As I'm writing this, five years after the fact, I thought she was finally history. Well, actually, I didn't think about her at all. However this morning, much to my surprise, she called and caught me at work.

Mrs. Thames was still, as she put it, "having trouble" over Gordon's death, and again I got the impression that she wanted absolution. She talked about how her husband and her daughter in Texas discouraged her from trying to get Gordon back to this continent, and also dismissively mentioned "Mark's little plan that probably wouldn't have worked anyway." There was no apparent awareness of *her* responsibility in all of this.

"That plan would have worked," I replied coolly. "Mark and I were working with a high-powered private eye and had already contacted Interpol. It would have worked."

A beat skipped.

"Now I feel worse about it," she said flatly.

"It's a shame, Mrs. Thames. I know of several people who were literally snatched from the jaws of death by the protease inhibitors. Gordon could have been one of them."

Her next remark gave me whiplash.

"Aruba is such a *wonderful* vacation spot!" she exclaimed brightly.

WHAT??? At first I thought I'd fallen into a parallel universe! The impact knocked the wind out of me.

As I sat there gasping from the whiplash, Mrs. Thames proceeded to tell me how Aruba was such a good tax haven and vacation spot and that I should go there. She cried poor a little (those pesky taxes and all that) but then told me of their *delightful* vacation house there and how I should look them up the next time I visited. I was so stunned by the abrupt change of topic, all I could manage was a weak "indeed."

She did mention that Victor contacted her a couple of months after Mark died to tell her the news, and she told him that she had heard. Mrs. Thames also advised him to move to the Midwest, change his name, and start over. I let her know about the lawsuit and how it left me with a sword of Damocles over my head.

THE EPILOGUE

Then there was the recap of how Mr. Thames was a psychopath she had chosen to live with all these years and how he had crushed her skull. (This, again, was the story of how she went through the windshield of the car. Years ago. And she's still married to him. She still has the tooth problem. His name is Mr. Thames.)

I also got the dish on Ruloph. It seems he was expecting to inherit the house and everything, but—pity!—it was all in Mrs. Thames's name. (She may be odious, but she isn't stupid.) I'm sure THAT was a rude surprise to him. Would he have hung around as long if he knew? And, more to the point, might Gordon still be alive because Ruloph had fled the scene? Mrs. Thames told me that she settled some money on Ruloph so he would go away.

There was a little more meaningless conversation, but all I really remember is my heart pounding and feeling really angry. Angry and disgusted. That fuckwit had no insight, nor desire to have insight, into how she herself allowed this situation. Bringing it to her attention was pointless.

She told me her phone number and email, and asked me to keep in touch. Like I'm going to do that.

And Robert:

Betty, Robert's wife, called me one day about six months after Mark died. It was nine thirty in the evening, which meant it was much later in Florida.

"Betty, what's wrong!?" I asked. There was a sick feeling in the pit of my stomach.

"It's Robert. He's dead."

Robert, after having a lovely day with the family and dinner, literally dropped over in his tracks. No warning. Nothing—just BOOM. I think it would be the best way to go, but it's an absolute shock for the people left behind.

What a gent, Robert. Last time I saw him, we were headed to the airport after Mark's affairs were closed down. We were in the car; it was sunny and warm for December, so I had the top down. We were chatting in the driveway before starting out. Robert thanked me for all my help and said how much he had enjoyed getting to know me better.

As I started the car, Robert looked over at me and said, "Ken, I'm not gay, but if I were gay, I would want to go out on a date with you. Take it as a compliment because that's how I intended it."

What a wonderful guy. A real gent. It just broke my heart that my one connection to Mark was gone. It somehow made Mark's death even more final.

And Victor:

Thankfully I don't hear from him. Last I heard was from a lawyer from the Hearst Corporation, asking for any information I could supply that could help them get their whopping legal fees out of him. After telling all I knew, I said, "I hope you find him and get the money!"

"We are the *HEARST Corporation*", he chuckled. "We'll get our money."

And finally, me:

As I said at the beginning, life really began for me on May 5, 1980, and I met Mark soon thereafter. In the sixteen years we knew each other, I grew up. Knowing Mark all that time was the one constant on that journey. He was sometimes more than a brother and sometimes less than a friend—but in the end, he was, indeed, the one constant in my life. Mark was there during my childhood and adolescence (*Act One*), distant while I was trying out my independence during my early adulthood (*Act Two*), and in a way, the aged parent I cared for (*Act Three*). Then the final curtain rang down on this particular show.

During Act One, I learned about seeing as an artist. Mark would tell me to not just look at something but to see it—take it in instead of just casting my eyes on something. This has enriched my creative life ever since.

THE EPILOGUE

Act Two taught me to accept that friends can have bad qualities, and one can get exasperated with them. One has to look at the person, warts and all, and really *see* them, and by seeing them clearly, decide whether one can continue with them or not. When I broke with Mark for that period of time, it was what I saw that made me know that I couldn't continue the friendship as it was. It didn't make me stop liking him or being concerned for him—

I saw that continuing as we were wasn't helping or changing things for either of us.

In the third act, I saw clearly that being a grown-up wasn't the glittering, cool, carefree existence that I had envisioned as a child. Sure, I had a spiffy car and evening clothes, hung around with glamorous people, went to the theater, opera, and restaurants—all the "grown-up" things I had dreamt about. But looking at this from the inside, I saw that the real measure of being a grown-up was something deeper and more profound. Along with the advantages of being an adult, I got a fuller understanding of the responsibilities, obligations, and unpleasant surprises that come with being grown up.

Instead of being a "grown-up," I'm all grown up now.

The most important thing I learned in Act Three was that doing the right thing is never easy, cheap, or popular. More importantly, doing the right thing is its own reward—sometimes it is the *only* reward.

I went to rescue Mark because I had made a promise to him. I had promised that when he was ready to leave Victor, I'd be there. I'd like to believe that it was knowing I'd be there when he was ready to leave that helped him to survive. When he called I knew that he was serious and that I had made a promise. It was the right thing to do. And *he was a friend*. Even though a long period of time had elapsed, this was a bond I hadn't broken. There was no question in my mind as to what to do.

But when it was all said and done, after all the struggle and trouble, I didn't even have my friend back for very long. Really he was present as I remembered him, in glimpses over his last few months, and totally during that last evening over dinner with his friends and me. I bitterly resent that I didn't get to keep him longer than I had him. I wanted him to restore his life, so I could have the old Mark back, the one who opened the window of my escape. So we both would be on the same side of that window. Then we both could have been peers. But life isn't fair. *Damn.*

But he died, and all I was left with was the knowledge that I had done the right thing. I had that and this experience, which strengthened me and will mark me forever. It has made me gutsier than I've ever thought possible and tougher, more open to taking big risks. There are big things I've done in my life since that have been made possible by the strength and power I claimed while helping Mark.

For me, this has to substitute for the applause and the bow after the final curtain and the fun after-party later, where everyone would congratulate me on my fine performance. It never works out that way in real life.

Final Curtain.

Made in the USA
Middletown, DE
06 February 2018